The Immigrant Heritage of America

Cecyle S. Neidle, *Editor*

Courtesy of the Norwegian-American Historical Association

The Restauration

The Norwegian-Americans

By ARLOW W. ANDERSEN

TWAYNE PUBLISHERS

A DIVISION OF G. K. HALL & CO., BOSTON

Library of Congress Cataloging in Publication Data

Andersen, Arlow William.
  The Norwegian-Americans.

  (The Immigrant heritage of America)
  Bibliography: pp. 251–61.
  1. Norwegians in the United States. I. Title.
E184.S2A43   917.3'06'3982   74-14651
ISBN 0–8057–3249–7

Contents

About the Author

Arlow W. Andersen was born to Norwegian immigrant parents in Neenah, Wisconsin, in 1906. Following graduation from the University of Minnesota and Northwestern University, Dr. Andersen served as professor of history in Kendall College (Evanston, Illinois), Jamestown College (Jamestown, North Dakota), McMurry College (Abilene, Texas), and, since 1964, the University of Wisconsin at Oshkosh. He has published two books. The first, *The Immigrant Takes His Stand*, evaluates the role of the pioneer Norwegian press in American public affairs before and during the Civil War. The second, *The Salt of the Earth*, is a history of the Norwegian-Danish Methodist Church in America, an organization in which his father was an active minister.

Among his articles published in various journals, several have appeared in the *Norwegian-American Studies*. The author serves on the board of publications of the Norwegian-American Historical Association and is a member of the Organization of American Historians, the American-Scandinavian Foundation, and the Society for the Advancement of Scandinavian Study. In 1960–61, a Fulbright grant enabled him to engage in research at the University of Oslo, concentrating on the attitudes of Norwegian newspapers toward American government and politics in the period 1875–1905. In World War II he served as an education officer with the Army Air Forces, concluding with a tour of duty in occupied Japan.

Preface

At this juncture in the history of the United States, with the bicentennial of the Declaration of Independence in the offing, Americans of Norwegian descent are also mindful of the sesquicentennial celebrations being planned for 1975 on both sides of the Atlantic. Norwegian group migration began in 1825 with the sailing of the sloop *Restauration* from Stavanger, Norway. In addition, the Norwegian-American Historical Association will observe its fiftieth anniversary in 1975. To this writer the many volumes published by the Association have provided invaluable source material.

Never is one more conscious of one's indebtedness to others than when one attempts to relate and interpret the experience of an ethnic group within the multinational American society. In our case, the name of Theodore C. Blegen, formerly dean of the graduate school of the University of Minnesota, stands preeminent. Not only was he the author of a highly exemplary two-volume work, *Norwegian Migration to America* (1931 and 1940), and of many valuable monographs, but he also personally inspired others to advance the study of Norwegian immigrant history.

I have been fortunate in having as readers and critics of the entire manuscript three well qualified persons. Kenneth O. Bjork, managing editor and president of the Norwegian-American Historical Association, has aided considerably in suggesting new insights. Erik J. Friis, director of publications for the American-Scandinavian Foundation and editor of its informative and attractive quarterly, *The American-Scandinavian Review*, read an early draft and is also the copy editor of this book. His pertinent comments on the contents and the emphasis of the total work are deeply appreciated. Cecyle S. Neidle serves as general editor of the series on "The Immigrant Heritage of America," of which this volume is a part. As one who understands, firsthand, the problems and the potentialities of writing in the field of American immigration, she has been very helpful in directing this effort.

For much detailed information I am beholden to numerous books and articles, most of them contained within the selected bibliography. For constructive commentary and advice on particular chapters the following have been generous in their cooperation: Carlton Qualey, formerly of Carleton College; Einar Haugen of Harvard University; Conrad Garmager, formerly Supreme President of the Sons of Norway; and Pastor Carl W. Schevenius of Minneapolis. Franklin D. Scott, formerly of Northwestern University and now curator of the Westergaard collection of Scandinavian works in the Honnold Library of the Claremont Colleges, has given constant encouragement to my studies. It is most gratifying to have his Foreword in the following pages.

It seems appropriate to acknowledge with reverence and appreciation my parents, Carl Andreas Andersen and Rakel Petrine Trockstad, who emigrated from Drammen, Norway, in 1895. For more than a quarter of a century they ministered to the spiritual needs of Norwegian congregations in the American Middle West. They taught me, in daily conversation, the Norwegian language and helped to instill an appreciation of Norwegian literature and of the Norwegian-American press.

This assignment was accepted with some hesitation. How can one write effectively and objectively concerning an immigrant people with whom one has been associated from childhood? And how can one improve upon the many impressive works already published in this field? One can only hope to supplement the good work of others. Perhaps those who read this saga should exercise the privilege of all eclectics. Let them choose what they wish from the smörgåsbord of chapters. For some there may be too much *lutefisk* or *gjetost*, and for others not enough perhaps. Hopefully, the story will serve as a contribution to the great American epic, which itself is enhanced by the dynamic pageant of immigration.

Our task has been one of selection and condensation of material from a growing body of literature dealing with Norwegians in American life. For any misinterpretations of the thoughts of others, and for the factual errors that inevitably creep in, I alone am responsible.

ARLOW W. ANDERSEN

University of Wisconsin
Oshkosh, Wisconsin

Foreword

Professor Andersen is mildly apologetic and protests the difficulties of writing on the history of his own people. He need not apologize or protest. Because he is one of them he can the more readily appreciate their ideas and values, their difficulties, their attitudes toward America. His historical training and his long and profound study of the Norwegians in America have developed in him not only insight into the circumstances of this major migration, but also a breadth of view. He understands this national movement in relation to others, and he places the entire immigration in the perspective of general American history. Putting migration in the context of broader historical trends is a service one all too seldom enjoys.

Why a book about the Norwegians? Are they different? Andersen is cautious. He indulges in no invidious comparisons, he makes no special case. He simply tells the story of this particular group of individuals, their background and their adaptation to the American scene, and lets the evidence lead where it will. Yet the thoughtful reader will inevitably ponder that evidence further and think of other national groups with which he is familiar. Similarities between people are greater than differences, but differences are nevertheless significant. Italians are *in general* different from Irishmen, even when they are transplanted, and Greeks are different from Germans. Their beliefs and customs are different, their attitudes and their physical makeup. Differences between Swedes and Norwegians may be less apparent and in individual cases nonexistent. Yet there are variations between Danes and Swedes and Norwegians engendered by tradition, by institutions, by economic circumstances and other factors. The conditions which generated emigration from Ireland were not the same as the conditions which pushed people from Germany or Poland or China. And in the reception areas conditions were different between cities and farms, between factories and offices; they were different for children than for adults, they were different in times of prosperity and in times of depression. Another of the manifold differences that becomes clear in this account is in the religious motivation behind emigration—strong among the "sloopers" of 1825, weak indeed at the end of the century. The process of migration may actually enhance differences by encouraging men in an alien environment to cling together with their own people and to emphasize values and institutions that they had previously taken for granted—the church, for instance.

Such factors as these, and many more, make it dangerous indeed to generalize about the processes of immigration. The problems and experiences of Russian Jews crowded into the unsanitary tenements of New York were fundamentally different from the types of hardships faced by Scandinavian settlers in the rural Midwest. And Rudolph Vecoli has shown that they were very different from the circumstances and the social attitudes and adjustments of the Italians in Chicago. Social scientists search indefatigably for the great truths that embrace all mankind. But some truths are confined within narrower limits. Generalizations may be partial truths that blind researchers to contradictory differences. Arlow Andersen has avoided such suspect and speculative conclusions. He realizes that valid generalization can take place only after a vast amount of specific evidence has been accumulated. He concentrates on the Norwegian example, and his judicious evaluation of that one group's experience creates a solid building block in what may eventually become a proper structure of generalization.

The topic of assimilation (or "Americanization") runs like a bright thread through the account of Andersen's book. And it tempts one into that risky field of generalization! We think of the Norwegian-Americans as excellent citizens. What makes of immigrants good citizens? Certainly not that overzealous love of birthplace that causes a person to mourn for years at having departed from his native heath. Not either that depth of alienation from the regime in his homeland that causes him to make of the United States a base for intrigue and rebellion abroad; nor such sense of shame for one's past that he cannot adjust to the opportunities of a new life. The Norwegian-Americans have been fortunate in that they have retained a profound love for the fjords and fields of the North while at the same time they have remained conscious of the fact that it was northern nature and economic conditions that impelled them to emigrate. It is of prime importance that these impelling forces were impersonal conditions rather than individual persecution or discrimination. Hence this group of immigrants from Northern Europe never felt called upon to join a Sinn Fein or a Zionist crusade. They loved their ancestral home in Norway, they took pride in their ancient heritage. Yet they recognized in America the chance for a better life and they appreciated that too. Without sorrowing too much they kept their love for things past along with thankfulness for the new.

The Japanese who settled in Hawaii are a good example of this thesis, and Daniel Inouye in his autobiographical *Journey to Washington* has provided a marvelous bit of corroboration. These Japanese-Americans carefully preserved their hallowed traditions; yet they were happy to be Americans. When their bitter time of testing arrived they proved to be remarkably loyal to their new country. The Norwegian-Americans, without having to endure the traumatic experience of the Japanese, had that same sense of complete indentification with "the land of their choice." Paul Knaplund is witness in his own life to the fact and some of the reasons for it:

As the [his own] children grew older their father saw America in a new light. The earth those children trod, the soil sifted through their little hands became to him more hallowed than the places where his ancestors had toiled and found their last resting place. The living were for him more significant than the dead. In the lives of his children his own life would continue.

(Moorings Old and New, 266)

Love for the motherland remained while a greater love was added. There was no conflict between past and present, only enhancement.

Another fascinating element in the story here presented is the penchant displayed by the Norwegian immigrants for reforming America. Some of them had been reformers at home and they remained reformers. Perhaps it was just because these sons of the Vikings could feel independent and proud that they could uninhibitedly both enjoy and criticize the country to which they had come. For almost without exception these apostles of improvement concentrated their efforts not on the Norway they had left behind but on the America to which they had come. They were social critics like Thorstein Veblen or political and labor leaders like Andrew Furuseth and Marcus Thrane (one of the few who continued to try to reform two countries). The Norwegian-Americans formed a solid backbone in the Populist and Farmer-Labor movements in the Upper Midwest. They had brought to America not only their full share of skills in engineering and business and education, but they brought also more than the usual quota of moral concern and sense of community responsibility. As Jon Wefald has pointed out (and he is cited herein) they eschewed the extreme individualistic and capitalistic ethic of frontier America; they thought in terms of the rural and sea-coast patterns of Norwegian society, of the necessity for mutual self-help in isolated communities, of long-established systems of communal ownership of forests and group exploitation of fisheries. Such customs known and approved established a basis for Norwegian-American social philosophy. It was therefore *not only* the agricultural conditions of the American West that produced the strong Norwegian-American participation in the protest movements of the late nineteenth and early twentieth centuries. These immigrants were applying on this side of the Atlantic the special kinds of ideals and methods that had been ingrained in them in their original homeland. This persistence of Old World traits and concepts is another of the intrinsic components of the Andersen narrative.

In numbers the Norwegian-Americans were large in proportion to the population of Norway. They were small proportionately in the population of the United States. But it is apparent throughout the breadth and diversity of this revealing survey that they have been of great consequence in the building of America.

FRANKLIN D. SCOTT

The Honnold Library for the
Claremont Colleges

CHAPTER 1

Norway: The Land They Left Behind

THE STORY OF WESTERN CIVILIZATION IS TO A GREAT EXTENT ONE of peoples on the move. Whether one considers the barbarian invasions of the declining Roman Empire, the adventuresome explorations and settlements of the Vikings, the Anglo-Saxon and Norman impacts upon Britain, the clashes between Christian crusaders and Moslem Saracens, or the mingling of the Asiatic Mongols with the medieval Russians, the effects are striking not only for the restless migrant peoples themselves but also for the more stable societies that felt the pressures of immigration, whether by sudden attack or by gradual infiltration.

This volume is concerned with a more recent "invasion," that of Norwegians who, as a part of the nineteenth-century European exodus, faced the uncertainties of leaving their familiar northern environment to settle in an America known to be both attractive and forbidding. While the effects of emigration upon the Scandinavian homeland is not our main theme, it is perhaps well to remember that among European countries only Ireland suffered greater losses than Norway in young manhood and womanhood in proportion to the home population. It is estimated that about a million Norwegians departed for America in the course of a century, down to the 1920s. The emigration of promising young folk drained Norway, at least temporarily, of incalculable human resources.

Our treatment of Norwegian immigration to America begins roughly with 1825, the year of the first group movement, from Stavanger on the west coast of Norway. Our opening chapter sets forth a panorama of nineteenth-century Norway. As one of several member states in the North Atlantic community, Norway was blessed more with scenic grandeur than with

[1]

valuable natural resources. Only three percent cultivable, she relied upon agriculture, timber, and fish for sustenance until, later in the century, railroad construction, mining, hydroelectric power, and especially shipping and shipbuilding injected new life into the economy. In the oversimplified words of one spokesman, "What would we be without the sea? A handful of people on a pile of rocks!" Prior to and during the industrial upswing, which was never sufficiently strong to stem the flow of emigrants, conditions in the homeland induced vast numbers of the sons and daughters of Norway to leave their country and to take up permanent residence in the overseas continent, in a land at once mysterious and familiar, thanks to *Amerikabreve* (America letters) and other reliable reports.

Norway shares the Scandinavian peninsula with Sweden, her neighbor to the east. The capital city of Oslo (Christiania before 1925) nestles at the head of the busy fjord of the same name in the south-central part of the country. On the west coast, fronting on the North Sea, are the port cities of Stavanger, Bergen, and Trondheim. Norway is a part of the Germanic world, where once barbarian tribes came to plunder and to make their homes. More specifically, she comprises a significant segment of the Scandinavian world. While Scandinavian political unity has never been lasting, it may be said that ethnic kinship, similar speech, and cultural and religious ties have determined a common Scandinavian history at times and common interests at many points.

Close relations with England and the United States have characterized the history of Norway. From the ninth to the eleventh centuries, Vikings, for reasons not fully known, set out from Scandinavian bays and fjords and made repeated contact with the British Isles. King Canute of Denmark ruled not only Norway but England as well. Descendants of Rollo the Norseman, who conquered Normandy, invaded England in the person of William the Conqueror in 1066. The Northmen, having first created with the Franks a new Norman civilization, thus set their stamp upon British institutions for all time.

The spirited lines of the Norwegian poet Aasmund Olavson Vinje (1818–1870), composed in tribute to the medieval explorers and conquerors from the North, may with some justifi-

cation be brushed off as an example of poetic license. Yet they
are not entirely devoid of historical meaning. The Wisconsin-
born Peer Strömme, litterateur and popular lecturer-politician,
has translated these lines as follows:

> He taught the Frenchman chivalry,
> And set his soul on fire;
> The Englishman to love the sea
> And wake the tuneful lyre.
>
> A captain, he, in days of yore,
> Disposing men and things;
> From Scotland to Messina's shore
> He made and unmade kings.

Communication with the United States was to become rather
intimate for the Northern kingdom. In 1814 Norwegian leaders
studied the new American Constitution, together with the
French document of 1791. Like the infant American nation,
Norway owed much politically to British precedent and practice.

In the Treaty of Kiel (1814) Denmark had ceded Norway to
the king of Sweden. In Swedish thinking the rationale was
simple. Sweden had lost Finland to Russia in 1808. Denmark
had been in alliance with Napoleon, the enemy of both Sweden
and Russia. Norway offered a natural compensation for the
loss of Finland.

Norwegian minds did not appreciate Swedish reasoning. They
were deeply disappointed over the apparent indifference of
Denmark toward the cession of Norway, which had been tied
like a province to the Danish realm since late in the fourteenth
century. This was the era of the Union of Kalmar, begun in
1397 under Queen Margaret of Denmark. Lasting union proved
impossible, partially because kingship was elective in Denmark
but hereditary in Norway. Sweden withdrew in 1523 under
Gustavus I. But Norway remained attached to the Danish
dynasty and government until her arbitrary transfer to the
royal house of Sweden in 1814.

The Norwegian petit-bourgeoisie and the *bønder*, or peasant
farmers, urged election of a Danish prince, Christian Fredrik,

and the formulation of a separate constitution and parliament. Their representatives met at Eidsvoll, some forty miles to the north of Christiania, and framed a constitution. Upon Christian Fredrik's election to the kingship, Sweden intervened militarily, whereupon the Danish prince yielded his briefly held throne.

Marshal Jean-Baptiste-Jules Bernadotte had been elected by the Swedes in 1810, to succeed the childless Carl XIII, whose death came in 1818. The erstwhile French military hero promised to abide by the terms of the Eidsvoll document, the fundamental law of Norway since that day. The Act of Union (1815) created a dual kingdom of Sweden-Norway. The new Norwegian Storting, or parliament, would be equal in power, theoretically, to the Swedish Riksdag.

If Norway experienced economic difficulties during the Napoleonic Wars, when her Danish connection aligned her involuntarily on the side of France, her plight after 1815 was hardly less serious. British navigation acts stifled the carrying trade in Scandinavian timber. Southern and Eastern Norway suffered most. West coast communities continued to thrive on fishing. Landless people found employment in an infant industry and in government roadbuilding projects. With a declining death rate, population had risen more rapidly than in most European countries in the past 150 years, from 440,000 in 1665 to 886,000 in 1815. The increase from 1815 to 1865 was 13.4 percent for each decade, again much above the continental average. It is understandable that 77,874 Norwegians emigrated, most of them to the United States, in the forty years after 1825.[1]

On the political and social fronts the peasant farmers saw some progress. True, the Storting remained under the control of the official class until 1830, but titles of nobility had been abolished in 1821, the earliest such action in the Scandinavian states. Not oblivious to the meaning of the July Revolution in Paris in 1830, King Carl XIV Johan (the former Marshal Bernadotte) heeded some demands, even if changes came slowly. Subsequently the Swedes yielded to the pressure of Ole Gabriel Ueland (1779–1870), a leading spokesman for the peasants in the parliament. His work stamps him as one of Norway's political giants. The poet Bjørnstjerne Bjørnson marked him as one who envisioned "the true government of the people" in much the same way as his great American contemporary, Abraham Lincoln.

While Ueland applied himself to political reform, Henrik Wergeland (1808–1845) strove to achieve social and economic improvements. Wergeland gave inspiration to agricultural and linguistic and prison reforms, as well as to temperance and sanitation. To slow down the incipient process of emigration he urged adequate housing for the working man. As a non-violent revolutionary, Wergeland entertained the idea of republicanism. His response to the concepts of the Enlightenment was matched by an equally genuine admiration for freedom as he saw it reflected in reports from America. Yet he greatly desired to better conditions in his beloved Norway, so that the *bønder* would not choose to emigrate. His last drama, *Fjeldstuen* (The Mountain Cabin) warned against unscrupulous emigration agents. Some hold that with Henrik Wergeland, and later with Bjørnson, each in his own time, Norwegian cultural history of the century is pretty well covered.

Progress along democratic lines became more marked in the second half of the nineteenth century. At the same time emigration reached maximum proportions. If there is a paradox here, how can it be explained? Why did more people become discontented in the very interval when Norway's economy was improving? The answer may lie in a revival of political liberalism following the repressive age of Metternich in Europe. In an economic sense a similar trend is observable, as in Britain, in the movement away from restrictive governmental regulations and toward free trade, the net result being for Norway and other maritime nations an upswing in shipping activity. There is also, it seems, a psychological tendency for men to expect and demand more when they have tasted a measure of success. The have-nots may occupy so low a rung on the economic ladder that they lose interest in climbing. And the haves may have had their hopes lifted to the point where only further gains will satisfy.

Norway's political achievements after 1850 were considerable. The death of Bernadotte in 1844 brought to the throne his son Oscar I (1844–1859), who was a bit more liberal in that he permitted Norway equal recognition in the Union coat of arms and allowed Norway's name to appear before Sweden's on Norwegian state papers. However, he and his successor, Carl XV (1859–1872), continued to appoint a Swedish statt-holder, a kind of governor-general, in Christiania. Since no comparable office existed in Stockholm, Norwegians regarded this functionary as a symbol of their inferiority in the partner-ship with Sweden.

Hopes for Norwegian farmers and laborers rose with the triumph of Johan Sverdrup (1816–1892) and Søren Jaabæk (1814–1894) in parliament and press. In the 1840s, some twenty years before Lincoln's Gettysburg Address, Sverdrup had em-ployed the phrase "Government of the people, by the people, and for the people." First elected to the Storting in 1851, he campaigned in favor of a jury system patterned after British and American institutions. Although relatively little was said in the Norwegian press concerning the American judiciary, Nicolai Grevstad, a former editor of Christiania's *Dagbladet* (The Daily Paper), classified some two hundred articles per-taining to the American jury system and achieved the satis-faction of having his study printed as a government document by action of the Storting. The fact that his observations were not questioned seriously in Norway lends support to the view that statesmen and editors alike were prepared for reform.[2]

Grevstad was in some ways exceptional. As editor from 1880 to 1883 of *Dagbladet*, an influential metropolitan journal which perpetuated the liberal Sverdrup tradition, he first scanned America from afar. As an immigrant and United States citizen after 1883, he skillfully employed the English idiom while writing for the *Minneapolis Tribune*. From 1892 to 1911 he served with distinction as editor of *Skandinaven* (The Scandinavian), the Chicago daily which probably exercised greater influence than any other journal among Americans of Scandinavian descent. The Republican administration of Wil-liam Howard Taft recognized his abilities, and his standing among Norwegian-Americans, by appointing him minister to Uruguay and Paraguay in 1911.

The argumentative Jaabæk, whose opponents sometimes called him Neibæk (No-bæk in contrast with Yes-bæk), joined Sverdrup in 1869. Successor to Ueland as an avowed friend of the peasant farmer, Jaabæk served in the Storting from 1845 to 1890, a record in Norwegian political annals. As editor and publisher of *Folketidende* (The People's News) from 1865 to 1880, he was pleased to reach a circulation of 17,000, high for that time, and to know that his journal was widely disseminated throughout Norway. He charged that the unresponsiveness of the Swedish king and government was to blame for the restlessness leading to emigration. He attacked religious intolerance, military conscription, alcoholism, highly restrictive voting qualifications, and other unbearable conditions. With no favorable governmental action in prospect, he extolled the virtues of America and propagandized more effectively than any other single person or agency on behalf of emigration.

Sverdrup, not without ambition for political preferment, fought the conservative leadership of Frederik Stang, who guided the Norwegian ministry from 1861 to 1880. With Jaabæk's help Sverdrup succeeded in getting annual meetings of Parliament, which had been meeting triennially. On the issue of whether the king's ministers should sit in Parliament and be responsible to that body, King Oscar II (1872–1905) reluctantly yielded. He was forced to name Sverdrup to head the cabinet in 1884. Thus responsible government was inaugurated, and in this manner a liberal regime triumphed for the first time. Not until 1888 did Johan Sverdrup meet with defeat at the polls. At that juncture he could look back upon no little achievement. In the liberal spirit, women had gained access to the University of Christiania and to the professions in the early 1880s. The suffrage was extended for the first time since 1814. Full manhood suffrage had to wait until 1898. Men who had savored Sverdrup's persuasiveness and eloquence as an orator, and were sympathetic with his aims, hailed him as the Gambetta, the Gladstone, of Norway.

A substantial fraction of the electorate of 1884 interpreted Sverdrup's victory as marking the end of domination by the official class. Equally important, they probably saw in liberal success a sign of the eventual demise of royal Swedish rule in Norway. In this hope they were encouraged in different ways by a number of persons of renown, among them Bjørnstjerne Bjørnson, Henrik Ibsen, Camilla Collett, Aasta Hansteen, Ivar

Aasen, Aasmund Vinje, and Arne Garborg. In the 1890s Fridtjof Nansen and Christian Michelsen, both politically nationalist, would gain popularity in circles where Swedish rule was being questioned.

The poet and novelist Bjørnson (1832–1910), though not narrowly nationalistic, championed the Sverdrup program. It was he who introduced in 1870 the flag-waving parades of children in celebration of the national day of independence, dating from May 17, 1814. Bjørnson also wrote the stirring lines of the national anthem, beginning with "Ja, vi elsker dette landet" (Yes, we love this country). Despite his later renunciation of some traditional Christian beliefs and the antagonism aroused thereby among the more pietistic, Bjørnson's stature among his fellow countrymen did not diminish seriously. He also lectured in the United States in 1880–1881 and spoke in glowing terms of opportunities for immigrant farmers. While clearly identified with Norwegian public affairs, Bjørnson came to be related to pan-Germanism and to republicanism, which endeared him to Germans on the one hand and to Frenchmen on the other, a valuable asset to Norway in her desire to win complete independence from dominant Sweden.

Henrik Ibsen (1828–1906) sounded forth as Norway's Shakespeare on themes of social significance. Free development of human personality was his main emphasis. More than any other man he brought Norway to the attention of the great powers. Theatergoers eagerly attended his plays in Berlin, Paris, London, and New York. Like his distinguished contemporary, Bjørnson, he deeply appreciated European culture. In fact, Ibsen resided abroad, most of the time in Italy, from the 1860s to the 1890s.

Ibsen's *A Doll's House* (1879) may well have alerted the Western world to the place of the modern woman in society. Already the ground had been prepared in Norway for participation of women in public life, in part as a result of American practices. Fredrika Bremer (1801–1865), the Swedish novelist who toured America and wrote *Homes in the New World* (1853), gave inspiration indirectly to the women's rights movement in Norway. Camilla Collett (1813–1895), author of *Amtmandens Døtre* (The Daughters of the County Governor) in

1855, and sister of Henrik Wergeland, the romantic poet and national hero, stressed the new role of her sex in Norway.

The influence of America upon Aasta Hansteen and, in turn, the impact of her writing and lecturing upon Norwegian audiences cannot go unnoticed. Her publication in 1878 of *Kvinden Skabet i Guds Billede* (Woman Created in God's Image) was followed by a nine-year stay in America, part of that period as correspondent for *Verdens Gang* (The Course of the World), a leading newspaper of Christiania. Her *Amerikabreve* confessed to an indescribable freedom in the New World.[3] In addition, Bjørnson returned from his America tour to speak with high praise for feminist leadership and for reform generally. Support for the women came also from Hans Tambs Lyche (1859–1898) and others in the newspaper world. Lyche had been employed by several journals in the Scandinavian countries, Jaabæk's *Folketidende* among them, before his departure for the United States in 1880. At the time of his death in Norway he was editing his own *Kringsjaa* (Survey), a periodical which brought the English-speaking world to Norway's attention.

Historians and philologists contributed their share to the national consciousness. Before his death Peter Andreas Munch (1810–1863) completed a multivolume *History of the Norwegian People*. He made patriots proud of medieval Norway and strengthened the sense of national continuity. His work revived respect for the Old Norse language. Henrik Ibsen followed with his *Pretenders*, a drama focusing upon the character of King Haakon IV (1218–1263). Similarly, Johan Ernst W. Sars (1835–1917) produced a monumental *Survey of the History of the Norwegian People* (1873). Upon Sverdrup's motion in the Parliament Sars was appointed professor in the University of Christiania, and the way was open to a wider influence upon the upcoming generation of intellectuals.[4]

Advocates of *landsmål*, the country language, did their part to make the people more sensitive to things Norwegian, to differentiate the Norwegian tongue from the Danish, and to draw a clearer line politically between Norway and Sweden. Not only the historian Munch, but a self-educated philologist, Ivar Aasen (1813–1896), attempted to restore a purely national language based upon Old Norse and local dialects, mainly from

Western Norway. Contrary to the spirit of Ibsen, who wrote in a Norwegian akin to Danish, Aasen by 1850 had published a grammar and a dictionary in *landsmål*. The poet Aasmund Vinje employed *landsmål* and was ably seconded by another poet and novelist, Arne Garborg (1851–1924). While the number of *landsmål* users remained small among Norway's men of letters, it is the opinion of T. K. Derry, the British historian, that "*landsmål* had become a shibboleth by which to distinguish the true democrat from the adherents of a language of foreign snobbery." Somehow the hopes of the *bønder* rose with the success of Aasen and Garborg. By law the new language was recognized as equal to the old, and Norway was saddled with a bilingual problem for which no satisfactory solution has yet been found.[5]

Apart from political conditions, why did Norwegians leave their country? Ingrid Semmingsen writes of the numerous influences playing upon adventuresome and discontented folk. Information-packed handbooks and travel guides are cited. They include in their number Ole Rynning's *Sandfærdige Beretning om Amerika* (True Account of America), published in Norway in 1838. In 1844 Johan Reinert Reiersen followed with a more detailed *Veiviser for de Norske Emigranter til de Forenede Nordamerikanske Stater og Texas* (Guide for Norwegian Emigrants to the United North American States and Texas). As a young man of 29, Reiersen founded *Christianssandsposten* in 1839 as a forum for discussion of emigration and of liberal reforms. Contrary to the opinions of his journalistic colleagues and to the views of Henrik Wergeland, he held that emigration was not harmful to Norway. A summer visit in the United States in 1843 proved so rewarding that he returned to settle permanently in 1845. He began publication of the monthly *Norge og Amerika*, intended to bind the two nations together. Despite the known shortcomings of the United States at mid-century, Norwegian colonists and their spokesmen usually sent favorable reports to the homeland.[6]

The early 1840s witnessed a significant trend in Norwegian departures for American shores, from 300 in 1840 to 1,600 in 1843. Hans Gasmann, one-time member of the Storting, sold his *gård* (farming estate) in 1842 preparatory to leaving for America. This momentous decision by a man of high station impressed his countrymen greatly. The return in the same year of Cleng Peerson, who had guided several emigrant parties and who proposed to continue in that endeavor, lent further encouragement to those who might be faint of heart. By 1845 the total number of *emigranter* was 6,200, nearly half of them from the single agricultural district of Bratsberg.[7]

Emigration agents also exerted tremendous pressure upon the footloose *bønder* and cotters in the valleys and uplands. Johan Holfeldt sought new members for Ole Bull's short-lived colony in Pennsylvania. The "New Norway" envisioned by the world-famed violinist never was realized. Bull (1810–1880) returned to his native land disappointed. In the words of Theodore C. Blegen, the historian of Norwegian immigration, "Thus ended Ole Bull's dream of a New Norway. Oleana is a tale of hope and disappointment; of comedy and tragedy; of idealism and villainy; of very human impulses, strivings, and actions." It is all but certain that Henrik Ibsen had the "dreamer-musician" in mind when he created the character of Peer Gynt.[8]

Another agent, Elias Stangeland, shares with Holfeldt the distinction of being the first in Norway. He represented an American transport company. In 1861 Oscar Malmborg, a Swede, served on behalf of the Illinois Central Railroad, then in search of passengers and freight along the northern section of its Chicago-to-New Orleans run. In 1862 American consuls were instructed to advertise employment opportunities. A federal law of 1864 (repealed in 1885) permitted contract labor. In 1864 *Bergensposten* called attention to mining possibilities in the Lake Superior region, with two-year contracts available. Abuses by agents were not uncommon. In 1869 the Norwegian government retaliated by requiring all emigration promoters to register with the local chiefs of police and to provide written contracts.[9]

The various states vied for immigrants. Wisconsin had its own commissioner of immigration in the 1850s. Minnesota followed in 1867, and Iowa in 1870. Ole C. Johnson, a Civil War officer in the nearly all-Norwegian Fifteenth Wisconsin Regiment and who had served as immigration commissioner in Minnesota, was sent by the Northern Pacific Railroad Company to Christiania in

1880. Next fall he led about 300 Scandinavians to North Dakota.[10]

Statistically, emigration fluctuated with the times. Prior to 1865 mainly rural folk departed. While men outnumbered women (535 to 465 per thousand), male emigration was not as heavy as in Europe generally. Family emigration was common. Children under twelve were therefore conspicuous, comprising about 32 percent of the aggregate number of those who crossed the Atlantic. Figures for Great Britain and Ireland indicate only 19 percent for the same age range. After 1865 the age bracket for adults dropped from the former 30–40 to 15–25. Family migration yielded noticeably to young men and women, with men outnumbering women even more than before 1860.[11]

On the industrial scene, labor unrest contributed relatively little in a quantitative way to Norwegian emigration. Yet men like Marcus Thrane (1817–1890) became self-chosen exiles in America. While still on Norwegian soil Thrane organized the labor movement, which today has its political counterpart in a strong Labor party. Of Thrane the distinguished historian Halvdan Koht remarks, "He was the first Norwegian socialist, and he was the one who made the year 1848 a year of revolution also in Norway. . . . Thrane's brief period of activity became a turning point in Norwegian history."[12] In 1854 Thrane was sentenced to prison for his radical views and for petitioning the king for redress of certain grievances of the working class. Released in 1858, he made his way five years later to America, where he carried on his work in the cause of socialism.[13]

It was not unusual for farmers and laborers to leave their Norwegian homeland in the 1860s. Whereas the decade of the 1850s had brought a degree of prosperity, the end of the Crimean War and the onset of competition with Russian grain spelled doom for the future. Once the American Civil War had come to an end, 15,500 Norse folk emigrated in 1866, and 18,000 in 1869, the peak number for that era. The agricultural crisis persisted for the remainder of the century. Another surge of emigration occurred in the late 1880s, with totals of 20,000 annually in 1887 and 1888. On the home front shipbuilding was declining. Shoemakers and others craftsmen were having to face the challenge of foreign machine-made goods. Eilert Sundt, the Norwegian sociologist of that generation, concluded that the greatest emigration took place among manual workers and day laborers. Trade unions, such as they were, were largely ineffective in relieving the plight of their members. Still later, after 1900, opportunities in the fishing industry were fewer. More capital was required with the advent of motor-driven boats, larger steamers, and expensive equipment. For those with an eye to the sea, there were greater inducements in American foreign and coastal trade.[14]

Together with political and economic developments, religious changes also constitute a part of the dynamics of Norwegian society. The Norwegians had undergone two major transitions in their religious organization. First came the gradual discarding of paganism in favor of Catholic Christianity, beginning around the year 1000. Second, a royal Danish proclamation of the sixteenth century introduced the Lutheran form of Protestantism, which was to take hold in northern Germany and in all of Scandinavia. Specifically, King Christian III of Denmark-Norway issued a charter in 1536 making Lutheranism official throughout his entire realm. As there were those who had murmured against the imposition of Rome in Scandinavian affairs, so there would be complaints of Danish intrusion in Norwegian church life, as in ecclesiastical appointments. Latin yielded to a seemingly foreign Danish in sermons, hymns, and scripture. To the end of the Danish period in Norway in 1814 there were not a few churchmen and layfolk whose enthusiasm for the Lutheran establishment was dampened by the knowledge that a king in Copenhagen headed their institution.

One authority analyzes the nineteenth century in Norway as one of "story-book proportions and a marvelous period of expansion on all fronts." He cites the religious reawakening particularly.[15] Prominent in that connection are the names of Hans Nielsen Hauge (1771–1824), Bishop Nicolai Frederik Severin Grundtvig (1783–1872), and Gisle Johnson (1822–1894). Simultaneous with the rise of the small farmers, Hauge's pietistic endeavors shook the political, business, and social worlds as well as the religious. Like John Wesley in England, this young man had his own strange religious experience, in 1796. Eight years of relatively uninterrupted lay preaching were followed by frequent arrests and imprisonments under the repressive terms of the Conventicle Ordinance of 1741, which enabled local clergy to suppress unorthodox religious gatherings. His evangelistic activities took him on foot to all corners of the land. He sought to lift the lowly peasant to a higher level of material prosperity and of spiritual well-being. Broken in health by long confinement, he died ten years after his release from prison.

Hauge wanted no separate church. Reforms must come from within the institution. Lutheranism was to be the mark of his followers, known as Haugeans. The role of laymen in the church was noticeably enhanced by his teaching and example. His hold upon the farming class did much to promote the concept of the dignity and equality of all men. Haugeanism, as puritanism, was matched by practical sense in agriculture, in industry, and even in politics. Three Haugeans were already present in the constitutional assembly at Eidsvoll in 1814. The farmer opposition bloc in the Storting owed much to Haugean leadership. In 1842 they and others were pleased with the formal repeal of the Conventicle Ordinance. On the other hand, Haugeans were disappointed with and alarmed over an act of 1845 which protected religious dissenters. Non-Lutheran bodies did not fall within the bounds of Haugean compassion.[16]

The influence of Bishop Grundtvig cannot be ignored. This Danish man of letters reacted strongly against the Enlightenment, with its accompanying rationalism and unbelief. He deplored formalism in religion. In time he doubted the infallibility of the Bible and advised, rather, adherence to the Apostles' Creed and to exemplary Christian living. Christianity meant to him an active participation in the varied affairs of life. He preferred feeling over doctrine, and personal judgment over unquestioning acceptance of authority. Grundtvig's disciple in Norway was W. A. Wexels, who ministered to the congregation of Our Saviour's Church of Christiania from 1819 to the year of his death in 1866.

Patriotism and religion merged in Grundtvig's thinking. He held that each nation had a special divine mission within civilization. Yet some peoples were more important in the fulfillment of God's designs. Historically the Jews, the Greeks, the Anglo-Saxons, and the Scandinavians were most outstanding. It is not strange that he authored *The Mythology of the North* and translated *Beowulf* into Danish. He implied that the Danes, together with other Scandinavians, inherited the mission of reestablishing peace and brotherhood among all mankind. The realization of this grand purpose was contingent, however, upon loyalty to one's own national language and traditions.

While home missionary activities and religious revivals accompanied the Grundtvigian movement, it was probably the folk high schools that made the strongest impact upon Denmark, and to a considerable extent upon Norway. Disdaining rote learning, the folk schools stressed vital Christianity, provided a sense of history, inculcated an appreciation of literature, and cemented a feeling of oneness through the method of group singing.

In Norway a religious awakening of the 1850s and 1860s is said to have surpassed the Haugean movement in its influence upon society and upon ecclesiastical development. Professor Gisle Johnson of the theological faculty of the University of Christiania stood at its center. His theology is described as Lutheran orthodoxy in modern dress. Overwhelmed in his younger days by the ideas of the Danish philosopher Søren Kierkegaard (1813–1855), he asserted on the one hand a strong Lutheran confession and on the other the liberty of the Christian man. He was opposed to Grundtvigianism, a force which in his opinion might well undermine the confessional tradition. The Johnsonian revival bridged the gap between social classes, bringing together the masses and the people of culture and official status.

Akin to the Grundtvigian movement of the time, in Norway as well as in Denmark, was the Inner Mission movement. The first *Indremission* association in Norway was formed in 1853. Prayer houses were to be instrumental in furthering its purposes, with emphasis upon lay leadership and participation in devotional exercises. A major victory came in the late 1880s when by royal proclamation laymen were permitted to speak in the churches.

To provide further excitement in the Norwegian religious realm there came eventually a wave of positivism, with stress upon cultural progress, religious skepticism, and "higher criticim" of the Bible. The people noticed that many of their heroes were drawn into the new intellectual stream. Among the spokesmen for positivism, whether they were known by that designation or not, were Bjørnstjerne Bjørnson, Henrik Ibsen, the national historian Ernst Sars, the Danish literary critic Georg Brandes, the advocate of a popular *landsmål* Arne Garborg, and the novelist Alexander Kielland.

The spiritual struggle was tied up with the political conflicts of the time. On the liberal side were the Grundtvigians, the low-church folk, the democratic revival groups, and the positivists, a rather strange company. On the conservative wing were arrayed most of the leading churchmen, themselves state officials. The issue was whether authoritarianism should prevail over free thought. Responses were various. On the one hand, a judgment-day mood dominated the 1880s. But a new theology came to the fore in the next decade. The cleavage was never healed. So deep was the division that *Menighetsfakultetet*, or the faculty of the congregations, separate from the university, was formed in 1908. Undoubtedly the proverbial man in the street, or on the farm, underwent inner turmoil as he witnessed Haugeans clashing with the state clergy, and scriptural theologians debating with Grundtvigians and "higher critics."

An aspect of religious life of direct concern to a small minority of Norwegian folk was the success of non-Lutheran activity. The line of descent is difficult to trace. It is highly probable, however, that the pietism of the Haugeans and others contributed toward, or reflected, a general yearning for personal salvation and sanctification. This desire was shown in the testimony of Norwegian sailors who, as prisoners of the British during the Napoleonic wars, were won to Quakerism by English missionaries who visited the prison ships. Seafaring Norsemen suffered at British hands in that instance because of the Danish, or Dano-Norwegian, alliance with the great Corsican. Upon their release at the close of the war they returned, many of them to Stavanger and its hinterland.

A second non-Lutheran activity was the Mormon mission, which encouraged and assisted converts in emigrating to Utah, the Mormon sanctuary. With proselyting already begun in Denmark, a Danish elder, Hans F. Petersen, entered Norway in 1851. Jailings and finings in various places testify to formidable official resistance to an unorthodox gospel which, by decision of the Supreme Court in 1853, was declared to be non-Christian and hence beyond the pale of the law's protection.[17]

Limited Mormon success must not be interpreted as complete failure. Over a long span of years numerous converts chose to flee to Zion, or Utah. Among the more influential missionaries in the early stages was Canute Peterson, who had been won over by the Saints in Illinois in 1842. He served briefly in the 1850s and again in the 1870s, the latter period as president of the entire Scandinavian mission, headquartered in Copenhagen. It is estimated that the total membership in Scandinavia in 1853 was 1,331. Of this number only 88 were Norwegians. The majority were Danes, 1,133 in all. As far as the half-century from 1850 to 1900 is concerned, an American scholar estimates a total of 22,653 Scandinavian Mormon emigrants, not including some 8,000 children under eight years of age. Danes led with 12,620, Swedes ranked second with 7,477, and Norwegians trailed with 2,556.[18]

A significant dissenter endeavor commenced with the coming of Methodism to Østfold, the southeastern section of Norway. There one Ole Peter Petersen, a sailor who enjoyed an intimate relationship with Olof Hedström, a Swedish Methodist clergyman who, ministering to Scandinavian seamen in the Bethelship Mission in New York harbor, established the first Methodist congregation in 1856 in Sarpsborg, near his birthplace, Fredrikstad. Among the first Methodist converts to withdraw from the state church was Andrew Haagensen who, with eleven others, gained the approval of the Church Department in Christiania to organize the Sarpsborg flock. So the dissenter law of 1845 worked to the advantage of the Methodists, if not the Mormons. Haagensen later became a prominent pastor and editor in the Norwegian-Danish Conference of the Methodist Episcopal Church in the United States. Petersen, on the other hand, rounded out a lifetime of service as pastor in Chicago, Brooklyn, and Milwaukee, where he died in 1901.[19]

Methodism, numerically, made modest yet somewhat impressive progress in Norway. By 1895 the Norway Conference, organized in 1876, claimed 4,736 members and over 3,000 probationers and "adherents," an indication that many attended Methodist services but retained their membership, for practical reasons, in the Lutheran establishment. Fifty-seven Sunday schools accommodated 5,728 pupils.[20] In contrast with the almost universal membership in the established church, Methodists and other dissenters were weak in numbers. Yet they joined with the Inner Mission, the Haugeans, and the Grundt-vigians to help modify rigid formalism and to give impetus to religious education for children through the medium of the Sunday school, an institution which was quickly adopted by the Lutheran congregations themselves.

With reference to reform, the name of Frederikke Nielsen, onetime nationally famous actress, comes to mind. As one who turned Methodist, she lectured before large audiences in Norway and the United States. In America alone she appeared in some 300 communities in twenty different states. Together with her countrywoman Aasta Hansteen, of women's rights fame, she contributed notably before her death in 1912 to Norwegian sentiment favoring woman suffrage. Concerning religious education in its broader sense, another woman of distinction, Elevine Heede, brought inspiration to Methodists and others in Norway through not only her original compositions but also translations of no less than 200 hymns then being sung by American Methodists. After 1874 she taught English in the Methodist theological school in Christiania. Her accomplishments brought an additional measure of American influence to bear upon Norwegian society as a whole.[21]

Vast numbers of Norwegians, more restless in some years than others, looked longingly to the New World. If this uneasiness applied to those of the Lutheran faith, it characterized non-Lutherans even more. The well-informed citizen could hardly fail to observe that Quaker families boarded the slooper *Restauration* (Restoration) at Stavanger in 1825, bound for America. It was clear also that Mormon believers were leaving regularly for the American Zion. Methodists, too, would constitute a part, however small, of Norway's emigrants. Naturally, the advent of religious toleration would reduce the flow of emigrants on purely religious grounds.

The changing character of Norwegian emigration has been cited. Relatively more young folk left the homeland as time went on. Interior districts lost heavily in man power. By 1915 a total of

754,500 had gone overseas since 1836. In the same period 137,500 entered Norway. The net loss in less than a century had been 617,000.[22]

Like the United States, Norway experienced a revival in industry, beginning about 1860. Lumbering became more specialized, with new paper and cellulose products. Processing and packing of fish improved. Shipping and railroad enterprises were revolutionized. Hydroelectric power replaced coal, of which the country had little. Farm prices rose, as did wages. Yet Norwegian youth continued to be enamored of economic opportunities abroad. It may well be, as Ingrid Semmingsen believes, that the newly created economic and social structures set people into motion, and that breakup became the watchword of the day.[23]

Popular restlessness is also dramatized in the struggle of Norway for complete separation from Sweden. The dual monarchy of 1814 came to an end in 1905. There is no conclusive evidence, however, that Norway's political yearnings in the decade or so prior to separation sparked an increase in emigration. It appears that the growing tension between the two Scandinavian states and the ultimate break in their partnership had no appreciable effect upon personal decisions, whether to remain at home or to strike out for America.

As the year 1905 approached there were new heroes. In the 1890s the arctic explorer Fridtjof Nansen (1861–1930) and the Bergen shipping magnate Christian Michelsen (1857–1925) replaced Sverdrup and Jaabæk, the activists of a former day. Bjørnson enjoyed considerable popularity, despite some tarnishing of his image. His outspoken ridicule of supernatural beliefs may have endeared him to those in intellectual circles but not to all of the common citizens of the parishes. Some wondered, too, whether his peace-mindedness might make him complacent as the day of political cleavage from the eastern Scandinavian neighbor came. Indicative of his vacillation is the fact that at one time he favored a republican constitution for Norway. In the autumn of 1905 he switched to preference for the monarchical structure.

The Scandinavian crisis brought prompt and sympathetic response from America, both from Norwegian immigrants and from native Americans. Bonds between relatives and friends on both sides of the water were strengthened. When news arrived of the unilateral termination of the Union on June 7 by the Parliament of Norway, a Chicago mass meeting of 5,000 Norwegian-Americans assured Prime Minister Christian Michelsen by telegram of their approval. Americans of Norwegian ancestry, the message read, were following the destinies of their fatherland with constant sympathy and solicitude. Changes in the government of Norway had been effected in "a dignified and deliberate manner," winning the respect of all mankind.

Reinforcing the felicitations were the words of editor Nicolai Grevstad of the Chicago journal, *Skandinaven*. Before a banquet audience in that city he emphasized that the interests of the Scandinavian countries would best be served by Norway's gaining the *de facto* freedom which constitutionally had been hers.[24]

Representative American periodicals expressed agreement with the Norwegian position. They generally saw the crisis through Norwegian eyes, in part because Norwegian sources of information predominated over Swedish. *The North American Review* pointed out that on May 23 the Norwegian Parliament unanimously endorsed a bill to provide for separate Norwegian consuls in foreign ports. King Oscar II's rejection of the measure induced the Norwegian ministers to resign. The king refused to accept their resignations. An *impasse* had been reached. The June 7 announcement of separation followed. The royal power ceased to be operative in Norway. *The Independent* published Bjørnson's explanation and quoted him as saying, "From the moment when, in 1821, we abolished all titles of nobility, down to 1884, when we rejected the absolute power of the king, the governing classes of Sweden have tried to exert an uninvited influence in our nation." Bjørnson viewed the dissolution as a happy outcome for both Sweden and Norway. William Dean Howells of *Harper's Monthly* stated that, relative to the consular issue, Norway owned a merchant marine larger than that of France and should be entitled to her own representation in the ports of the world. Lyman Abbott of *The Outlook*, known to be an intimate friend of President Theodore Roosevelt, for whom he may have been a mouthpiece, suggested that the real reason for the separation was not legalistic. It lay, rather, in the essentially democratic framework of Norwegian society. Howells echoed Abbott's sentiments.[25]

For Norway a necessary corollary to the separation question was the choice of a form of government. Of the American commentators in the monarchy-versus-republic debate, Theodore Stanton of *The Independent* comprehended the issue better than most. As a Paris correspondent who enjoyed the acquaintance of Norwegian republican advocates residing there, he played a large part in aiding them during the eventful summer of 1905. But in the end Stanton faced realities. Norway would do best to remain a monarchy and to insure good relations with Great Britain, possibly as a protective measure against Russia. It was gratifying to know, he said, that Fridtjof Nansen was serving in London as Norway's confidential agent. (Nansen was shortly to become Norway's first minister to Britain.) Stanton spoke of "the ingrained democratic and republican character of the Norwegian people." He contended that the "perversion of the real sentiment of Norway," a republican sentiment no less, could have been prevented if the French and American republics had given timely support. It is noteworthy that American correspondents and editors heavily favored an independent Norway, with or without royalty. Nothing in the American response could be interpreted as detrimental to cordial Norwegian-American relations and to a continued flow of emigrants across the Atlantic.[26]

The press in Norway reacted in its own way to the impending changes in the Scandinavian world. With unconcealed preference it discoursed on the monarchical framework of government. Often comments from American sources accompanied the editorials. Not until October 30, well after the June 7 resolution in Christiania, did the United States government indicate that diplomatic relations would be established. Norwegian newsmen seldom, if ever, denounced Uncle Sam for delaying official recognition of their new state. Few, if any, suggested that the great republic overseas owed anything to old Norway. Rather, Norwegian spokesmen expressed the gratitude of their country for all good will shown by Americans and by the sons and daughters now residing under the Stars and Stripes.

On August 13, 1905, Norwegian men confirmed the decision for separation by an overwhelming vote, 368,208 for and only

184 against. On November 12 and 13 they again went to the polls, not specifically to determine whether monarchy should prevail but to decide whether Prince Carl of Denmark should ascend the throne of Norway. The verdict favored Carl, who proceeded to reign as Haakon VII. Norwegians had chosen freely and, at the same time, had preserved their respect for the republican experiment being carried on in the United States.

In the crisis of 1905 it was first generally realized that Norwegian-Americans constituted a tremendous reservoir of good will for the fatherland. In Trondheim, in the cathedral of which the coronation ceremony would take place in 1906, a prominent journal appealed for appreciation of Norwegians abroad who had encouraged Norway and for the creation of an organization that would bind Norsemen throughout the world more closely. Many of Norwegian ancestry in America traveled to Trondheim for the crowning of Haakon VII. The founding of *Nordmanns-Forbundet* (The League of Norwegians) in 1907 symbolized their loyalty to the spirit of Norway. By 1914 the organization claimed 42,000 members from both sides of the ocean and from distant places on the globe.[27]

The explanation for the mass exodus from the soil to the cities and to America's prairies is not obscure. In the nineteenth century land titles resided in heads of families, under a system called *odelsret* (alodial right). Upon the owner's death there was no subdivision of the land. The eldest son usually inherited the property, leaving younger sons without the means of subsistence. Another disadvantaged class were the *husmenn* (cotters), or smallholders, who paid rent to the farmer in work rather than in money or in kind. In the course of time there was less demand for their services and more need for land. In 1903 with governmental approval a special bank was established for cotters, enabling them to buy farms. But most of the cotters had already departed the country. Whereas in 1845 they constituted 26 percent of the population, in 1920 all but 3 percent had taken flight to the cities or to America. A sizable fraction of the *bønder* (peasant landowners) had done likewise.

During a Liberal ministry in Norway, from 1908 and well into World War I, emigration subsided slightly. However, not until the American quota system took effect in 1921 and 1924 was there a sharp decline. Meanwhile, in 1908 Norwegian commercial and industrial interests attempted to slow down the stream of emigration through an internal colonization scheme supported by *Selskabet til Emigrationens Indskrænkning* (The Society for the Limitation of Emigration), following a Swedish pattern of a year or two earlier. This belated provision for land proved to be of minor consequence.[28]

Many factors and forces had persuaded the people of Norway to transport themselves and possessions, and eventually their citizenship, to the United States. Apart from mainly economic considerations, a mysterious desire for movement characterized the nineteenth century in the Northern lands. The Treaty of Kiel, with its Swedish-Danish determination of Norway's future, produced a feeling of inferiority on the part of a people who seemed to have been manipulated like pawns in an international chess game. The rise of national leaders among poets and peasants spread a romantic veil over the country. Conversely, the shortcomings of romanticism, or the snail-like progress toward national fulfillment, brought disappointment to the less patient elements in Norwegian society. Favorable reports from America were bound to accentuate the sensitivities of an already uneasy nation, short on agricultural soil and on industrial opportunity, especially by American standards. The push of Norway and the pull of America worked together at that point. To many who departed their native shores, universal manhood suffrage and prospects for women's rights in the New World were enticing. Others appreciated the absence of an official class in America. Still others, whose loyalty to the Lutheran Church was somewhat strained, preferred to practice their faith under less restrictive conditions. For religious nonconformists the appeal of the United States was even stronger. Finally, and probably foremost, America letters from the forerunners created distinct personal ties with family and friends who, like as not, would succumb to the beckonings of their trusted brothers, sisters, and onetime neighbors now living abroad.

CHAPTER 2

The Crossing and the Reception

AN IMMIGRANT LEAVETAKING HAD ITS NOSTALGIC SIDE, AS IN this farewell song:

> Farewell, valley that I cherish,
> Farewell, church and trees and home,
> Farewell parson, farewell parish,
> Farewell kith and kin, my own,
> Lovely gardens, walks of beauty,—
> Would to God this were undone!—
> Home, you stay me in my duty,
> Calling, "Leave me not, my son!"

For those who recently entered upon pioneer life there might be words less kind, yet not completely lacking in gratitude:[1]

> Blessed land, farewell forever,
> Stern thy ways, severe thy hand,
> Bread denied to fair endeavor,
> Still I honor Motherland.
> All things vanish—care and sorrow
> Pass, their marks engraved on me,
> Yet my soul fronts each tomorrow
> Glad, refreshed with thought of thee.

The Atlantic voyage of the nineteenth century has been the theme of countless narratives by those who shared its joys and its trials. Scholars too have given it consideration, as a prelude to the immigrant experience. It was in midpassage that the emigrant turned immigrant, about to enter his adopted country and to begin a new life. The old country never faded completely into the past, but the immigrant envisioned the new from the

[24]

very inception of his America dream. Many eventful years lay ahead, beyond the voyage and the landing on an unfamiliar and distant shore. No small part of the experience was the reception at the port of entry. Often treated like a number rather than as a person, the stranger was not likely to recall the occasion with unmingled pleasure. His letters and diaries are, in most instances, ominously silent on the Castle Garden or Ellis Island episode terminating the long journey. But there is no doubt that private agencies and governmental authorities, including the State of New York and the United States, attempted to provide for the immigrants' needs, as well as to sift out the undesirables.

With emphasis upon commercial gain, some sailing-vessel captains and shipmasters paid little heed to the wishes or comforts of passengers, except insofar as it suited the owners to compete successfully with other lines or vessels. Fares were of necessity kept within reason, not only because of competition but because westbound freight was generally light. There was ample space for human cargo. Raw materials, such as timber, cotton, and tobacco, made up the bulk of the eastbound Atlantic traffic. Between 1815 and 1846, in the prosperity following the Napoleonic wars, Liverpool-to-New York fares dropped from twelve English pounds to only three. But passenger accommodations, especially in the steerage, were Spartan.[2]

Conditions on British packets were miserable at times. Fourteen Norwegian emigrants of 1853 framed a joint letter to *Morgenbladet* of Christiania complaining of abuses of various kinds. Teeth were knocked out or bruises and broken bones were inflicted by brutal sailors whose orders, given in English, were not understood by the passengers from the North. Food was thrown to the half-starved voyagers who fought for it in animal fashion. Bunks were lice-ridden. Threats of assault were made against the women. "If we were to tell all the bloody events we saw," they wrote, "it would fill several volumes."[3]

For many passengers bound for the new land, however, the ocean experience was not a major ordeal but a thrilling adventure. Ships became more seaworthy and better manned as the nineteenth century wore on. Whether through European shrewdness or Yankee ingenuity, the mid-century sea odyssey became both safer and speedier. As a result of the benefits acquired through long navigational experience, seamen improved their knowledge and their skills. Packet vessels and clipper ships, more streamlined in construction, carried mail and light freight and followed more regular schedules. Advantage was taken of new lighthouses and buoys. A coast guard was developing. The factor of age among the passengers also contributed toward a low mortality rate. Migrants were usually in their best years physically, able to withstand the rigors of transplantation from one continent to another. Despite occasional disastrous voyages of Irish travelers and others, deaths in the 1840s and 1850s declined to about one-half of one percent of the people on board.[4]

One explanation for the rapid increase in emigration is the improvement in marine transportation. The steamer of 1880 appealed more strongly than the sailing vessel of 1840 to those bent upon crossing the North Atlantic. If it be true that, as late as 1863, sailing ships carried 55 percent of all European immigrants, the percentage was equally high for Norwegian passengers, and even higher for the North Sea traffic. Not until the inauguration of travel service by the Danish-owned Thingvalla Line (1879), the Scandinavian-American Line (1902), and the Norwegian-America Line (1910) did Scandinavians have access to steamer transportation from Copenhagen or Christiania. Before that, for the ocean voyage full use was made of the British lines—the Inman, the Cunard, the White Star, and the Allan. The British Wilson Line carried Norwegian passengers across the North Sea to Hull, from which port the travelers proceeded by rail westward to Liverpool, the principal British port of embarkation for America-bound steamers. Until well toward the close of the century an alternative to the North Sea crossing was a Danish or Norwegian brig.

As a center for emigrant activity few European ports could match Liverpool. There the steamship companies provided overnight lodging for their humble clients. At times both lodging houses and ships were booked to capacity, and many weary and anxious sojourners roamed the streets. But at last the ship was boarded, the anchor lifted, and the passengers assigned to their respective duties, whether for emergencies or for routine chores. When the first meal was in preparation and the steamer was well under way, the discomforts and anxieties of leavetaking from the shores of Britain were momentarily forgotten. By evening the tired Atlantic travelers were ready to occupy the narrow sleeping quarters, shelf-like berths six feet long, two feet wide, and two and one-half feet high. On the British and Scandinavian sides the laws pertaining to passenger limitations were more lenient than on the American side. The United States law of 1819 allowed no more than two passengers for each five tons of vessel. *Restauration* of 1825 ran afoul of this provision and was spared a heavy fine by the personal intervention of President John Quincy Adams. To some travelers the sea was unkind, the time unbearably long, and the food deplorable, becoming less palatable with every circuit of the sun. The average length of time for a sailing vessel on the Liverpool–New York route was 44 days, reduced sharply by early steamers to thirteen days. But some trips were longer and some shorter.

Personal experiences of the immigrants varied as much as the weather itself. In 1840 a Norwegian bark, the *Emilie*, sailed from Drammen, a port on an arm of the Christianiafjord south of the capital city. Its destination was New York via Göteborg (Gothenburg), Sweden. The inevitable storms were encountered, but Captain Thomas Anchersen was more solicitous than most men of his rank for the welfare of his charges. Before leaving Drammen he had supplied himself with remedies for the most common diseases. He stopped in the English Channel and also on the Newfoundland Banks in order that passengers, satiated with dried and salted food, might fish for fresh cod. He arranged for prayers and devotional singing on deck every evening. When the ship hove in to New York he accompanied his people up the Hudson and on the Erie Canal as far as Schenectady, not neglecting to entertain the entire company with a sumptuous dinner in Albany.[5]

Knud Langeland, who in 1847 founded *Nordlyset* (The Northern Light), the first exclusively Norwegian newspaper in the United States, sailed from Bergen on Norway's west coast in 1843. After a restless wait of two weeks, with food supplies running low, the 52 passengers boarded the brig and enjoyed pleasant sailing for a few days, thanks to the helpful east wind. Most of the emigrants had sufficient money, many of them as much as $1,000, says Langeland, and the assurance through letters of meeting relatives and friends in America. Adverse winds, storm, and sickness took their toll eventually. There were several burials at sea, with the customary singing of a hymn before each body, wrapped in sailcloth, was allowed to glide off into the deep.

At last, within 200 miles of New York, an American pilot came aboard, the signal for much hustling about and, like as not, for full sail ahead. In preparation for quarantine the ship anchored off the marine hospital on Staten Island. Seven or eight passengers were removed. Langeland, though not ill himself, remained at the hospital for several days as an interpreter, since none of the patients could speak or understand English. On board the vessel with Langeland was Even Heg, an early settler in Muskego, about twenty miles west of Milwaukee. In future years many a new arrival would be the guest of the Hegs while a search was made for a permanent home. Even Heg was to be the father of Hans Christian Heg, subsequently colonel of the nearly all-Norwegian Fifteenth Wisconsin Regiment in the Civil War.[6]

In the interests of comfort and safety United States authorities dropped the two-for-five ratio in 1847 and declared a minimum deck area of fourteen square feet for each passenger and a height of six and one-half feet between decks. Captains and owners thereupon frequently elected to put in at Quebec in Canada, where regulations governing passenger accommodations were less stringent. Coincidentally, the Quebec destination benefited passengers as well. Fares were cheaper on Canada-bound vessels, since captains were surer of returning, eastbound, with full cargoes of lumber.

Nevertheless, the American act of 1847 proved helpful to the immigrants. Under the more commodious conditions provided by this particular legislation a young Lutheran pastor and his wife, Vilhelm and Elisabeth Koren, bound for the Koshkonong settlement in Wisconsin, boarded the German packet *Rhein* at Hamburg in 1853. They had come from Norway and had spent a week as house guests of the Swedish-Norwegian consul in Hamburg. There was much that smacked of elegance on their Atlantic trip. The detailed diary of Elisabeth Koren, who was well educated, breathes refinement and good taste. Not many would read Dickens while others retreated to their berths below for relief from seasickness and from the violent jerking and pitching of the ship. Eleven passengers died before the English Channel was cleared. The captain felt obliged to put in at Portsmouth, where a doctor came aboard. For several days there were opportunities for those in good health to go ashore and enjoy mingling with the English people and seeing their wares. Once in motion again, this female passenger of sturdy stomach was able to relish soup brought by the steward, balance the tureen while her companions helped themselves, spear roast chicken that seemed to be alive on a plate, and finish the meal off with gravy, peas, beets, and bread pudding. She and her clergyman husband occupied a first-class stateroom, set apart from the thirty or so second-class and about 200 steerage passengers.

After slow headway, the American coastline finally came into view. New York officials cared for the sick, fumigated the vessel, but allowed some like the Korens to come and go from ship to shore. From New York the way led into Iowa, where the Korens were to assume leadership in the activities of the pioneer church among Norwegian immigrants for many years.[7]

Often the destination of immigrant vessels was Quebec rather than New York. Much discomfort and embarrassment were thereby avoided, but there might be hardship on the journey into the interior, from Quebec to the Great Lakes and the upper Middle West. The future historian Laurence M. Larson departed from Norway in 1870, when he was not quite two years of age. Gleaning the details of the voyage and the arrival from older members of the family group, he describes a 49-day Atlantic passage by sail. With storm and overcrowding, the experience was distressing enough. More was to follow before the Iowa destination was reached. At Grand Haven, Michigan, (possibly Ludington, he says) they boarded a cargo vessel bound for Milwaukee. The ship had recently discharged a load of cattle and had not been cleaned. A thunderstorm drove the passengers below on a warm summer night. The filth and stench were almost unbearable.[8]

While the federal government continued to enact legislation in the 1850s calling for proper ventilation on board ship and to set higher standards for personal cleanliness and food preparation, state authorities and civic leaders in New York City became more disturbed over abuses perpetrated against the newcomers and more sensitive to their needs. To supplement the unofficial assistance of organizations like New York's German Society (1784) and Irish Society (1844), as well as the Scandinavian Society (1844), the state legislature adopted a measure creating a Board of Commissioners of Emigration (rather than immigration) on May 5, 1847. Six of its ten members were to be appointed by the state governor. The other four were ex officio: the mayors of New York and Brooklyn and the presidents of the German and Irish societies.

Uppermost in the minds of the commissioners was the securing of a permanent landing depot and receiving station. In the interval from 1847 to 1855 there was much opposition when it became known that the board had their eyes on Castle Garden. The site of federal Fort Clinton until 1807, the island was ceded in 1822 to New York City. Residents of the great metropolis complained that the Battery, on the southern edge of Manhattan, would become a haven for penniless and shiftless derelicts and that property values would fall. Runners charged that their "legitimate" business would suffer. The *New York Daily Times* denounced the establishment of an immigrant depot at the proposed site as a desecration of a cultural center whose main hall had witnessed many memorable lectures and concerts. But after several years of heated discussion the state legislature designated Castle Garden as the official reception center.[9]

The establishment of Castle Garden, located on a small island a few feet off the south shore of Manhattan, was expected to benefit immigrants, shippers, captains, and the New York community as a whole. It was the official receiving and processing center for the State of New York. Sickness and distress, it was hoped, would be mitigated. Fewer people would become public charges. Determination of financial status and ultimate destination of the immigrant would be facilitated. The bands of outlaws that had preyed upon the unsuspecting and uninformed arrivals would tend to disintegrate but not enough, as it turned out, to prevent occasional physical attacks upon immigrants by runners still in the employ of booking agents and boardinghouse owners.

Meanwhile, the services of the Garden did expand into twelve useful areas ranging from the boarding, landing, and registering departments to railroad service, city baggage delivery, personal letter writing, money exchange and, in 1867, a labor exchange. The labor unit, for lack of funds, was discontinued after eight years. More efficient service was provided by the emigrant societies, for incoming Germans and Irish particularly.[10]

The scourge of mistreatment of the future citizens of America never abated completely. In 1871 Isador Kjellberg, a Swedish journalist, initiated a campaign against runners, a class of *homo sapiens* supposedly exterminated by the law. Mass meetings of Scandinavian-Americans considered the problem. Conditions worsened by 1887, partly because of fluctuations in the labor market and in part because of space limitations at Castle Garden when the volume of immigration soared. President Grover Cleveland's administration began an investigation.

In time Castle Garden, confined to its mere three acres, was found to be unsuitable for the large volume of immigration. State regulation was also seen to be inadequate, at least at New York. An immigration act of 1891 inaugurated an era of federal regulation. Already a joint congressional committee had approved Ellis Island, a mile south of Manhattan Island, as the new receiving center. Castle Garden was converted into a municipal aquarium in 1896 and was established as Castle Clinton National Monument in 1950, reverting to its earlier name of Fort Clinton. The original fort was partially razed in 1941.

Prior to the selection of Ellis Island for immigrant processing the island had been but a small dot in New York Bay. As long ago as 1808 the United States had purchased it from New York State, which in turn had received it from one Samuel Ellis. It was first used as a fort, then as a powder arsenal. Dumpings from the ballast of ships added perceptibly to the acreage. Once an area of only 3.3 acres, the soils of many nations enlarged it to 21 acres. From 1892 to 1943 about 90 percent of the immigrants entered at that station. In 1943 the immigration facilities were transferred to Manhattan, reducing the role of Ellis Island to a detention station for aliens and deportees, until 1954.

One young Norseman of twenty-one recalls his Ellis Island experience as degrading. Paul Knaplund, later an eminent his-

torian, departed from his far northern home near the Lofoten
fisheries in 1906. On the Cunard Line's *Caronia* he came to New
York. He had already encountered much excitement. At Trondheim, where the coastal steamer docked, "a band of agents representing the various trans-Atlantic steamship companies pounced
on the small flock of emigrants." The Wilson Line gave him a
rough North Sea voyage to Hull. In Liverpool the omnipresent
"hawkers, money-changers, and panderers" confronted him. And
at Ellis Island he was tricked into buying an unwanted package
of food. But the crowning insult, which he mentions twice, was
the disdainful glance of a Negro charwoman as she surveyed
the motley immigrant horde.[11]

In his charming little autobiography Fiorello La Guardia,
the late mayor of New York, presents one of the few firsthand
accounts of an Ellis Island official. He served as an interpreter
there for three years while he attended law school. Immigration
laws were strictly enforced, he says, in the period 1907–1910.
New arrivals, the majority from Southern and Eastern Europe,
were often found to be physically unfit. Heartrending scenes
occurred frequently. Families or individual members were compelled to return to their homeland until 1919, when Uncle Sam
required that physical examinations should be given at European
ports of embarkation. In spite of some irregularities by immigration center personnel and some corruption by the police, La
Guardia felt that most of the Ellis Island staff were reliable and
considerate. At a time when about 5,000 immigrants were pro-
cessed daily, it seems not surprising that he saw many cases of
drunkenness and was aware of prostitution as a way of life, as
well as of traffic in white slavery.[12]

Mayor La Guardia makes no specific reference to Scandinavian immigrants, nor does Edward Corsi, whose chronicle of
Ellis Island covers more than his years of service there. From
1931 to 1934 Corsi held the office of Commissioner of Immigration and Naturalization for the New York District. With vivid
memories of his own reception there in 1907 as an Italian boy
of ten, he proceeded from tenement living on New York's East
Side to earn a degree in law and an appointment as immigration
commissioner by President Herbert Hoover.

Corsi's sympathy for the oppressed and the underprivileged

is clear. His father, once an editor of a liberal newspaper in southern Italy, was forced into political exile by the Italian conservatives. So popular was he that, without campaigning, he was elected to Parliament from Tuscany. He died while about to deliver his acceptance speech. In the spirit of his father, Edward Corsi did much to make procedures at Ellis Island more flexible. He emphasized the intent of the law rather than the narrow literal interpretation. As one who had traveled in the company of 1,600 Italians and had shared with them the awe-inspiring sights of the famous statue in the harbor and of the towering skyscrapers of the big city, he found it natural to look upon the alien as a human being.[13]

Corsi had no successor as Commissioner at Ellis Island. The quota system of 1924 had drastically reduced the number of aliens entering the United States. Although favored by the law, Scandinavians and other Northern and Western Europeans failed to respond as they had in former years. Southern and Eastern Europeans were practically excluded, as were Asiatics and Africans.

Another class of immigrant needs to be mentioned. The Norwegian seaman who decided to desert his vessel in an American port often took up residence in New York or elsewhere. He knew that Yankee shipowners paid higher wages than a Scandinavian master could afford. It is estimated that in 1887 about 25 percent of the crewmen on long-distance American merchant vessels were of Scandinavian descent, mainly Norwegian, and that the percentage was even higher in the coastal trade. The captain of the *Restauration* had set the precedent, though not for desertion, when he chose to sell his ship and to enter the American merchant marine service.[14]

The seaman who left ship in New York, whether as deserter or not, was fortunate if he could locate an agency where his needs could be met. Some were agencies of the church, Lutheran and otherwise. As early as 1845, ten years before the opening of Castle Garden, the Methodist Episcopal Church appointed Swedish-born Olof G. Hedström to the chaplaincy of the Bethel Ship *John Wesley* in New York harbor. The labors of Hedström and his associates as missionaries, advisers, and friends to the nautical sons of Scandinavia, for the most part Norwegian, exceeded in scope the work of the Scandinavian Society of 1844. Hedström declared that some 1,200 Scandinavian seamen visited the port of New York during the year 1850 and that 4,000 emigrants had arrived from the Scandinavian countries. With the aid of his assistants he regularly boarded the merchant vessels and preached and dispensed Bibles and other religious literature. On occasion he preached aboard four vessels in a single day. Many listeners, among them some who would remain in America, came ashore and attended his meetings. Hedström's name became a byword in Scandinavian homes on both sides of the ocean. He died in 1877 at the age of 74.[15]

In 1864 Lutherans in Norway founded the Norwegian Seamen's Mission; its first station was established in London and other stations were added over the years in the principal ports of the world. It was the heyday of the sailing vessel and of the Norwegian merchant marine. The fleet had expanded steadily in the 1850s. By 1860 only Great Britain, the United States, France, and Italy had fleets larger than Norway's. During the next twenty years Norway moved into third place, ahead of France, Italy, and the rising German empire. The advent of steam lowered Norway's ranking, but the work of the seamen's mission continued, among those who gave up the life of the sea as well as among those who remained.[16]

In the philosophical words of Gunnar Christie Wasberg, the historian of the Norwegian Seamen's Mission, one is overwhelmed by a feeling of timelessness when one encounters the sea:

The inexorable rhythm, the constant switch from crisis to idyll, witness to that which has been and to that which will be. The sea was before man and will perhaps be after him. The sea rolls on. The thought of only the thin deck between man and the powers of the sea fascinated our forefathers and conjured up for them deep thoughts. The sea is ever unchanging in spite of man's conquest of other forces of nature.

Equally poetic are the lines of the Dane Holger Drachmann as he depicts in *Fresh Breeze* the vicissitudes of venturesome travelers on the turbulent waters:[17]

All night long we've been a-rolling,
To the rocking sea no check.
Would we stood on four controlling
Balance like our cat on deck.

Sunbeams laugh and clouds are weeping,
Showers beat the ocean's flanks,
While *Thingvalla*, onward sweeping,
Nears New Foundland's foggy banks.

Fog, our dreaded foe's before us,
But our friend, the chief, guards o'er us.
Luck be with him on the main,
Out and home and out again!

But the day is near at hand now
When our merry trip is done;
Cast for roads unknown we land now
And another trip's begun.

Ocean-wells, our wishes heeding,
Speed us on the flag to hail,
Flag that never is misleading
Tho' some hopeful ones may fail.

"Smallness" shall possess us never!
Freedom over us forever!
Forward by that flag we'll soar!
Homeward—may be nevermore!

For the vast majority of seafarers the Atlantic interlude was never erased from the mind but, with the passing years, it faded into the complex perspective of American life. The voyagers dismissed from their minds the long and stormy trip and saw the green heights of Brooklyn while their ships lay at anchor off Castle Garden or Ellis Island. Untold thousands of restless Norwegians faced hopefully westward with the assurance that their railroad tickets, their baggage, and their persons were safe and intact, thanks to the essential services of the personnel employed at the port of entry. Most of the argonauts from the world of yesterday would realize the hopes for success in fair degree, not without trial and tribulation, but with confidence that abundant patience and constant application of energy would bring the better life that they were seeking.

CHAPTER 3

The Land to Which They Came

IMMIGRANTS ARRIVED IN AMERICA IN VARIOUS STATES OF READINESS to meet the challenges of a new society. For most there was the necessity of learning a new language. People from the English-speaking world had no such problem. They came ready-made, as it were, for participation and leadership in American affairs. But for Norwegians and others the language barrier proved to be formidable. A ballad excerpt of the time puts it aptly:[1]

> The new speech, it was tough to acquire,
> And we often got into a mess.
> When a Yankee your name would inquire,
> You'd solemnly answer him, "Yes."

There were other problems, some of which are examined in the following chapters. For example, how could one learn about the United States, its history, its economic advantages, its schools and churches, its governmental machinery, and the role of politics?

For up-to-date information on religion and politics the pioneer Norwegian press was a distinct asset. Prior to the Civil War a small but influential secular press helped not only to keep readers abreast of goings-on in Norway but also to alert them to the history of the new nation and to the political issues of the day. During the politically charged 1850s Wisconsin newspapers like *Nordlyset* (The Northern Light), *Democraten*, and *Emigranten* provided bipartisan coverage. It should be remembered, however, that the editors were usually more than a step ahead of their subscribers in their political education.

Few of the settlers could wrestle with matters of state and national concern until their immediate problems as pioneers had been solved. Men and women alike were compelled, first of all,

[37]

to adjust to New World conditions. Gro Svendsen, an early settler near Estherville, Iowa, spoke for many women when she wrote to kinfolk in Norway, "Life here is altogether different from life in our mountain valley. One must readjust oneself and learn everything all over again, even to the preparation of food. We are told that the women in America have much leisure time, but I haven't yet met any woman who thought so."[2]

Authorities on American immigrant history estimate, mainly on the strength of census records, that since the first tabulation of 1790 some 36,000,000 to 40,000,000 aliens have entered the United States. The vast majority arrived in the second half of the nineteenth century and the first decade of the twentieth. Of this mass movement the Norwegians were but a small part. The end of the century-long mass migration to America practically coincides with the inauguration of the national origins quota system of the 1920s.

Norwegian immigration figures, however small in comparison with the total for European and other immigrants, are of special concern here. For Norway the estimates of the foreign office in Oslo are adequate for our purpose. Between 1836 and 1928 these are some representative years:[3]

1849	4,000	1893	18,500
1857	7,300	1903	26,800
1861	8,500	1910	18,800
1866	15,300	1923	18,800
1869	18,000	1927	12,600
1882	28,500	1928	8,000

The total immigration of Norwegians covered by the period 1836–1928 reached approximately 850,000 persons. As in the case of many European countries, the peak year was 1882.

The immigrant was more than a number. He absorbed, sometimes inadvertently, the elements of American history. He learned that in the eighteenth century England had defeated France in the struggle for North America. Then the English colonies won their freedom, making a reality of the Declaration of Independence. Following the War of Independence, new incentive was given to all sorts of activity, not the least significant of which was the extension of the cotton planters' domain westward. With it, unfortunately, came further development of the system of black slavery.

The expansion-minded War Hawks of 1812 failed in their avowed intention to seize Canada from England and Florida from Spain, but territories and states were added rapidly to the original Union. The fact that the newer political units in the West were not the creators but the creatures of the national government enhanced the prestige and augmented the power of the administration in Washington, D. C., far beyond the expectations of the founding fathers.

The Sloopers of 1825 from Stavanger, Norway, and those who followed them in the 1830s thus arrived in a country which was on the move. The *Restauration* passengers, in large part Quaker sympathizers, sought freedom from religious discrimination in their native land. They arrived in New York and proceeded up the Hudson and some distance westward on the newly opened Erie Canal. Indeed, they passed the vessel carrying Governor DeWitt Clinton and his official party from Buffalo on Lake Erie to the mouth of the Hudson, where two barrels of fresh lake water were ceremoniously emptied into the briny waters of the Atlantic. The canal-building mania of the 1830s was in the offing. But canals in general deteriorated as railroads, beginning with the Baltimore and Ohio (1830), stretched farther and farther inland.

Political and territorial changes came rapidly as the human tide moved relentlessly westward. While Canada fell outside the scope of American settlement, ample compensation was found in the admission of Louisiana, Indiana, Illinois, and Mississippi, all by the year 1819. Shortly thereafter the trans-Mississippi area, broadly identical with the Louisiana Purchase of 1803, beckoned both cotton planters and wheat growers. The Missouri Compromise (1820) brought Missouri and Maine into the family of states, one slave and one free, and determined the geographical limits of the slavery system until 1850. Thanks to the discovery of gold and the resultant influx of miners and hangers-on, California entered as a free state in the Compromise of 1850. As a part of the same measure the slave trade was abolished in the District of Columbia, the site of the nation's capital. Slave owners found some satisfaction in the enactment of a new fugitive-slave law calling for stricter enforcement. The State of Wisconsin, already the home of many Norwegians, disregarded the new law. Instead of returning escaped slaves with dispatch, Wisconsin offered asylum to those who fled from Southern plantations.

The immigrants from Northern Europe accepted the United States Constitution, the republican framework of government, and the political party system without serious mental reservations. As long as the spirit of democracy had ample room in which to thrive there was seldom any argument. Though not really discontented with monarchy as such, the new Norwegian-Americans accepted a popularly based presidency, with its fixed term of office, and a clear delineation between legislative, executive, and judicial powers. Norwegian menfolk, especially, eagerly sought United States citizenship, through the process of naturalization.

The American Whig party of 1834–1854 was reputed to be nativist, hence not much interested in improving the lot of the alien. Perhaps also its espousal of a strong central government and a United States Bank estranged the party from the new arrivals, who saw in state and local banks a freer flow of currency and a moderate inflationary economy, all to the good of immigrant-debtors who wished to pay off their creditors. In the second quarter of the century the people from the European North usually voted for Democratic candidates, who claimed to be carrying on the tradition of Thomas Jefferson and, later, the spirit of Andrew Jackson, the first genuine Westerner to occupy the White House.

Possibly the very name "Democrat" appealed strongly to the newcomers. And had not the admission of the first Western states, Kentucky and Tennessee, brought universal manhood suffrage, while the Whiggish Eastern states hesitated to apply the principle of equality of all men? A Wisconsin settler summed it up in a fashion when he wrote his son in Norway to the effect that Whigs favored long-term office-holding, while Democrats preferred terms of not more than four years. Whigs demanded a long period of residence, said he, for the privilege of voting. For Democrats a six-month period would suffice. But the

Koshkonong, Wisconsin, father confessed to a divided loyalty. "Although I am a Democrat in thought," he explained, "I favor many of the Whig principles."[4]

In the political perspective of midwestern Norwegians the new Republican party soon had two notable accomplishments to its credit. First, the free-soil element of the organization introduced proposals for confining the practice of slavery to its existing limits, with hopes of its eventual disappearance. Related to free-soil aims was encouragement of immigration of Europeans, who would augment substantially the free population of America. Second, the Republican leadership, not satisfied with the price of $1.25 an acre for government land, advocated free homesteads of 160 acres each for genuine settlers, whether of American or European birth. A Republican Congress passed the desired Homestead Act in 1862. The free-soil aspect of the Republican program spared the party the stigma of nativism. Many Americans of Scandinavian blood shifted their allegiance from the Democrats to the Republicans after 1854.

Habit and custom played their parts in determining the extent of immigrant participation in politics. Knud Langeland of *Nordlyset* once remarked concerning his weekly publication, "As a political paper it had come too soon. The first immigrant population was composed of people from rural communities who by and large were not accustomed to reading anything but their religious books. Many of them even considered it a sin to read political papers."[5]

Adam Løvenskjold, Swedish-Norwegian consul general, agreed with Langeland that the Norwegian potential for politics was quite negligible. In commenting upon his travels among 7,500 of his former countrymen living in Wisconsin in 1847, he stated that their ignorance reached such proportions that other national groups called them "Norwegian Indians." But the emissary from Scandinavia might well have been voicing the common displeasure of his government over the heavy emigration of promising young folk. By way of contrast, the judgment of Laurence M. Larson, a Norwegian-born historian in America, merits consideration. "The Norseman is by nature a politician," declared Larson. "In the gray dawn of Northern history he emerges as a sovereign freeman with a full share in the management of local concerns. His descendants came to the West with a training which has not been allowed to grow stale."[6]

There is probably no paradox in these seemingly conflicting points of view, each of which contains more than a grain of truth. However, in view of the rather impressive degree of political activity of Norwegian-Americans within but a few years after the negative observations of the late 1840s, Larson's reference to a tradition of participation in government is more revealing of the forthcoming role of the immigrants in American life.

Sectional issues pivoting on slavery loomed large at mid-century. Only temporarily did the Compromise of 1850 settle the outstanding questions of the contending proslavery and antislavery forces. The decade leading up to the war for Southern independence was characterized by a series of emotion-laden crises. Among other things, nativism raised its head in the guise of the Supreme Order of the Star-Spangled Banner and in its political counterpart, the Know-Nothing faction.

With anti-foreign organizations frowning upon the Irish and the Germans, whether because of their Catholicism, their unbroken loyalty to their European homelands, or their personal habits and customs, the lines were drawn between desirable and undesirable aliens in the upper Mississippi Valley and elsewhere. Scandinavians, fewer in number in the cities and not very conspicuous in the rural areas, escaped much of the venom of anti-foreignism.

Disturbing events of the 1850s turned the thoughts of all Americans, even the nativists, to more urgent matters. No book succeeded as well as that of Harriet Beecher Stowe's *Uncle Tom's Cabin* in accentuating sectional division. In the South her humanitarian propaganda led many to believe that Northerners were bent upon immediate emancipation of the Negroes, with no compensation whatsoever to slave owners. The people of the North, on the other hand, now envisioned countless Simon Legrees scattered throughout the cotton belt. Fact and fiction became indistinguishable. The mental pictures of both Southerners and Northerners were viciously distorted.

Following the discovery that three United States ministers abroad in European capitals were suggesting, in the so-called

Ostend Manifesto, the purchase or seizure of Cuba by the federal government as a possible slave state came the Kansas-Nebraska Act of 1854. Its provisions for popular sovereignty with reference to slavery extension into the territories reopened the sensitive question. Quickly the new Republican party took its stand for non-extension. From this point on Republicans and Democrats were at odds on the slavery issue. For most immigrants the Republican position was right. The Irish, however, fearful of future competition from freed Negroes in the labor market, continued to support the Democrats. Also some Missouri Synod Lutherans, both German and Scandinavian, justified slavery on biblical grounds and remained in the Democratic camp.

Two developments of 1857 brought consternation, especially to the people of the Northern states. Not only was the nation afflicted by a major panic, but the Supreme Court decision in the Dred Scott case further emphasized a division along slavery and antislavery lines. The panic was of short duration, yet severe enough to deter many potential emigrants from leaving Europe.

Chief Justice Roger B. Taney's announcement of the majority opinion of the court in the case of freedom or slavery for a black man, Dred Scott, confirmed the fears of abolitionists and non-extensionists. Scott, the descendant of generations of slaves, lived with his master in Missouri, a slave state by virtue of the Missouri Compromise of 1820. Together they moved to free territory, and they eventually returned to Missouri. Taney first announced that Scott, as a slave, had no legal right of appeal. Scott's residence in free territory did not make him free. The verdict gave comfort to the proslavery element, who now could anticipate expansion of the plantation system with slave labor into the territories without legal interference. It was into the territories, especially north of the parallel of 36 degrees and 30 minutes, the Missouri Compromise line, that legions of freedom-loving immigrants were destined to migrate.

In the wake of the climactic Supreme Court decision came the senatorial elections of 1858. Abraham Lincoln, Republican candidate in Illinois, challenged the incumbent, Stephen A. Douglas, a Democrat. The less politically experienced lawyer from downstate Illinois seemed to be no match for the polished

"Little Giant," as Douglas was called. But Lincoln forced his eloquent opponent to choose between two irreconcilable principles. Should the residents of a territory like Kansas or Nebraska have the legal right to determine by ballot whether slavery should be allowed, or was the high court of the land correct in affirming the legality of slavery in a territory, irrespective of the will of a majority of its people? Douglas hedged on the question. His concession to popular sovereignty, while it cost him little in Illinois in the race for reelection to the U. S. Senate, lost him much stature in the South. Two years later, in his bid for the office of President of the United States, he won fewer votes than either the victorious Lincoln or the Southern Democrat, John C. Breckinridge.

The Southern leadership had determined that if Lincoln, whom they labeled a "Black Republican," won the election in 1860 they would promptly secede from the United States. Hence the new President was confronted with a *fait accompli* upon his inauguration in March of 1861. Lincoln met the challenge by calling up federal troops to restore unity. The Southern government, under the presidency of Jefferson Davis, likewise called for enlistments, in the name of the Confederate States of America. A "civil" war had begun, a conflict which from the Southern point of view was not an armed confrontation between citizens of one nation but rather a struggle for independence of one nation from another.

To most Americans the slavery issue sufficed to explain the war. Their thinking is understandable. Diverging sectional interests seemed to revert inevitably to the status of the black man in an age that was becoming increasingly humanitarian. Few were conscious of the influence of extremists as a primary cause of the break. Little appreciation was shown by Northerners for the rise of Southern nationalism, cultural or political. Southern gentlemen, on the other hand, proceeded as though the "peculiar institution" of slavery was deathless, despite signs of its eventual disappearance. Forces of various kinds were at work, but the titanic personalities capable of compromise were lacking at the crucial moment when hostilities were about to commence. Henry Clay, Horace Greeley, and Daniel Webster, the men of 1850, were gone.

At the critical juncture when Abraham Lincoln stepped upon the national stage his virtues were not generally known, and least of all in the South. He was not an abolitionist, and the South would have done well to perceive it. Nor was he pro-slavery. From the time when as a young man he had witnessed a slave auction in New Orleans and had vowed to hit "that thing" hard, he never condoned human bondage. More recently, in the senatorial campaign of 1858, his "house divided" speech marked him as one who championed the cause of a free people, black, red, or white. For all of this the North showed its appreciation in the election returns of 1860, realizing at the same time that his party was not committed to do more than prevent the continued spread of slavery.

As far as can be ascertained, the chief executive who was destined to martyrdom in the cause of national unity believed in the gradual emancipation of the unfree blacks and in a fair monetary compensation to their owners. War developments precipitated a different kind of decision. The Union government cherished the goodwill of humanitarians everywhere, at home and abroad. Hence the Emancipation Proclamation of January 1, 1863, called officially for the liberation of blacks in the South as rapidly as Union generals found it possible to comply in their advance into Confederate territory. By this device the relatively small number of Northern abolitionists and the larger contingent of antislavery folk, more moderate in their demands, were at least partially satisfied.

Lincoln's public position on slavery coincided with the Republican platform statement, which declared for non-extension in the territories. In this purpose most immigrants concurred. In particular, most Scandinavian-Americans, not least the Swedes, gave their support to the Republicans, whose standard bearer was in many ways a man of their own mold. Thus from the soil of the Middle West and from a humble log-cabin environment arose a national leader in what is widely recognized as the greatest crisis in the history of the United States.

National politics cannot be disengaged completely from the lives of ordinary citizens. Even Gro Svendsen and other immigrants of her condition, bound to the homestead and the cattle, displayed at times a lively interest in the larger public issues.

Home and church and school (an English school in her case) came first for the pioneer mother. Yet like others she was highly conscious of the Civil War and its import. As her husband marched in the army of General William T. Sherman she felt like "a lonely frightened bird," she said. She was proud of him. Her letter to relatives in Hallingdal, her home in Norway, explained that he returned as "an honorable soldier." At the age of 37 she died, in 1878, after giving birth to her tenth child. Had she lived longer there is every evidence that she would have been caught up in the cultural activities and reform movements of the last quarter of the century. There could be no other Gro Svendsen, but there were many like her.

CHAPTER 4

The Immigrants Move Westward

THE GRANDEUR OF THE AMERICAN EPIC IS ENHANCED BY THE parallel tale of the absorption of the immigrants, their participation in the movement westward, and their permanent settlement of the frontier. In the process of immigration and continued movement there was much success, both for the individual and for the nation, but accompanied by pain and pleasure in generous proportions.

As early as the seventeenth century a few Norwegians inhabited the Dutch colony of New Netherland (called New York after 1664). Anneken Henriksen from Bergen married Jan Arentzen van der Bilt in 1650, thus giving life to what would become the wealthy and powerful Vanderbilts of the nineteenth century. Another *Bergenser,* Hans Hansen, acquired extensive property on Long Island and became the progenitor of a line of Bergens, the family name. Claes Carstensen, originally Claus perhaps, served as an interpreter for the Dutch and the Indians in the Hudson River Valley. And there were others. Most of the early Norwegians came by way of Holland on Dutch vessels in the 1630s. The Moravian cemetery in Bethlehem, Pennsylvania, bears silent testimony to the presence of many Norwegian converts in the eighteenth century.[1]

Norwegian group migration began, as has been noted, with the sailing of the sloop *Restauration.* Its passengers had evidently been encouraged to emigrate by America-bound Germans, some 500 religious separatists who were forced into Bergen for repairs to their damaged ship in 1817. Led by Cleng Peerson, who had explored upper New York State and other areas in the early 1820s, the Stavanger folk, many of them Quakers or Quaker adherents, departed from their country on July 4, 1825. They

[47]

landed in New York on October 9, a date observed since 1964 by presidential proclamation as Leif Erikson Day.[2]

Cleng Peerson was born near Stavanger in 1783. A chronic traveler, he appears to have become dissatisfied with the church in Norway. Although he was not a member of the Slooper party, and probably was not an avowed Friend, his hand may be seen at almost every turn in the initial emigration venture. Not only did he explore the land to be bought and settled upon in America. He also recommended to Captain Lars Olsen Helland of the *Restauration* that a vessel be purchased in Norway, loaded with goods as well as with passengers, and sold in New York. The vessel eventually did carry a cargo of rod iron and was sold, but at less than cost.[3]

Whatever the official church relationship of the original Sloopers, their leaders and others had forsaken the church of their fathers. Already the teachings of Hans Nielsen Hauge had prepared them for acceptance of the faith of the Society of Friends. Both Haugeanism and Quakerism stressed personal piety, a spiritual outlook on life, and a simple form of worship. Lars Larsen, a carpenter by trade, assumed the leadership of the group. Like many a seaman, he had been taken prisoner by the British during the Napoleonic wars, when Britain and Denmark-Norway were technically at war. Until the Treaty of Kiel facilitated his release in 1814, he remained a prisoner on board the British prison ships. There the Norwegians yielded to the persuasive missionary efforts of English Quakers. Eventually, in 1818, the converts and their wives organized a Quaker Society in their native city of Stavanger. It is recorded that as many as 200 persons attended one of their sessions. However, most of them retained their Lutheran connection.

The Sloopers first settled on the shores of Lake Ontario in Kendall and Orleans Counties, New York. The center of their settlement lay about 35 miles northeast of Rochester. The Erie Canal had been opened to traffic in 1825, linking East and West, and a boom period was in prospect. Through the services of an American Quaker and land agent, Joseph Fellows, they were able to purchase land on installments covering a period of ten years. Not all of the buyers were able to meet their payments, however, nor were the plots of land of uniform size.

Clearly, the immigrants from Stavanger were under economic pressures. As free farmers and artisans their financial predicament is revealed in a letter addressed by Peerson and seven Sloopers to the Harmony Society of Frederick Rapp requesting a loan of $1,600. By implication the letter also suggests that the passengers on the Norwegian Mayflower were not unfavorably inclined toward communitarian living.[4]

The majority of the Kendall settlers soon made their way westward to the Fox River country of northern Illinois. It is significant that Lars Larsen, the carpenter and born leader, remained in New York State. After he built a permanent home in 1827 in Rochester, he and his wife Martha provided a way station for many later arrivals on their journey to the Illinois settlements.[5]

Especially important in speeding Norwegian immigration to New York State and the American interior were the letters of Gjert G. Hovland, who arrived in the Kendall settlement in 1831. Knud Langeland, an emigrant of 1843, refers to the tremendous popular interest of Hovland's letters in the villages and valleys of western Norway. Newspapers did their part in disseminating Hovland's personal information on various practical matters. Some believe that with his letters the great debate on emigration began in Norway. Of particular importance was his epistle of April 22, 1835, which carried this message: "Nothing has made me more happy and contented than the fact that we left Norway and journeyed to this country. We have gained more since our arrival here than I did during all the time I resided in Norway." Hovland purchased fifty acres of land in the Kendall settlement, then sold it in 1834 on the eve of his departure for the Fox River settlement in Illinois. He spoke favorably of the set price of $1.25 an acre for public land in the West. His words in praise of America reverberated throughout Norway into the 1840s.[6]

Most of the Sloopers found land too expensive in New York State and again followed the lead of Cleng Peerson, who now saw alluring possibilities in a proposed Illinois and Michigan Canal. The projected waterway, never built, would provide a navigational nexus between the Great Lakes and the Gulf of Mexico, with heavy reliance upon the natural route of the Illinois and Mississippi Rivers. Northern Illinois would benefit economically, it was thought, by the impending canal development. Hence, all but a few of the self-chosen exiles from the Kendall colony established the Fox River settlement in 1834 near Ottawa, La Salle County, about 75 miles west of Chicago.

In the saga of Norwegian settlement in America the Fox River colony holds the distinction of being the point of origin for almost all Norwegian concentrations, which in the course of time fanned out to the north and west into Wisconsin, Minnesota, the Dakotas, and Iowa. The arrival of two brigs in 1836 with some 160 passengers, also inclined toward Quakerism, augmented the numbers of the Illinois community. Conversely, the Kendall settlement declined. In 1838, when Ole Rynning wrote his *True Account of America,* he remarked of the New York settlement that only two or three families remained. Lars Larsen himself had been urging immigrants to seek land in Illinois or points farther west. In this suggestion he was not alone, since thousands of native Americans were migrating from western New York to the region of the Great Lakes.[7]

Notwithstanding the basic agricultural concerns of Norwegian venturers to the heartland of America, there were thousands who stopped in Chicago, hub of the national railroad system and of Great Lakes navigation. Multitudes regarded the city as simply the gateway to the West, yet a considerable number remained there. A few of the immigrants of 1836 appear to have made their homes in Chicago, which during the next year was chartered as a town. At the moment there was only limited comfort in seeing "a midget town of wooden boxes, struggling like a few old, brown teeth, on the flat gums of the river's mouth opening to the Lake."[8]

In Chicago an entire community of *Vossings* came into being. These people originated from the region of Voss, east of Bergen. Among them was Erik Endreson Rude, later to be identified with the founding of the Winneshiek County settlement in northeastern Iowa. Another new face from Voss was that of Iver Lawson (originally Lassen or Larsen). He was to become the father of Victor F. Lawson, who in 1876 would found the *Chicago Daily News.* Scarcely noticed at the time was John Anderson, a lad who came in 1846 to the rising city where *Skandinaven,* strongest among Norwegian journals for over half a century, would be published under his direction after 1866. Census data attest to the popularity of Chicago. In 1850 the Norwegian contingent was 562. In 1860 there were 1,573.[9]

More fertile land beckoned Norwegian immigrants to the southeastern corner of Wisconsin Territory. Beginning in 1838, settlement began at Jefferson Prairie in Rock County. The defeat of Chief Black Hawk in 1832 had reduced the Indian menace. The Pre-Emption Act of 1841 also gave encouragement to northern migration, inasmuch as it offered opportunity for acquiring land at the prevailing price, set by the government, before it was surveyed and readied for sale. The mere fact that Wisconsin was growing gave further impetus to settlement. Wisconsin statehood was to come in 1848.

The first known Norwegian settler in Wisconsin was Ole Knudsen Nattestad of Jefferson Prairie. Thanks to the arrival of several Fox River families from Illinois, Jefferson Prairie could claim 407 people by 1850. Some twenty miles southwest of Milwaukee there developed the settlement of Muskego, to which Søren Bache of Drammen, Norway, made his way in 1839. A party led by Even Heg augmented the numbers in Muskego in 1840. While Heg's "hotel," a commodious barn, often provided temporary residence for newly arrived Norsemen, his intimate friend Søren Bache disappointed the immigrants by leaving for Norway permanently in 1847. The Muskego venture resulted in no large-scale establishment. Malaria and cholera took their tolls. Koshkonong, farther to the west, offered inducements more essential to health and prosperity.[10]

Whatever the motive for Bache's return, on many occasions sickness or death were sources of despair. Homesickness also claimed its casualties. In the lines of a dialogue of 1846,[11]

> If in Wisconsin old worries languish,
> If fortune rolls all my debts away,
> What's the good, if my mind's in anguish?
> If longing gnaws me each bitter day?

In the early stages of Muskego's growth a Danish pastor, Claus Lauritsen Clausen (1820–1892), played a stellar role. His life in America was to be shared more with the Norwegian element than the Danish. His contributions as colonizer, newspaper editor, and Civil War chaplain mark him as a person of lasting eminence in the annals of Norwegian America. In Norway, which he visited for the sake of his health, he had come under the influence of Hans Nielsen Hauge's followers. There he met a Haugean layman, T. O. Bache, father of Søren Bache. It was the beginning of a lifelong friendship. Upon returning to Denmark from Norway Clausen was invited to accompany a missionary to America. The older Bache arranged for his reception in Muskego. Friends in Europe advised him to seek ordination at the hands of a German Lutheran pastor in America, there being no ordained Norwegian pastors available. In the coming years questions were raised as to the validity of the ordination.[12]

In 1850 Clausen and several colleagues explored southern Minnesota and northern Iowa, with an eye to suitable land for settlement. From the Rock Prairie community of Wisconsin a caravan of about 75 people, with forty covered wagons and 200 cattle, set forth in 1853 with Iowa as their destination. The venture may have been the largest of its kind in the Norwegian-American experience, reminiscent of the Danish Mormon trek to Utah. Thousands of land seekers were to follow. The Reverend and Mrs. Vilhelm Koren, fresh from Norway, fixed their abode in Winneshiek County, Iowa. Elisabeth Koren remarks in her diary in the spring of 1854: "I think the whole population of Wisconsin must be moving west. A young man who came here yesterday with greetings from Pastor Preus had passed more than 300 wagon-loads of Norwegians, the greater part bound for Minnesota—some few for Pastor Clausen's."[13]

In Iowa Clausen aided settlers in their disputes with claim jumpers and applied himself to establishing the town of St. Ansgar, named for the patron saint who brought Christianity to Denmark in the ninth century. Despite the richer and less expensive soil in Minnesota, the St. Ansgar colony continued to grow. It became a dispersion point for landseekers in Iowa and Minnesota, thanks to Clausen's vision. His mission in America assumed new significance as immigration totals swelled. In 1843 the annual Norwegian figure first reached 1,000. From then on, the yearly immigration totals increased steadily.

An understanding of Norwegian settlement in the 1840s and

of the role of leading personalities in the process is aided considerably by a series of travel letters of 1847–1848. Ole Munch Raeder, a scholar bent upon studying the American jury system, published his observations in Norway. On a Norwegian government stipend the young Raeder visited Wisconsin in the company of Consul General Adam Løvenskjold. While the results of his examination of American jurisprudence did not bear fruit until 1887, in the reform ministry of Johan Sverdrup, his letters served to illuminate prospective emigrants and others on conditions in the New World.[14]

Raeder speaks of Johan Reinert Reiersen, onetime founder and editor of *Christianssandsposten*, who explored America in 1843 for suitable locations for settlement and, like Raeder, published a guide for emigrants. Reiersen inspired the creation of several colonies in Texas in 1847. In addition to his printed guide, he left several letters which came to light long after his death in 1864. They express his sincere hope that caravans would follow in his wake and declare that the glorious West was deserving of nothing less than an organized exodus from Norway.[15]

Raeder, the lawyer from Norway, was somewhat unusual in that, while he accurately portrayed frontier conditions, he emphasized the role of Norwegian cooks and maids in American private homes. He surmised that the young ladies, "respected and almost loved," created an image of "morality, sobriety, and natural ability" that reflected most favorably upon the Norwegian people as a whole. In Madison, Wisconsin, he believed, there was hardly a house in which Norwegian women were not employed. In the century or more of written commentary upon immigrant life too little has been said in praise of the sterling qualities of Scandinavians and others as domestics.[16]

Prior to the opening of the Civil War, Norwegians moved into the Upper Midwest. They were made to feel welcome by special immigration legislation in Wisconsin. While their concentration was mainly in the southeastern corner of the Badger State, a scattered few made their way farther north. Sons and daughters of Norway were also moving at that time into western Wisconsin, to the counties lying along the east bank of the Mississippi River.[17]

Together with thousands of native Americans, the Norwegians pressed on from Wisconsin into Iowa, where the northeastern section proved most suitable to an agricultural life. For the entire state the population was estimated at 675,000 in 1860. Of that number slightly better than 8,000 were of Norwegian heritage. Letters from the Iowa settlements appeared frequently in the columns of *Emigranten*. Almost invariably they bespoke the advantages of the area.

In all probability the first Norwegian to arrive in the future corn state of Iowa was Ole Valle in 1846, the year in which Iowa received the status of statehood. His report to friends in the Koshkonong settlement of Wisconsin induced others to come in 1848. Shortly Wisconsin's Dane and Racine Counties were sacrificing a bit of their strength to the new Washington Prairie settlement in Iowa, so that by 1860 in Winneshiek County alone there were 4,207 Norwegians. The total for all of northeastern Iowa at that date was 6,403. From this corner of the state many families were to move westward and northward into Minnesota and the Dakotas.[18]

Claus Clausen's St. Ansgar colony in Iowa, totaling 500 Norwegians by 1860, contributed directly to settlement in Minnesota. The vanguard of the Norwegians arrived in 1851 from Muskego. So heavy was the eventual influx into the "glorious new Scandinavia," as the Swedish visitor Fredrika Bremer called Minnesota in her *Homes in the New World*, that the census of 1860 could record 11,893 Norwegians. Treaties with the Sioux Indians prepared the way for Americans into southern Minnesota. The "iron horse" lent assistance to the migration when it first crossed the Mississippi River in 1854. The Gopher State, like others, made its official bid for alien stocks through an immigration commission. Many of Norwegian origin found permanent residence in Minneapolis, which would one day assume the characteristics of a second Christiania, or Oslo.[19]

According to records, Dakota Territory received its first Norwegian inhabitants in 1858, an omen of the day when a fair-sized segment of the Norwegian population would forsake America's green fields and water courses for semi-arid country. In the winter of 1860–1861 *Emigranten* announced, "There are about

150 Norwegian and Danish families around the town of Vermillion (South Dakota) and up along the Missouri River."[20]

One also reads of argonauts in California, beginning with a gold-seeking expedition emanating from north of Trondheim, Norway, in 1850. Favorable reports in *Nordlyset* fanned the interest of readers in America. Numerous farmers and artisans in the Middle West responded. Some stayed in California, although they most often failed to find the elusive precious metal in paying quantities. Sparse though the Norwegian population of California may have been, numbers gradually swelled from 124 (only one woman) in 1850 to 5,060 in 1900. In 1860 more than 75 percent of the Norse element in San Francisco resided within six blocks of the wharves, proof of the eternal attraction of the sea and of possibilities for a decent livelihood. They formed the beginnings of a coastal fleet.[21]

Among the several forerunners in California were men of diverse talents and careers. Benjamin A. Henriksen purchased lots in San Francisco in 1849, dug wells upon his property, and sold drinking water at a dollar a barrel. George C. Johnson traded in iron, steel, and hardware and in 1856 became consul for the government of Sweden-Norway. Peder Saether (Peter Sather) rose to prominence in banking and left a fortune to the University of California at Berkeley. Jon Thoresen Rue, better known as Snowshoe Thompson, carried the mail on a regular schedule through the Sierra Nevada Mountains. His fabulous exploits of 1856–1861 helped to lay out the route of the Central Pacific Railroad.[22]

Texas appealed to a limited number of Norwegians. Glowing descriptions by Johan R. Reiersen, Mrs. Elise Waerenskjold, and Cleng Peerson produced little result. Reiersen conducted a party from Norway to New Orleans in 1844. Elise Waerenskjold, a newcomer of 1846, gave credence to Reiersen's optimistic account in her personal correspondence. Partially through her influence, Norwegians eventually selected a site to be known as Four Mile Prairie, a few miles southwest of Dallas. Contagious disease in Brownsboro had turned them toward Dallas. A larger settlement had developed in the vicinity of Waco by 1851. Meanwhile, in 1849 and again in 1850, Cleng Peerson made his appearance in the state. Through *Democraten* of Racine, Wisconsin, he addressed words of encouragement to his countrymen in the North, chiding them for their clannish concentration. In 1860 the Norwegian population of Texas stood at 321.[23]

While there were features of communal living in the Norwegian-American settlements, Oleana, a colonization project in Potter County, northern Pennsylvania, is the only known attempt by Norwegians to establish an ideal community, in the spirit of Charles Fourier of France or Henry Thoreau of New England. Romanticism and economic instability squelched this effort by Ole Bull (1810–1880), the famed Norwegian violinist. Bull had gained a European reputation for his artistry with the bow before he made his debut in America in 1843. The New World gripped him and affected his music. Having become disenchanted with the new national theater in Norway, he spent five years in America, in the 1850s. The exuberant concert artist declared his intention to "found a new Norway, consecrated to liberty, baptized with independence, and protected by the Union's mighty flag." All of this was to take place in Pennsylvania, where he purchased 120,000 acres of land.

News of Bull's transaction was hard to believe in Norway, a country desperately short of tillable soil. Norwegian settlers arrived, and buildings were brought under construction. The distinguished promoter came and went between concert tours, not realizing the hardship of his colonists on what proved to be less fertile ground than in other parts of the state. He reneged on the wage contract with his workers. Many began to leave Oleana. The story broke in the Norwegian press on both sides of the Atlantic. One journal sarcastically admitted that the music master had a way with the violin but suggested that his bow was unsuited to leveling the earth, moving mountains, or clearing primeval forests. More humiliating to the musical genius was a song composed in Norway entitled "Oleana." The satirical lines were sung throughout the homeland in ridicule of the spurious hopes held out by the naïve violinist. A few verses will suffice to convey the message of this familiar tune:.

> In Oleana, that's where I'd like to be,
>   and not drag the chains of slavery in Norway.
> Ole—Ole—Ole—oh! Oleana!
> Ole—Ole—Ole—oh! Oleana!

In Oleana they give you land for nothing,
    and the grain just pops out of the ground.
Golly, that's easy.
Ole—Ole—Ole—oh! etc.

And the salmon, they leap like mad in the rivers,
    and hop into the kettles, and cry out for a cover.

And little roasted piggies rush about the streets
    politely inquiring if you wish for ham.

Crisis came to Oleana. It was discovered that Ole Bull had been the victim of fraud in the land sale. Fortunately, immigrants could still face westward, where the black-loamed upper Mississippi Valley beckoned. Not many remained in the East.[24]

Canada did her part in promoting immigration. In 1857 the department of agriculture appointed Christopher Closter, a Stavanger native, as emigrant agent. Closter's promises of prosperity in the Gaspé Peninsula of the lower St. Lawrence Valley were seriously challenged in Norway. His colonization scheme failed. Yet estimates are that, of the nearly 47,000 Norwegians who entered the United States between 1854 and 1865, some 44,000 came indirectly by way of Canada. Lower fares and, for shipowners, fewer restrictions provide the explanation. The vast majority of these early comers proceeded to the American Upper Midwest. Permanent occupation of the Canadian provinces far to the west came later.[25]

That a large proportion of the new Americans were identified with one or another Protestant communion, or with Mormonism, should not rule out the economic motive in emigration. On the contrary, for most of the restless, material factors weighed most heavily in the decision to migrate. With unsatisfactory working conditions in Europe, and with America letters, travel accounts, and pamphlet guides repeatedly pointing up the advantages of the Mississippi Valley breadbasket, the pull became irresistible. Often the America letters contained welcome remittances of money, and sometimes prepaid tickets, intended for passage of relatives from Norway to New York or Quebec.

This is the story, in brief, of the vanguard of a national group which, in the latter part of the nineteenth century, would find the next generation, whether foreign-born or American-born, swelling the modest pre-1860 immigrant population. On the whole, it is a tale of hardship borne by young people who, for various reasons, turned their backs upon Europe and sought fulfillment of their lives in America. Their steps normally led into the interior of the continent, a reminder of Charles Dickens's observation during his American tour that few Americans longed for heaven. They simply went farther west. Pioneer immigrants trekked and traveled with the rest. Their response to institutions and events during future American territorial expansion and national growth is a topic to be considered.

CHAPTER 5

The Pioneer Press: Politics and Slavery

NORWEGIAN IMMIGRANTS OF THE MIDDLE OF THE NINETEENTH century generally took an active interest in American public affairs. The mid-century movement in Norway for increased participation by the *bønder* (peasant farmers) in government made them more aware of political conditions and problems in their adopted country. Newcomers liked the republican form of government. Ole Munch Raeder, the pioneer observer of the 1840s, spoke for many later arrivals when he extolled the virtues of American democracy, marveled at the coexistence of state and national governments, and prophesied a bright future for America.[1]

The Norwegian-American novelist Ole Rölvaag, author of *Giants in the Earth*, universally regarded as a masterpiece of immigrant fiction, may be correct in ascribing to the earlier arrivals from Norway a different motivation and intention from the later comers. He once declared that in the first immigration period, from 1825 to the 1870s, large numbers emigrated from the small communities of Norway solely for economic reasons. In some cases even bread was wanting. Therefore they accepted America, with its better prospects for a livelihood, as their permanent home. They may have retained a sentimental interest in the land of their birth, but they soon thought of themselves as Americans. Their children were all but lost to the homeland of their parents. To Rölvaag, who in his college teaching career met hundreds of second-generation Norwegians, their haste in identifying with America was deplorable. And their feeling of identity with America spelled a keen interest in American politics as well.

As to the extent of participation, let letters and newspapers speak for themselves. An early Norwegian settler in New York

State informed his friends in Norway that "when assemblies
are held here to elect officers who are to serve the country,
the vote of the common man carries equal authority and influence with that of the rich and powerful man. A farmer has just
as much freedom as an official." A second letter bore this message: "I wish that there were more institutions as good over the
whole world as there are here: good laws and a good system,
and we are ruled by a good government."[2]

Words of praise continued to flow. With a comprehension
of American affairs gained from an extended period of residence,
and with no small measure of spread-eagleism, Johan R. Reiersen,
founder of the first Norwegian settlement in Texas, wrote in
1852, when the slavery issue had been resolved temporarily in
the Compromise of 1850,[3]

I have learned to love this country to which I have migrated
more than my old fatherland, which I can never reflect upon with
dear longing, and from my standpoint I consider the old monarchical,
aristocratic, and hierarchical institutions as some contemptible play-
things which human intelligence ought to be ashamed of. I feel free
and independent among a free people who are not chained to old
conditions of social position and caste, and I feel proud to belong to
a mighty nation, whose institutions are bound to rule the entire
civilized world because they rest upon principles which reason alone
can recognize as just.

Although immigrants from the European North generally
approved of American governmental forms and procedures,
there were exceptions. A Wisconsin Norwegian, after twelve
years in that area, disdained politics in 1856 because of its ill
repute. He confessed to having no interest whatsoever in being
an American citizen. In his opinion everything tended toward
anarchy and revolution. Political parties were tearing one another
asunder. Everyone wished to govern, and in the end there would
be no government. "I choose to remain out of politics," he
concluded.[4]

In scanning immigrant correspondence one is more likely to
find not a defeatist attitude but a constructive political concern,
short of running for public office. Knud S. Arker, the Wisconsin
pioneer mentioned earlier, associated Whigs with a preference

for long-term officeholding. They wished to prevent aliens from voting by requiring many years of residence. And they stood for a high tariff. The Koshkonong settler thought better of the Democrats, since they favored shorter terms for public officials, a six-month residence requirement for voting, a boon to immigrants, and free trade.[5]

There are signs of conservatism in the letter of Arker. Was he voicing the original Whig dissent against President Andrew Jackson's authoritarianism? Or was the territorial expansionist policy of James K. Polk, a Democrat, unacceptable to him? One wonders. If in accordance with the more restrictive Whig immigration policy he feared an inundation of the nation by mass German and Irish immigration, he was speaking rather early. Nativism was to become more intense in the 1850s.

In examining pioneer Norwegian-American newspapers, as compared with immigrant letters, one is impressed by their understanding of American problems and their partisan political objectives. To be sure, the press gave prominent coverage to news from Norway, but much attention was devoted also to issues near at hand. *Nordlyset* (The Northern Light), first published on July 29, 1847, in the Muskego settlement, southwest of Milwaukee, serves to illustrate this political involvement. As a Free-Soil organ under James Denoon Reymert's editorship, the very first number carried a Norwegian translation of the Declaration of Independence. Subsequently, as in *Emigranten* and similar journals, there were translations of the United States Constitution and other documents of national import. Before *Nordlyset* ceased publication in 1851 it had done much to promote understanding of American institutions among Norwegians in the new land.[6]

In 1847 the Norwegian element of Racine County, Wisconsin, elected as their delegate to the state constitutional convention none other than editor Reymert of *Nordlyset*. His career became in large part political, as a Democratic state assemblyman and senator in the 1850s. Unlike most Scandinavian immigrants, he refused to join the Republican party. He did not, however, favor Negro slavery.

Strongest of the early Norwegian papers was *Emigranten* (The Emigrant), a weekly beginning on January 23, 1852, near Inmansville, in Rock County, Wisconsin. Its debut coincided with the state's official encouragement of immigration. *Emigranten* was published by the Scandinavian Press Association, composed mainly of Lutheran pastors, among them the first editor, Danish-born Claus Lauritsen Clausen. The Association elected Reymert president.

In the number one issue of *Emigranten* Clausen explained that he aimed to "hurry the process of Americanization." He expressed the desire of the immigrants to emancipate themselves from "the degrading bondage of ignorance" regarding privileges and duties of citizenship under the American flag. Next to the financial burden of publication, Clausen believed that the worst obstacle for him to overcome was the general Scandinavian indifference to newspapers of any description. To subscribe to such printed matter was a luxury never thought of by most people of the European North. With reference to politics, Clausen declared, "Our views and principles are Democratic . . . knowing that the majority of our people agree with us in our strong predilection for those principles." Clausen held the editorial reins only briefly, from January to August.[7]

In 1854 *Emigranten* turned Republican. Meanwhile Clausen had journeyed to St. Ansgar, Iowa, where he was persuaded to serve in public office. His neighbors, mostly Norwegians, chose their Danish leader justice of the peace. Next he won election to the state's house of representatives. In *Emigranten* he reported, "My chief consideration is the hope of uniting all our countrymen here in northern Iowa in the Republican party." Sensing disapproval from his pastoral colleagues, who hinted that his ministerial duties were being neglected, he declined to run for reelection.[8]

Norwegian newcomers, though aware of America's shortcomings, were grateful for the freedom afforded them in the new country. They were sensitive to the differences between true and counterfeit democracy. Political turmoil and a growing immigrant constituency opened the way for a partisan and thriving press, which turned for the most part from a Democratic-Free-Soil position to a Republican-Free-Soil perspective. Political discussion and voting preceded actual office-holding. Two factors would in time propel Norwegian-Americans into public office. One was the mastery of the English language, an indispensable tool. The other was the reputation for patriotism acquired through military service in the Civil War.

In the 1850s Norwegians were examining themselves as an ethnic group within the panorama of national stocks in America. In their America letters and in their press they made known their displeasure with unqualified office-seeking countrymen. They directed a like disfavor against the nativist Know-Nothings and against politically ambitious German and Irish immigrants. Norwegians tended to be satisfied to settle down in communities of their own nationality, which was hardly advantagous politically. Strengthened by the spirit of nationalism in nineteenth-century Norway, they inadvertently gave their Yankee neighbors an impression of Old World loyalty. In the opinion of an authority on Swedish immigration, Norwegian solidarity had no counterpart among the Swedes, who left Sweden when national feeling was at a low ebb.[9]

For their clannishness the Norwegians paid a price. The Wisconsin state constitutional convention of 1846 provided a forum for a heated debate on their readiness to carry the responsibilities of citizenship. One member declared that Negroes were more entitled to vote than the Norwegians. The convention did adopt an amendment, however, authorizing the printing of 5,000 copies of the new state constitution in the Norwegian language, as well as in German. But in the process another Yankee delegate sarcastically suggested that the Winnebago and Chippewa tribes were worthy of equal consideration, as far as translations were concerned![10]

At mid-century the American people stood upon the threshold of a nativist decade, symbolized in the Know-Nothing movement which cried out for stricter naturalization laws. By 1855 the Know-Nothings controlled the governorships and legislatures of several New England states and of New York and California. The Middle West, where Scandinavians were concentrated, was less affected. The anti-foreign crusaders chose as their primary targets the more numerous Irish and German populations, both heavily Roman Catholic.

Republicans and Democrats vied for the Scandinavian vote. Neither party wished to be stigmatized as anti-foreign. Much to the embarrassment of Republicans nationwide, the Republican lawmakers of Massachusetts proposed in 1859 to amend their state constitution so as to prevent naturalized citizens from voting until two years after they had obtained United States citizenship. Federal law required immigrants to reside in the country for five years in order to become citizens through the naturalization process. Under the proposed change the alien population of Massachusetts, therefore, would not be allowed to cast their ballots for at least seven years from the time of their arrival at Castle Garden or other ports of entry. Scandinavians and Germans reacted solidly against the Massachusetts plan, and the Republican party was obliged to guarantee that there would be no discrimination against Americans of foreign birth, either in voting or in obtaining free homesteads. Lincoln himself deemed it expedient to assure the future citizens of his disapproval of the Massachusetts idea.[11]

Scandinavians tended to feel as one people when they considered their position in American society. In 1857 *Emigranten* editorialized on the need for Scandinavian candidates for public office in Wisconsin. No descendant from the European North then sat in the state legislature. Only three were holding county offices at that time. A Scandinavian mass meeting in Chicago in 1859 resulted in a resolution to secure municipal and county positions for their kinsmen.[12]

More successful in achieving political recognition than their Chicago relatives were the Norwegians of Wisconsin. In 1859 three of their countrymen were being weighed as possible candidates for state office. *Emigranten* remained unpledged to any of them, however, since all were or had been Democrats. A fourth man, Hans C. Heg, was nominated by the Republicans and elected to the office of State prison inspector. *Emigranten* supported Heg, whose name would soon become more familiar as colonel of the Fifteenth Wisconsin Regiment in the Civil War.

Norsemen of the Badger State scored another victory in 1859 in the election of Knud Langeland to the state assembly. Langeland himself had devoted his energies to the election of Heg, whom he had known for sixteen years, since they arrived as fellow passengers in New York. "Countrymen," he said, "we have the Scandinavian name to take care of."[13]

Yet the sons of Scandinavia, while evaluating their American posture, had reason to feel discouraged over their limited participation in politics on other than local and county levels. The language barrier constantly intruded. Rivalry among religious groups played havoc with the prospects of a more complete unity. Poor transportation, especially in rural areas, made for isolation and difficulty of involvement in political roles. Social life suffered for the same reason. In view of the many disadvantages, it is significant that some progress was made in officeholding.

Within the limitations of their language problem and their handicaps in attending political meetings, the new Americans from Norway came to grips with the issues of the antebellum period. Their editorial leaders, usually the original Americanizers, helped to enhance the American image both in America and in Europe. Some were voices calling for political action. Others found the strife and back-biting of the 1850s repugnant, but they would not be denied their opportunity to be heard and considered on questions of public concern.

Immigrant newspapers kept their readers abreast of the movements of the day. They took political stands. Langeland and Clausen, Democratic at first, later espoused Republican principles. James Reymert and Carl M. Reese, on the contrary, continued on the Democratic course, though they were not in sympathy with the Southern Democracy and the institution of slavery.

A salient factor in the political progress of the Norwegian-Americans was the need of participation in government, beyond the casting of ballots, if certain reforms were to be achieved. Above all, Negro slavery, still economically profitable to Southern planters, was being attacked on humanitarian grounds within the context of a Western civilization which gave lip service to the idea of human equality.

Among the people of Norwegian descent there were diverse opinions and sometimes sharp exchanges on the question of the black man's bondage. The few representatives of Norway who settled in the American South quickly learned to accept the "peculiar institution" as natural, economically necessary, biblically supported, and constitutionally justifiable. Only a few of their countrymen in the Northern free states adopted the Southern point of view. Of the same persuasion, and resorting mainly to scripture and theology for their argument, were a small but influential body of Lutheran pastors, a group which in turn had come under the spell of the proslavery professors in the German Missouri Synod. Another faction, comprised of Scandinavian Mormon proselytes, regarded slavery somewhat indifferently or they accepted the institution as proof of the black man's natural inferiority, within the plan of the Almighty. But proslavery Scandinavians, whether of Missouri or Utah origin, never had the satisfaction of being in a majority among their own immigrant stock.

Typical of the Norwegian arrivals before 1860 on the slavery issue was the traveler Ole Rynning, who in 1838 reported "the infamous slave traffic" to be in "ugly contrast to this freedom and equality which justly constitute the pride of the Americans." With remarkable foresight Rynning predicted "bloody civil disputes," which might end in secession. His words were widely disseminated in the Scandinavian lands.[14]

In the late 1840s several signs of concern over the number one issue of the day are discernible. One evidence was the gathering of some Wisconsin Norwegians under the Free-Soil banner. Another was a statement by an immigrant group, possibly the earliest of its kind, which appeared in a church ordinance adopted by Pastor Elling Eielsen and his flock. It denounced slavery as "a frightful sin" and asserted that Negroes were "redeemed by the same blood" as men of other races. The Ellingians, as they were known, pledged themselves to work toward complete liberation of the slaves. A third indication of this trend toward emancipation may be seen in the proposals of Norwegians in three Wisconsin counties—Racine, Walworth, and Waukesha. All urged approval, but to no avail, of a provision for equal suffrage for Negroes in the new state constitution.[15]

Prophetic of Norwegian antislavery agitation in the 1850s were the frequent criticisms and accusations in *Nordlyset* and *Democraten*. *Nordlyset* gave editorial space to a suggestion that the Northwest Ordinance of 1787, which forbade slavery in the Old Northwest, should be extended to cover California and Western areas. It accused the South of deliberately spreading the slavery blight into the territories and predicted a dissolution of the Union unless preventive measures were taken.[16]

Knud Langeland expressed concern in *Democraten* when Millard Fillmore fell heir to the White House upon the death of President Zachary Taylor in 1850. "The country has reason to expect of this Whig of the North," he said, "that he will do his best to stop this worst of all national plagues." Fillmore was known to side with the advocates of the Compromise of 1850 which, among its several provisions, called for speedy return of fugitive slaves to their masters and for popular sovereignty as the approved method of solving the slavery question in the newly developing Southwest. Favorable to the North in the Compromise was the admission of California as a free state and the end of slave-trading in the District of Columbia, the home of the nation's capital. But Langeland denounced the Compromise as being hazardous to the Union. He held that it could lead only to estrangement of the two sections.[17]

Emigranten, foremost of the Norwegian news media in the 1850s, reflected most consistently the thinking of this immigrant group. Even before the rise of the Republican party it asserted itself against slavery. Editorially, Knud Fleischer in the period 1854–1857 reacted almost passionately against the Kansas-Nebraska Act of 1854. The act raised the specter of slavery creeping into all territories through popular vote. Conceding that "the rotten institution does not lie within the power of the present generation to abolish," he prophesied ultimate collapse of the evil system and announced his support of Republican John C. Frémont for President in 1856.[18]

As an aside to the Wisconsin story, Norwegian political activity in Chicago in the 1850s was of relatively minor consequence. A portent of things to come may be seen, however, in the support given Frémont by Iver Lawson, originally a member of the Fox River colony. Lawson later served as a Republican representative in the Illinois state assembly.

Carl F. Solberg had hardly taken Fleischer's chair in *Emigranten* when he declared that, for the sake of their political and civil independence, Norwegians should strive to forestall the extension of "damnable slavery" beyond the Mississippi. Similar pleas followed in rapid succession during the balance of the year 1857, the same year in which the climactic Dred Scott case came before the United States Supreme Court. The Court decided that the Missouri Compromise of 1820, which had banned slavery north of the latitude of 36 degrees and 30 minutes in the Louisiana Territory, was unconstitutional. Moreover, slaves should be regarded as property, not as citizens. Dred Scott had no right to sue. The decision raised the ire of Republicans. Solberg of *Emigranten* was no exception. The rival Democrats suddenly became anathema. Solberg sent a kick in their direction by urging voting privileges for Wisconsin's Negroes, of which there were but a few.[19]

Speaking for Norwegian Democrats, the minority within an ethnic minority, *Den Norske Amerikaner* argued that constitutionally the Southern commonwealths were within their rights in maintaining a slave economy and society. To editor Charles M. Reese (originally Carl M. Riise) the Douglas doctrine of popular sovereignty demonstrated the best in democracy. "It is high time," he stated, "that the bleeding-Kansas farce played itself out," a clear reference to overdramatization by would-be friends of the blacks. *Den Norske Amerikaner* was succeeded by *Nordstjernen* (The North Star), under the auspices of a Scandinavian Democratic Press Association. Reese, still editor, declared his position in the first issue. In contrast with the "Modern Black Republicans," who spurned the popular-sovereignty doctrine, the Democrats had found the key to a peaceful settlement of the "agitating question of African slavery" in the United States.[20]

Norwegian-Americans stood by Republican candidates again in 1860. *Emigranten,* the most familiar messenger in Norwegian communities, assumed the lead in their behalf. It found itself unable to endorse a fellow countryman, James D. Reymert, a Wisconsin Democrat, for a seat in the federal House of Representatives. It mattered little that Reymert professed to be against slavery. He failed to secure the backing of Scandinavians in Wisconsin.[21]

Charles Reese, once a Douglas man, lost faith in the "Little Giant" from Illinois. As helmsman for a new Chicago paper, *Folkebladet,* he clarified his changed position as a Republican. "The struggle this fall will be simply between Freedom and Slavery," he explained, "and where is the man in the North who can for a moment be undecided as to which side to take."

From now on, he vowed, he would be found battling for "Freedom, Free Speech, and Free Territory." Although of Danish descent, Reese addressed himself mainly to Norwegians.[22]

One important element among Norwegian immigrants remained Democratic and proslavery. As has been mentioned, a number of influential ministers of the Norwegian Lutheran Synod had caught the spirit of the German Missouri Synod, largely domiciled in the slave state of Missouri. Professor Laurentius Larsen of the faculty of Concordia Seminary in St. Louis had been converted to the Missouri view. The seminary prepared candidates for Missouri Synod pulpits and served temporarily for early Norwegian candidates as well. More than a few Norwegian clergy thus came to be convinced of the soundness of the Southern position on the pressing issue of the times. Remaining unconvinced was Claus L. Clausen, former editor of *Emigranten*. He voiced his disapproval of slavery until his resignation from the synod in 1868.[23]

The closing of Concordia Seminary upon the outbreak of the Civil War heightened the slavery controversy among Norwegian-Americans. Professor Larsen's sympathetic attitude toward the Southern states prompted *Emigranten* to challenge him. But the "Missouri" ministers were not to be moved. In synodical session at Luther Valley, Wisconsin, in 1861 they framed a resolution declaring that slavery "in and by itself" was not sinful. Laymen who were present disagreed. The lay position was mainly humanitarian, not theological. Clausen concurred with the laymen in charging the ministers with sophistry, insofar as they were attempting to draw a distinction between slavery as sin and slavery as evil.[24]

In the ensuing debate between Clausen and the Larson school of thinkers, *Emigranten* and Chicago's *Skandinaven* stood by Clausen. Scandinavian immigrants generally were with him also. Still, the Norwegian Synod reaffirmed its decision in 1868, when the victory of the Union Army had seemingly resolved the issue. The following year, however, the Synod condemned "American slavery" but not slavery *per se*.

What was unusual in the slavery dispute was the fact that it grew in intensity only after the Civil War began and that it occurred among an ethnic group hitherto almost unacquainted with slavery and, in their hearts, almost unanimously against it. For the Synod leaders the central reality was the Word of God. For Clausen and the vast majority of Norsemen in America the focal point of consideration was the brutality of American slavery. Clausen's involvement in the emancipation crusade was to draw him into the war as an army chaplain.

Lest the relatively small contingent of semi-isolated Norwegian Mormons in Utah be forgotten, it should be explained that the tenets of their faith determined their posture on all political and social matters. What one author calls "the anti-Negro doctrine" is therefore explainable on reputedly historical grounds. The Book of Abraham, a part of the Mormon scriptures, speaks of the curse of Ham, by his marriage to a Negress. Yet the Book of Mormon extols racial equality. Brigham Young struck a compromise in his "white theocracy" in the West. Men of mixed or pure Negro blood, said Young, might be Mormon members, but none should be advanced to the status of the priesthood. So the Latter Day Saints gave the appearance of straddling the important issue of the 1850s.[25]

Although the votes of the foreign-born probably did not put Lincoln into the White House, it is all but certain that a very large segment of Scandinavian-Americans voted Republican, as a vote against the extension of slavery. The Swedes, guided by *Hemlandet,* their leading journal, had been rapidly turning Republican. The only Swedish proslavery group of any consequence was to be found in the small Texas settlements.

Leading Norwegian-American newspapers were definitely antislavery. Yet the circulation of smaller Democratic papers is proof of disunity within the ranks. An outright generalization is unwarranted, mainly because the influence of the Missouri-trained ministers of the Norwegian Synod cannot be accurately gauged and probably never will be known.

On the other hand, the impact of the proslavery Missouri Synod leadership upon the Norwegian element in America should not be overestimated. Lay opposition was demonstrated at the very time when the Synod was declaring slavery in itself to be no sin. Synodical intellectuals were arguing on theological and scriptural grounds, which had little appeal to many less philosophically inclined Norwegian church members. The latter considered the problem of slavery from a contemporary and realistic point of view. The fact that the identical leaders of the Norwegian *ecclesia* admitted the American institution to be sinful indicates that at heart they abhorred chattel slavery as it was practiced in the South. Norwegian immigrants, more divided in opinion than the Swedes, were nevertheless predominantly antislavery.

CHAPTER 6

Sword and Pen in War and Reconstruction

IN THE WAR BETWEEN THE STATES BOTH SIDES EXPECTED AN EARLY
victory. Enlistments were for short terms, only three months at
the outset. The initial military advantage lay with the Con-
federacy, whose constituents believed that not only their way
of life but also their homes and families were in danger. The
psychological factor of defense was coupled with an efficient,
though smaller, army with a high percentage of West Point graduates among its officers. Their men were accustomed to giving
orders, to horseback riding, and to the out-of-doors. Knowledge
of the Southern terrain, where most of the battles would be
fought, was an asset. Finally, there was the superb leadership,
as man and soldier, of General Robert E. Lee.

For the Union a war of long duration carried greater promise
of victory. With more than token assistance from immigrant
volunteers, some of whom were actually recruited at Castle
Garden, the North possessed superior manpower and a greater
potential for producing food and medical supplies and for manufacturing clothing, weapons, and munitions. East-west railroad
lines proved to be of strategic military value. The Union navy
blockaded the enemy coast. Most important for the North was
that intangible substance called time, for as the years came and
went the North gained momentum and strength, while the
South suffered decline.

In view of their lesser numbers, the military contribution of
Norwegian immigrants in the struggle between the sections
cannot be considered of major importance. Yet it is significant
that they provided probably a higher percentage of soldiers, in
proportion to the Norwegian-American population, than did the
native Americans. One reason for their strong response to the
call of the Union was that their age range fell within the mili-

tary requirements. Many had arrived as young men from Norway and were still in their prime physically.[1]

Norwegian immigrants joined the colors in the North, and a few in the South, often choosing a particular regiment or company. The most distinguished unit in the military annals of Norwegian America is the Fifteenth Wisconsin Regiment, commanded by Colonel Hans Christian Heg.

Heg's prewar career indicates a high potential for political activity. Born in Norway in 1829, he emigrated with his parents in 1840. As we have seen, the Heg family settled in the Muskego community, Wisconsin Territory, where the father, Even Heg, supplied the funds in large part for *Nordlyset*, the pioneer journalistic venture. In the offices of that press young Hans first became familiar with American politics. In 1859 he was elected, as previously noted, to the office of state prison commissioner. He was the first man of Scandinavian origin, of nineteenth-century vintage, to hold an elective position on the state level.

Heg declined a second term as state prison commissioner and chose instead to organize a Scandinavian regiment for the war. Carl F. Solberg of *Emigranten* called for volunteers. The two men had understood each other in this matter for some time. Solberg quotes Heg as having said on one occasion, "The men who conduct this war are the men who will conduct affairs after it is over. If we are going to have any influence then, we must get into the war."[2]

Heg's enthusiasm shone in his personal appeal in *Emigranten*: "Let us band together and deliver untarnished to posterity the old and honorable name of Norsemen." On October 1, 1861, he was commissioned as colonel. In December the Fifteenth Wisconsin Regiment assembled at Camp Randall in Madison. By March 2, 1862, a contingent of almost 900 men departed for active duty. The vast majority were Norwegians. Of the total regimental roster, 128 answered to the name of Ole.[3]

There were notable exceptions to the otherwise Norwegian complexion of the Fifteenth Wisconsin Regiment. Majors Hans Borchsenius and Charles Reese were of Danish descent. Captain Joseph Mathiesen was also Danish, while Captain Charles Gustafson was Swedish. Lieutenant Henry Siegel was German, but born and reared in Norway. Major George Wilson, of English blood, was born in Hamburg, Germany, and grew up in Christiania. Lieutenant Colonel Jones, a native American, had a Norwegian wife and spoke her language. And Lieutenant Colonel David McKee was of Scottish descent.[4]

Waldemar Ager presents the diary of Private Bersven (Ben) Nelson of the Fifteenth Wisconsin Regiment. Some of his experiences may illustrate the life of the immigrant soldier.[5] Young Bersven left North Norway in 1861 with his parents and ten brothers and sisters. His father took up land near Eau Claire, Wisconsin. In November of 1861 a Sergeant O. R. Dahl, himself a recent arrival from Norway, came to the Eau Claire community to recruit men for Colonel Heg's regiment. He indicated that there was a bounty of $300.00 and that the soldiers' pay would be $13.00 per month. Free clothing and meals were included. By mid-December Dahl had enlisted 22 men. The way then led to Camp Randall.

Together with two other Wisconsin regiments, the Fifteenth left for the South. In Chicago, the first train stop of any importance, they were honored by an assembly of Norwegians, who presented to them a silk flag bearing the figure of the Norwegian lion, to add to their regimental colors and their battle flag. From Cairo, Illinois, they crossed the Mississippi to Missouri. In April they captured Island No. 10 in the Mississippi River. Some would remain on garrison duty there for the duration of the war. In June they moved to Tennessee. Ben was ordered back to Island No. 10 to join the guard, who chose him as their cook. With rice and milk (hard to get) he managed to provide *velling*, a gruel of rare delicacy in the situation. Sickness and a few deaths reduced the number of men stationed on the island. An army medical officer advised Ben to take a thirty-day leave. His family welcomed home a man who had dropped from 200 pounds to only 165.

In May, 1864, Private Nelson became a member of the brigade of General Augustus Willich, who commanded four regiments: the Fifteenth Wisconsin, the Fifteenth Ohio, the Eighth Kansas, and the Thirty-Second Indiana. In the battle at New Hope Church, in Tennessee, the Norwegian regiment lost 92 men. Ben looked forward to December 20, the terminal date for his enlistment. But it got to be February, 1865, before he and others were ordered to proceed to Chattanooga to turn in their weapons and to receive their honorable discharge papers. They returned to their Wisconsin homes. The war was still in progress.

Bersven Nelson was not with the main body of the Fifteenth Wisconsin at all times. Waldemar Ager fills in the story of the regiment. Temporarily, on October 8, 1862, they felt the thrill of victory at Perrysville, an indecisive battle. Confederates got revenge in late December at Stone's River, but on January 2, 1863, they were driven back. Six months later, on July 3, Heg was placed in command of the Third Brigade of Jefferson C. Davis's division, a hint of eventual promotion to general. Heg's brigade was the first to cross the Tennessee River in the advance against the elusive General Braxton Bragg, on August 17.[6]

To conclude Ager's summary, in the climactic engagement of September 18–20, 1863, at Chickamauga, in the vicinity of Chattanooga but located in the northwest corner of Georgia, the regiment lost over half of its personnel. The greatest single casualty was the death of Colonel Heg himself. Thirty-two of those taken prisoner eventually died in Andersonville Prison, in Georgia, where inmates succumbed by the thousands. Buried daily in long ditches were the bodies of Union soldiers. The last to die in Andersonville, Ager remarks, was Knud Hanson, a Norwegian of the First Wisconsin Cavalry Regiment. He was laid in grave number 12,848, a sad commentary on the multitudes who died needlessly.

A few escaped after their capture at Chickamauga. Lieutenant Colonel Ole C. Johnson and his companions, first confined at Libby Prison, cut a hole in the floor of the cattle car taking them to Andersonville. They lowered themselves to the ground and luckily were spared injury or death from the moving train. Johnson lost some buttons from his uniform. He had succeeded to the command of the Fifteenth Wisconsin when Heg was elevated to brigade chief.[7]

As the Union armies advanced, more prisoners arrived at Andersonville. They were plundered almost every night by fellow prisoners. Anarchy reigned. The better element finally organized themselves into "Regulators" and prison officials allowed them to try and to punish offenders. Six were sentenced to hang by the Regulator court for robbery and murder. Most offenders were "scum from New York." Of the 30,000 prisoners in Andersonville in the summer of 1864, the majority watched the hanging and doubtless were much sobered by the experience. At the end of April, 1865, after General Robert E. Lee's surrender, numerous survivors were released and allowed to seek assistance in Union camps. Some walked barefoot for months. Weary soldiers testified to suffering more from lack of sanitation and shelter than from hunger. According to one soldier's recollection, 43 members of the Fifteenth Wisconsin died in Andersonville, and fourteen in all other prisons.[8]

Complete agreement on casualty figures is lacking, but all sources reveal that the Grim Reaper accomplished more through sickness than through combat. By the time the Fifteenth Wisconsin was mustered out in Chattanooga in 1865, after marching with General William T. Sherman to Atlanta, about one-third of the original number had been killed, or had died of wounds or disease. Their regimental casualties were substantially heavier than the average in the Union Army. Ager presents statistics for the Wisconsin regiments that were hardest hit and suggests that more Norwegians in uniform might have survived the war had they not felt disinclined to go on sick call. Insecure in the use of the English language, they shied away from hospitals. These are the figures:[9]

	Men	Losses	Percentage
Fifteenth Wisconsin	905	299	33.04
Twenty-Fifth Wisconsin	1,420	418	29.44
Seventh Wisconsin	1,794	391	21.79
Eleventh Wisconsin	1,735	343	19.70

The role of the Norwegian-American soldier in the East is best reflected in the experiences of Company I of the First New York Regiment of Volunteers (Infantry). A two-year enlistment period began in 1861. Many who were mustered out in May, 1863, reenlisted in other units. What Heg was to the Wisconsin Norwegians, Hans Balling (Ole Peder Hansen Balling) was to the Norwegians in the State of New York. Starting as captain, he advanced to the rank of lieutenant colonel in another New York regiment, the 145th. After being wounded at Fredericksburg, he was honorably discharged in January, 1863. Balling was a person of unusual talent. He returned to a successful career in portrait painting. Among his subjects were Abraham Lincoln and several Union generals.[10]

It may not be possible to determine the exact number of Norwegian Americans in uniform. A mere counting of names is unreliable, simply because in many instances the names failed to prove a man's national origin. But Norwegian soldiers alone, nationwide, probably numbered close to 6,000. If some 1,500 Swedes and a like number of Danes are added to the Norwegian strength, the total number of Scandinavians in the Civil war approached 9,000.

As has been observed, a few Danes fought with the Fifteenth Wisconsin Regiment. Conspicuous among them, though not fighting, was chaplain Claus L. Clausen, whose contact with Norwegian pioneers in the Middle West was of long standing. Apparently he was the personal choice of Colonel Heg, but the ten company commanders were given the opportunity of approving his appointment. Company K, under Captain Mons Grinager, honored him by calling themselves Clausen's Guards. Commissioned in December, 1861, Clausen resigned in November of the following year because of shock suffered in a bomb explosion on Island No. 10.

A footnote, so to speak, on Clausen appears in Ager's reference to the sergeant who acted in the capacity of chaplain for the duration of the war. John Henry (Johan Henrik) Johnson, already a Methodist lay preacher, enlisted with the Fifteenth Wisconsin. When Clausen resigned, the officers recommended Johnson to replace him. Since he lacked ordination, he retained the rank of sergeant, carried arms, and engaged in combat. He was known to slip away from camp on occasion to preach to the Negroes, who welcomed him enthusiastically. Following the war, Johnson served with distinction as pastor, editor, district superintendent, and three time-delegate to the General Conference of the larger Methodist Episcopal Church.[11]

Emigranten spoke well of the Lincoln administration. Editor Solberg spent several months behind the Union lines in the South, as a correspondent for his paper. In 1863 he was urging the prosecution of the war, with preservation of the Union as the primary consideration. He defended Lincoln in his affair with the Ohio Democrats who, led by Clement L. Vallandigham, a so-called Copperhead, opposed the war.[12]

Most Norwegian-Americans scorned the Copperheads, the peace Democrats residing in the North. The hateful label may have been wrongly applied in some instances. Rasmus B. Anderson, later prominent in Norwegian affairs in the Middle West and a professor of Scandinavian literature in the University of Wisconsin, tells of the town of Decorah, Iowa, going wild upon hearing the news of Lee's surrender. But up the hill at Luther College, steeped in the proslavery theology of the Missouri Synod, all was quiet and dark. Professors were searching for students in the crowds down below and ordering them up to the dormitory. Citizens revived talk about Copperheadism and called a mass meeting at the court house. Professor Laur. Larsen and other faculty members explained their attitude at the meeting. Their replies were accepted as satisfactory.[13]

In the judgment of Waldemar Ager, the war revolved on the issue of slavery, as far as most Norwegian immigrants were concerned. It became a kind of holy war, with moral objectives rather than political. There is much evidence to support Ager's position. One typical Norwegian couple addressed these lines to relatives in Norway:[14]

The cause of the war between the Northern Republican states and the Southern Democratic states is that the Southern states want to spread slavery over all the civilized American states and to abolish their good laws and government. . . . We Northerners are against the Southern states because of their heathenish slavery and un-Christian behavior in the same.

A second Norwegian settler repeated the common charge that the Democratic platform, identified with Southern interests, was "of such a nature that it sought to extend slavery over the entire *Yunaitisstet* [sic] or nearly over all America."[15]

But one does not always find clear expression of purpose. "The battle hymn of the Republic" with its stirring "Mine eyes have seen the glory" appears to have been far removed from the mundane thoughts of the common soldier. From field or camp, where the war was closer and where issues were dimmed by the minutiae and hubbub of military life, bits of rhyme were often sung to while away the dragging time or to relieve the tedium of the march. This was one of them:[16]

> Old Rosy [Rosecrans] is the man;
> By him we all will stand.
> The glorious Union we'll restore.
> The Negroes we don't care anything for!

Some saw slavery as the lesser evil. The possibility of permanent disunion was the other. To men like Colonel Hans Heg the structure of government and the preservation of the Union were paramount. In that perspective, he was unhappy with the "many reckless and dishonest politicians" who were "mostly in the Army as officers." He supposed, hopefully it seems, that many of these gaudy reprobates would be killed off. If European-born Americans failed to comprehend the objectives of the war as intelligently as Heg, they were perhaps no more confused than their Yankee neighbors, caught up in the emotional propaganda of the time. If they had understood President Lincoln, they would have known of his primary concern to save the United States of America as one nation.[17]

Lincoln's assassination drew expressions of genuine sorrow from many quarters. It may be gathered from the myriad of letters and editorials that his interests and aims, insofar as they were understood, were shared by the great majority of Scandinavian immigrants. No force did as much as the Civil War to identify the sons of Norway with American life and American problems. Long and sustained association with Union troops under varied field conditions quickened the Norwegian boys in blue to a more vivid consciousness of the meaning of United States citizenship. Their kin who remained at home in Wisconsin, Minnesota, or New York, hoping for victory, likewise merged their interests with those of the nation as a whole. It is understandable that in the postwar reconstruction period they watched with keen anticipation the course of events under the victorious Republicans and sought to assume more active roles in the country whose integrity they had defended.

Peace brought problems of its own. Normal conditions must be restored, if possible, in the seceded states. Relations between the executive and the legislative branches of the federal government needed reinforcement. Upon Lincoln's sudden death, Vice President Andrew Johnson succeeded to the presidential office. His plans for political reconstruction, like Lincoln's, were predicated upon the thesis that the South had not actually seceded. He favored readmission of the wayward states on condition that ten percent of the voters as of 1860 in a Southern state would swear allegiance to the United States, and that Southern state conventions would invalidate the ordinances of secession, abolish slavery, and repudiate the state debts incurred from the war. The Southern states acted favorably upon this plan.

When Congress, dominated by Radical Republicans, met in December, 1865, it established its own reconstruction committee, in defiance of President Johnson. The Norwegian-American press sided with Congress. It reflected suspicion of the "tailor President" who before the war had voiced himself in opposition to abolitionists. Johnson vetoed the Freedman's Bureau bill, designed to provide for the care and education of Negroes for two years. Already in operation, the Freedmen's Bureau, which was rumored to provide "forty acres and a mule" for every head of a Negro household, was administered by Edwin M. Stanton, Secretary of War. Not averse to aiding the helpless former slaves, Johnson complained that the bill did not do enough for them. It guaranteed no legal protection for blacks and included no system of land distribution or of long-term credit.

In general, Norwegian-American newspapers took an anti-administration stand. *Emigranten* attacked the President as one who obstructed the well-intended legislation of Congress. *Fædrelandet*, a new Republican journal founded in La Crosse, Wisconsin, argued that the "rebel states" might well wait a year or two for representation in Congress. *Skandinaven* wondered whether the American people were content to fold their hands and permit an ambitious little man to play his own game.[18]

Tension against Johnson mounted in the fall of 1866. The immigrant press stated that the question before the people in the forthcoming congressional elections was whether the republic should be ruled by the party that saved it from destruction or by the party that attempted to destroy it. It claimed that the President had dismissed loyal Republican officials and was encouraging the people of the South to take up arms again. Editors prophesied that even the Southern rebels whom Johnson had befriended would forsake him in the next presidential election.[19]

The year 1868 brought opportunity not to Johnson but to Ulysses S. Grant. As a war hero, the general rode into office mainly on the strength of his popularity. Leading Scandinavian newspapers stood by the Republican party, as they had been doing since the late 1850s. *Skandinaven* exercised conspicuous restraint, however, in supporting Grant's election. *Nordisk Folkeblad* (Northern People's Gazette) of Rochester, Minnesota, and later of Minneapolis, took pride in Grant's triumph. *Fædrelandet og Emigranten*, the result of a merger of two papers, joined Republicans in urging a firm hand against the racist activities of the Ku Klux Klan.[20]

Grant's shortcomings as President were known to the Norwegian immigrants, but they continued to respect him until the scandals of the administration came to light. Perhaps it was their Old World tradition of reverence for authority that determined their attitude toward Grant. Knud Langeland of *Skandinaven* refused to give unqualified support to him, however. In the event of a complete demise of the Democratic party, he would prefer a division of the Republicans into two parties, in order to preserve the two-party system. New issues of sufficient popular interest and national importance might be faced without the Democratic organization. He gave guarded approval to Grant's reelection. "He is a perfect man," he wrote, "who does not fail in something." Let the Senate be the watchdog, confirming or rejecting Grant's appointments henceforth. "We just about know now what we have, while with a new man we would be more uncertain." It was a lukewarm recommendation.[21]

Langeland's mild insistence that a two-party system should be maintained was borne out in 1872 in a manner different from what he had anticipated. Southern whites were returning to leadership, displacing both carpetbaggers from the North and the incumbent Negro politicians. The Democratic party of Jefferson and Jackson did not die. On the other hand, a dissenting wing known as Liberal Republicans formed a separate party, with a willingness to cease waving the bloody shirt, reminiscent of the war. Among their aims were also civil service reform and a downward revision of the tariff. With Horace Greeley, editor of the *New York Tribune*, as their common standard bearer, the Liberal Republicans and the Democrats campaigned against the distinguished veteran in the White House, and lost.

No startling change in political perspective occurred in 1872 among Norwegian-Americans, if the press is used as a barometer. Langeland had left *Skandinaven* to become editor of *Amerika*, a new Chicago publication. He saw no real issue in the campaign. He had suspected Greeley of faddism and inconsistency, in view of his onetime reputation as a high-tariff advocate and an abolitionist. The Liberal Republican cry for amnesty left Langeland cold. "A little more reconstruction and a little less amnesty would be better for these ex-rebels who still have not learned to respect the right to vote." He was referring to Southern white intimidation of blacks at the polls.[22]

A Norwegian weekly, *Minnesota*, gave its support to Greeley, making more of Grant's vices than of Greeley's virtues. *Minnesota* accused the Radical Republicans of making political capital out of sectional bitterness remaining from the war. It charged that Grant's military record was utilized by his friends to conceal his ineptitude as President. And the corruption of Grant's administration was coming to light. *Minnesota* specifically mentioned his acceptance of gifts, his nepotism, and his retention of officials known to be dishonest.[23]

Perhaps no gauge of Norwegian-American political opinion is more accurate than Chicago's *Skandinaven*. Repeatedly it denounced the Republican party for its reluctant support of Scandinavian candidates for public office in Minnesota and Wisconsin. It declared its independence of either of the major political parties. While expressing the hope that Grant would not choose to run for a third term in 1876, *Skandinaven* withheld any recommendation of a successor in Washington.[24]

When Governor Rutherford B. Hayes of Ohio and Governor Samuel J. Tilden of New York were named by their respective parties to enter the presidential race in 1876, *Skandinaven* quickly spoke out in favor of Hayes, the Republican. His military and political careers were favorably presented. The paper identified him with civil service reform and with a program of strict moral integrity in government. *Skandinaven* wasted no sympathy on Tilden and the Democrats. It leveled numerous charges against Tilden. His pacifism had verged upon Copperheadism during the war. He was responding hypocritically to public demands for reform. Desire for power was his obsession. At the age of 63 he was old and infirm. His left arm was partially lame. He was more than half-blind in one eye. He had not married. His religion called for dancing around the golden calf. Truly this was an American election year![25]

On the eve of the election of 1876 *Skandinaven* made a final effort to identify Tilden with the former rebels. Jefferson Davis, once President of the Confederate States of America, was reported to have written from London hoping for a Tilden victory. There was talk of Davis being named secretary of war in Tilden's cabinet. "What possibilities!" exclaimed *Skandinaven*. "A rebel Congress in Washington, Lincoln treacherously murdered, Stanton dead, and Jeff. [*sic*] in his place." Dual electoral returns from four states kept the country in suspense until almost inauguration day. In the last moment Hayes was declared to be the winner. In general, Norwegians were satisfied that the better man had won.[26]

Norwegian-Americans for the most part concurred in the Radical Republican program of the postwar period. Readmission of the Southern states could wait. The Congress might be justified in controlling the President. Fathers, sons, husbands, and sweethearts had given their lives in the great effort to save the Union. Seldom had Norwegians, or Scandinavians, faced each other as enemies on the firing line. The vast majority responded therefore as Northerners whenever the war issue was raised. Only a small minority, dissatisfied with President Grant, joined the Liberal Republicans.

CHAPTER 7

In the Maelstrom of Reform

WHEN THE WINNEBAGO COUNTY REPUBLICAN CONVENTION OF 1876 met in Benson Grove, Iowa, and erupted into a riot, a changed attitude of Norwegian-Americans was apparent in relation not only to local political responsibility but also toward national affairs. Admittedly, some Norwegians had moved rapidly toward Americanization. Some were Civil War veterans and could not easily be ignored as prospects for political leadership. According to rumor, a gang of native Americans were prepared to break up the convention of October 21. Most important of the offices to be filled was that of county treasurer. There were three strong candidates, two of them of Norwegian descent. A rotten apple thrown at a Norwegian bystander produced a free-for-all and some bloody faces. Norwegian farmers went to the polls in November determined to elect men of their own national origin. They succeeded. In the next forty years, down to World War I, Norwegians usually held the more strategic offices. Of 31 men elected to Winnebago County positions in that interval of time, only four were native Americans.[1]

Granted that nativist barbs were directed more against the Germans and the Irish, and later against the so-called New Immigration from Southern and Eastern Europe, Norwegians did not go unscathed, as the Benson Grove incident illustrates. Until the movement for stricter federal supervision of immigration reached its peak in the late 1890's, all foreign-born Americans were prime targets for unwarranted charges of un-Americanism.

Norwegians were perhaps no threat to American economic standards, to the religious beliefs and institutions of the land, or to American social customs. They were seldom to blame for following corrupt political bosses, as urban immigrants might

[84]

often do. Nor as farmers did they contribute noticeably to industrial unemployment and unrest. The Roman Catholic Church, suspected as a foreign danger but enjoying great success in the organization of new dioceses and in the erection of countless parochial schools, did not appeal to Norwegians any more than to their Yankee neighbors. But Norwegians suffered from a general American dislike for all hyphenates, an attitude which did not limit itself to specific national groups. They were bound to feel humiliation and discrimination in a country whose people were being classified as either Yankees or foreigners.[2]

A review of the final quarter of the nineteenth century verifies that nativist verbal onslaughts played a large part in the emergence of distinct national groupings in American politics. Signs of ethnic solidarity prompted both the Republican and the Democratic parties to create in the 1880s special "nationalities divisions," their purpose being to corral the immigrant vote.

For the newer Americans bewildering dismay often characterized the last two decades of the nineteenth century. In desperation many of them supported farmers' alliances, the Greenback program for cheaper money, and the People's party. Augmenting the economic discontent of the farmers and laborers were events that boded ill for the future of the entire population. It was widely believed that a radical German immigrant threw the bomb that killed eight Chicago policemen in Haymarket Square in 1886. By way of backlash, the press, the politicians, and the general public agreed that there must be a quarantine on socialists and anarchists. When the Bureau of the Census announced in 1890 that, for practical purposes, the long taken-for-granted Western frontier no longer existed, there was further cause for alarm. The strident cry was that the public domain could absorb no more immigrants. Depression led to the panic of 1893 and culminated in the Pullman strike of 1894. Again, let the government beware of allowing hordes of unskilled, illiterate, and radical Europeans to enter the portals of Ellis Island. But as prosperity returned, and tensions relaxed, the movement for immigration restriction subsided.

Around mid-century and beyond, the newly admitted states were eager for immigrants. Iowa beckoned Scandinavians through a state board of immigration, to which the governor appointed

Claus L. Clausen, the Danish Lutheran pastor and erstwhile Civil War chaplain. Railroad owners did their bit to encourage the populating of the West. The operations of James J. Hill and his Great Northern Railway were especially fruitful, with ocean transportation, railroad travel expense, and even farm land being provided for many a Norwegian newcomer in North Dakota. The Burlington Line assisted notably in attracting the Swedes to Iowa and Nebraska, and the Northern Pacific introduced tens of thousands of Scandinavians to Minnesota, the Dakotas, and the Pacific Northwest. The transcontinental lines deserve much of the credit for bringing 788,000 persons from Europe in the single year of 1882, among them 105,000 Scandinavians. Numerically, Norwegian America grew tremendously in the period from 1880 to 1914. Growth in numbers stimulated the founding of churches, promoted the creation of social and literary societies, inspired further growth of the press, and gave rise to a professional class.

In many ways Norwegians found nineteenth-century America to their liking. There was real satisfaction in coming to a thinly settled West, where agricultural land was cheap, abundant, and fertile. For many immigrants the result was a degree of prosperity that they had never dreamed of in Europe. The claim has been made that Norwegians practically monopolized the Great Lakes shipping industry in the 1880s. Duluth and Superior became centers of the lumber trade, while the timber and fish of the states of Washington and Oregon drew more Norwegians than did salubrious California. Puget Sound and the salmon fisheries were central in the lives of Norsemen in the far Northwest. After the Puget Sound banks were fished out, Alaska attracted the sons of Norway for its gold mining and its maritime opportunities. Even in Gloucester, Massachusetts, at the eastern end of the American continent, 1,000 of its 6,000 fishermen in 1898 were of Scandinavian origin.[3]

Labor-management relations were strained in the last quarter of the century. A major depression in the 1870s aggravated this relationship. It mattered little to the captains of finance that labor was underpaid and overworked. The "robber barons" may well have accepted not only Charles Darwin's theory of biological evolution but also the idea that the processes of nature should be undisturbed in human relations as well. In short, social and economic Darwinism prevailed, the very condition which Thorstein Veblen, the son of Norwegian immigrant parents in Wisconsin, later decried in his provocative *Theory of the Leisure Class.*

Immigrants, like their Yankee neighbors, hoped to employ the ballot as an instrument for social reform. A recent study, covering the quarter century prior to World War I, presents the view that, contrary to the belief that European peasant immigrants were by nature conservative and nonprogressive, Norwegians of the peasant class "became radical reformers in the period of Populism and Progressivism." They were especially desirous of regulating industrial capitalism through governmental controls. Their affiliation with the Republican party, in the sense of complete loyalty, has been exaggerated.[4]

The findings of Jon Wefald, cited above, are convincing. Just as the peasants in Norway did much to shape the course of modern Norwegian history, so their brothers who had emigrated carried with them a yearning for social improvement. Agreeing with Veblen, whose academically-couched philosophy defied their comprehension, they condemned absentee ownership, whether in land or in industry. It is not surprising that consumer and producer cooperatives eventually flourished in Minnesota, the New Scandinavia.[5]

That most Norwegians sought the land, and not the shop or the factory, cannot be doubted. As late as 1920, 52 percent of all Norwegian-born and 65.4 percent of those of Norwegian descent resided in agricultural areas. Their peasant-farmer heritage proved to be no handicap in the transition from Norwegian to American. Their personal desires, carried from Northern Europe, achieved a fair degree of fulfillment in the New Norway of the Upper Middle West.[6]

Political radicalism on the part of first- and second-generation Americans from Norway was, however, not much in evidence until the last fifteen or twenty years of the century. Some began their political careers as regular Republicans and later turned progressive. Nils P. Haugen was nominated railroad commissioner in Wisconsin's state Republican convention in 1881. He was elected and went on to hold that office with distinction until 1887, when he began the first of four terms in the House of Representatives. But in Haugen can be seen something more than a party man. He showed a definite inclination for reform legislation, demonstrated in a personal way by his refusal to accept free railroad transportation. Haugen declined to run for a fifth term in Congress and was approached by Robert M. LaFollette, later Progressive Republican governor, in the matter of running for the office of governor in Wisconsin. Opposition from regular Republicans cost Haugen the nomination. As state tax commissioner from 1901 to 1921 he saw his reform policy generally prevail.[7]

Norwegian-American political ideologies covered a spectrum ranging from socialism to moderate Republicanism. A socialist journal, *Gaa Paa* (Forward), published in Minneapolis after 1902, was the only one of its kind. Most Norwegian newspapers were moderate in their demands for progress. The larger number attached themselves to the Republican party, commonly identified with human freedom and with national unity. But there may have been an additional factor in the case of the immigrants from the European North. Much as they may have sympathized with Liberals in their homeland, and hence with the Democrats in the United States, they tired of voting Democratic in Wisconsin and Minnesota elections, where they invariably ended up on the losing side.

The numbers are impressive. By conservative estimate, there were 1,650,000 people of Norwegian descent in America, according to the Census of 1910. This figure includes those with only one parent of Norwegian extraction. Martin Ulvestad, in his encyclopedic two-volume work, declares that between 1847 and 1905, Norwegians held 2,221 county offices and sent 669 of their countrymen to the respective state legislatures. They elected four state governors and four lieutenant governors, not to forget eight state secretaries, seven state treasurers, three United States senators, and twelve Congressmen. Minnesota ranked first with 893 county officers, 259 state legislators, one governor (Knute Nelson), one United States senator (Knute Nelson), and six Congressmen. North Dakota came second, with Wisconsin and South Dakota trailing. Norwegian political contributions in Illinois and New York were almost negligible, in view of the relatively small percentage of their ethnic descent and their weakness at the polls in those states.[8]

For verification of Norwegian participation in American politics North Dakota, an agricultural state, serves as an excellent example. There the number of politically oriented newspapers, Republican in the main, came and went. Of these, *Normanden* (The Norwegian) of Grand Forks voiced most effectively the farmers' grievances and hopes from its beginning in 1887 to its termination in 1954. Like other nominally Republican weeklies, it was caught up in the agrarian crusade of the 1890s.[9]

The name of Marcus Thrane (1817–1890) calls to mind a different kind of immigrant, a leader in the drive for the rights of the workingman in an industrial society which had suddenly produced new social problems. Thrane's significance as originator of the Norwegian labor movement, and in a real sense founder of today's Labor party in Norway, has been cited. His socialistic views in the revolutionary year of 1848 brought him eight years of imprisonment and an eventual release in 1858.

The second of the two chapters in the life of Thrane was lived out in America. From the day of his arrival at Castle Garden in 1863, America was his abode. Through a Chicago weekly, *Marcus Thranes Norske Amerikaner*, he asserted himself on behalf of the workingman in 1866. It was a small beginning. He supported the demand for the eight-hour working day and, rather strangely for one suspected of atheism, paid tribute to the Sermon on the Mount. He sold out in the same year to *Skandinaven*, then about to begin its long and influential venture in immigrant journalism.[10]

In 1869 Thrane launched a new organ, *Dagslyset* (Daylight). a philosophical-religious monthly as he called it. A Thomas Paine credo provided the theme for one issue: "My fatherland is the world, and my religion is to do good." Thrane believed that the new American Labor Reform party and the Social Democratic party in Europe were similar in their aims. He appreciated their fraternal internationalism. He scorned the "priestly caste" and "money power." He complimented Søren Jaabæk. agrarian leader and parliamentarian in Norway, for equating workers with clergymen in social importance. Subsequent issues of *Dagslyset* contained a platform for a proposed Radical Reform party. The paper appeared less frequently in the 1870s. It succumbed to the panic of 1873. When it came to life once more in 1875, Thrane's editorial responsibilities were assumed by a Scandinavian freethinkers' society of Chicago. His final venture in journalism came as co-editor of *Den Nye Tid* (The New Age), founded in 1878 in Chicago. Louis Pio, a Danish socialist, was his partner for a time.[11]

The year 1883 found Thrane back in Norway on a visit. He met with little cordiality. The police were alerted to watch his movements. He carried with him 10,000 copies of a pamphlet bearing the suspicious title *Norge som Republik* (Norway as a Republic). When he proposed to speak on the lights and shadows of America, the Christiania *Arbeidersamfund* (Workers' Society) refused him permission to use their meeting hall. Later, in a statement to American friends, he confessed that the Conservative party in Norway treated him more respectfully than did the Liberals. He returned to Eau Claire, Wisconsin, where his son Arthur had begun a medical practice. From 1880 to 1884 he served as land agent for James J. Hill's Great Northern Railroad and enjoyed the luxury of a free pass. From the time of his death in 1890 until 1949 his earthly remains were undisturbed. As mentioned earlier, the Labor government of Norway arranged to have his bones transferred to Our Savior's Cemetery in Oslo, beside those of Ibsen, Bjørnson, and other great Norwegian personages. Delivering the eulogy on that occasion, the one-hundreth anniversary of the beginning of an organized labor movement in Norway, was Halvdan Koht, brilliant historian and wartime foreign minister of the 1940s.[12]

Marcus Thrane's career in Norway and America is both varied and pathetic. With unbelievable energy he wrote numerous articles, poems, and plays. He flew a black flag outside his son's home on November 11 in 1888 and 1889, "the republic's day of shame," as Thrane explained it. His reference was to the hanging of four professed anarchists, following the Haymarket affair of 1886 in Chicago. Thrane admired the American governmental system, but he appears to have lost confidence in it due to the display of hardheartedness and snobbery by the wealthy. To the end he befriended the workingman. In his time he was radical. Today he would be called a progressive.[13]

One can readily understand Thrane's impatience with the snail-like progress of the labor movement in America, and with the indifference of his countrymen, the Norwegians, before the period of political activism began, in the 1890s. As farmers rather than city workers, Norwegians in America would be affected and would respond with their fellow sufferers in times of agricultural distress. Yet for the cultural programs of the Grange, or Patrons of Husbandry, there was only limited appeal to a foreign-born people who self-consciously shied away from meetings conducted in the English language. Moreover, for Norwegian Lutherans, church activities claimed priority over those of secular stamp.

Agrarian discontent expressed itself before 1890. The plight of Norwegian-American farmers is discernible in a personal way in the political philosophy and participation of Knute Nelson (1843–1923). Once an emigrant from Voss in Norway at the age of six, he enlisted twelve years later in the Fourth Wisconsin Infantry Regiment. Upon being released from the army, he studied law in the University of Wisconsin and was admitted to the state bar. After a year in the state legislature he moved to Alexandria, Minnesota. Nelson sat in the Minnesota state senate and served as Republican presidential elector for the state in 1880, as Knud Langeland was doing in the neighboring state of Wisconsin.[14]

The score of years from 1880 on were marked by sizable political gains for Norwegian-Americans in the upper Mississippi Valley. Knute Nelson inaugurated this era of successful Norse candidacies by his election to the House of Representatives in 1882. Reelection came twice, with convincing majorities. It was enough to draw the attention of Republican leaders, who were disturbed over the Scandinavian shift toward Populism. In any event, Nelson was nominated and elected to the governorship of Minnesota in 1892, and reelected in 1894.

Already as a congressman in Washington, Nelson cautioned against excesses by labor, capital, or manufacturing interests. "True wisdom and statesmanship," he said, "lie in diffusing rather than in concentrating. Big cities may become dangerous monopolies, as well as big railroads and big men." Yet his Republican affiliation exposed him to criticism by Farmers' Alliance

Norwegians, whose strength lay in the one-crop area of western Minnesota and eastern North Dakota. They frankly called him a tool of his party.[15]

Granted that Nelson, as a Republican, deprived himself of grass-roots support in Minnesota, his popularity with Chicago's *Skandinaven*, nominally Republican, and with the Norwegian-American press as a whole was undiminished. In fact, the press reflected more of the reform spirit than did the politicians. In the early 1890s Nicolai Grevstad of *Skandinaven*, himself of humble origin in Norway, professed to be shocked over the "profound indifference of Chicago's rich industrialists toward the poor and the unemployed." The Populist *Nye Normanden* (The New Norwegian) of Minneapolis deplored federal intervention with troops in the Pullman strike of 1894, charging that the law, the judges, and the Winchester rifles defended capitalists at the expense of the workers. At the same time the American press stressed rugged individualism, all to the advantage of the industrial magnates.[16]

The nineties, not as gay as commonly supposed, were characterized by the rise of giant corporations, despite the passage of the Sherman Anti-Trust Act at the beginning of the decade. In self-defense the People's party and the Democrats merged in 1896. Yet electoral votes for William Jennings Bryan, standard bearer for the combined parties and avowed friend of the little man, were hard to come by even in the Upper Midwest states. And the ballots of a relatively small number of Norwegian immigrants and of their progeny born in America could hardly be determinative in the climactic struggle with the financial interests of the East, represented in the Republican candidate, William B. McKinley.

It is significant that in 1896 *Skandinaven* was decrying the sweatshop, and *Amerika*, a Republican journal of Madison, Wisconsin, was urging that "silver have equal rights with gold." Ole Amundsen Buslett of *Amerika* serialized William H. Harvey's *Coin's Financial School*, the Bible of the Populists and the accepted argument for a bimetallic standard of currency. *Decorah-Posten* in Iowa, true to its intended purpose, took no active part in the campaign. Its Republican leanings were indicated, however, in the announcement that McKinley's "great victory" was an omen of better times. Reform was a common feature in Norwegian-American journalism. In 1912, for example, *Decorah-Posten* hinted that Republicans would have done better to nominate the progressive Theodore Roosevelt instead of the stodgy William Howard Taft.[17]

A revival of nativism followed the Haymarket episode. It manifested itself in the American Protective Association (1887) and the Immigration Restriction League (1894). Directed against Roman Catholics and Eastern and Southern Europeans, as well as against radicals, the new nativism lacked effectiveness for want of a clear objective. Some patriotic proponents urged a literacy test for screening undesirables. Others pressed for recognition of "Nordic" supremacy, a boon to the older immigration. The Statue of Liberty, erected in 1886 in New York harbor as a gift from the people of France, seemed to symbolize rejection rather than welcome for Europe's "huddled masses yearning to be free."

Racial theories derived from Social Darwinism gained in popularity before the turn of the century. Anti-foreignism was the inevitable result. It had not helped that since 1880 there occurred a tremendous increase in Southern and Eastern European immigration. In the decade of the 1860s, of the total immigration only 1.5 percent arrived from Europe's South and East, and 87.8 percent from North and West. In contrast, the figures for 1901–1910 were 70.8 percent from the South and East, and 21.7 percent from the North and West.[18]

Suspicion and disdain were often directed against the newer arrivals by the older, as well as by native-born Americans. Not infrequently Norwegian immigrants feared the impact of an unfamiliar alien population upon established customs and institutions. Hjalmar Hjorth Boyesen on several occasions let his feelings be known, in criticism of unrestricted immigration. In two separate articles he emphasized the constructive aspects of Scandinavian immigration on the one hand and, on the other, the negative contributions of what he considered to be unassimilable peoples from economically undernourished and politically unstable European lands.[19]

Boyesen had arrived in the United States at the age of twenty-one. He differed from his Scandinavian countrymen in that his life was lived in the East, largely among Americans of British stock. He quickly mastered the English language and eventually became professor of European literature at Cornell University and Columbia University. Never did he publish in the Norwegian language, whether in his realistic novels or in his historical essays. His Scandinavianism showed through in an article praising the qualities of the peoples of the European North. Swedes and Norwegians, he said, "come here with no millennial expectations" but bring "qualities of perseverance, thrift, and a sturdy sense of independence." Their interest in public affairs was commendable. Apart from their national vice of drunkenness, imported from Scandinavia, and their clannishness, they were among the elements who found it easy to adjust to American conditions. Boyesen complimented President Grover Cleveland, a Democrat, for his appointment of Rasmus B. Anderson, a specialist in Norwegian language and literature, as minister to Denmark. Anderson was the first Norseman to be so honored. Boyesen did not limit his criticism of ethnic groups to the new arrivals alone. Perhaps in part because of long association with Yankee stock, he relegated Irish-Americans to a lower category. Norwegians, he believed, could hardly be anything but Republican, as long as the Irish were Democratic. "The Norsemen and the Celt will, I fancy, never pull together," he concluded.

Boyesen opened his attack upon the so-called unassimilables in 1887 with an assertion that American cities were "filling up with a turbulent foreign proletariat, clamoring for *panem et circenses*, as in the days of ancient Rome, and threatening the existence of the republic if their demands remain unheeded." Again, his reference was to the unruly element conspicuous in the Haymarket affair of the previous year. He feared that the American people would retaliate with violence against the "foreign mischief-makers." Brute force, he warned, might imperil the very democratic institutions which it was attempting to protect. The better solution was strict government control of immigration. Boyesen agreed with prominent eugenically-minded writers of the day, men like Francis Amasa Walker, a political economist who at one time directed the Bureau of the Census. Walker was warning that foreign ethnic strains were replacing the original Anglo-Saxon stock.[20]

In support of immigration restrictionists, a Congressional commission reported in 1907 on the status and implications of unrestricted immigration. The majority of this Dillingham Commission agreed that the new immigrants were illiterate and unskilled, that they came initially as single males, and that they were transient, clannish, and disinterested in becoming useful American citizens. Little recognition was given by the commission to the fact that the older immigrants arrived with the same handicaps. Unfortunately, the misconceptions of the report persisted and found their way into legend. In defense of the report, however, it is probably true that the peoples of the British Isles, including Ireland, and of Germany and the Scandinavian states were more familiar with representative government and democratic procedures than were the majority of immigrants dealt with in the report. Norwegians fell into this category. They felt at home in the new land from the start, except for the language barrier, and were able to participate in local government almost immediately.

It was perhaps this last factor, a relatively quick identification with community concerns, that led the Wisconsin sociologist Edward Alsworth Ross to elaborate upon Scandinavian virtues. "In point of literacy they lead the world," he began. In intellectual capacity and in physical traits they were superior. Norwegians had never known "the steam-roller of feudalism." As peasants they had held their farms under odel tenure, that is, free from tenurial rights of an overlord, and could order the king himself off their land. In politics they reflected "moral ideas." The considered public office to be a public trust. Constructive programs attracted them. They opposed the "interests," not least the brewing interest of the German-Americans. So said Ross in his onesided tribute. His article appeared in 1914, the year of Norway's centennial observance of separate constitutional status. Whether the eminent social scientist framed his essay with that in mind is not known.[21]

Temperance was also an issue that came to the fore at this time. A substantial number of Norwegian-American newspapers participated in the movement for total abstinence in the use of alcoholic beverages. Their reasons for joining the so-called temperance forces were varied. Religious implications do not seem to have been foremost in their thinking. At any rate, Norwegian pastors in America gave little assistance to the effort to dethrone John Barleycorn. On the contrary, they viewed with suspicion the secret order of Good Templars, whose membership rolls were mounting. Secret societies were thought to be in competition with the church. While non-Lutheran pastors held the same view regarding secret societies, they were more likely to side with the stated social aims of their church bodies, which often included the elimination of the drinking evil.

The Civil War and its aftermath lifted the moral restraints upon personal behavior. Separation from the old country also relieved many an isolated Norwegian farmer or disconsolate workingman from the social pressures that had prevailed in Norway. Frustration, induced by hard times and by disillusionment in the period of uncontrolled industrial expansion, made the bottle a convenient outlet for self-indulgence and momentary satisfaction. Drunkenness prevailed among Norwegians in America in greater degree than in the home country.

Ethnic and political forces also provoked anti-saloon attacks in the press. To a large proportion of the Germans and the Irish in America, beer drinking came as naturally as breathing. They observed Saturday nights and Sundays in traditional European fashion, with *gemütlichkeit*. Occasionally a German or an Irish band disturbed the Protestant services of worship in Chicago or other metropolitan centers as they paraded on cobblestone streets, in apparent disregard of the rights of others. With this in mind, *Skandinaven* expressed concern over the possibility of a repeal of the Sunday closing law in Chicago. To add insult to injury, half of the Germans and nearly all of the Irish voted Democratic regularly, putting them at odds with the predominantly Republican Norwegians. Temperance advocates shared the feeling that saloon keepers and politics were a bad combination. Tales about New York's Democratic Tammany organization were kept alive. Political bossism on state levels and municipal corruption reigned. Demon Rum seemed to be a part of this unholy alliance.[22]

Whatever the reasons for teetotalism, they were seldom spelled out completely. Undoubtedly, the harmful effects of alcoholism on individual persons, families, and entire communities were noted. Something must be done to protect a people in dispersion, like the Norwegian immigrants, from their own excesses. Furthermore, there was much to be said for preserving the Norwegian name in an American society given increasingly to inebriation and crime. It was with these objectives in mind that Waldemar Ager established his weekly *Reform* in Eau Claire, Wisconsin, in 1890 and continued to draw his bill of particulars against the saloon and the tavern until his death in 1941.

In North Dakota politics the temperance issue ranked high. The Grand Forks *Normanden*, leading Norwegian-American paper in the state, had been established in 1887 specifically for that purpose and continued its commitment to that ideal down to 1954, the year of its final edition. *Afholds-Basunen* (The Temperance Trumpet) of Hillsboro cooperated in the temperance fight from 1887 to 1896 and was influential, with *Normanden*, in adoption of a prohibition clause in the state constitution of 1889.[23]

As a rule, the Norwegian-American press, however temperance-oriented, devoted itself mainly to other issues. *Skandinaven* and *Minneapolis Tidende*, for example, read widely throughout Norwegian communities of the Great Lakes region and farther to the west, identified themselves with the reformist wing of the Republican party, but they did not limit themselves to the function of temperance organs. On the other hand, few Norwegian journals sneered at the idea of prohibition, whether in the form of local ordinances or of state laws.

On the subject of women's rights, little was said in the nineteenth century. Perhaps here the Danish-Norwegian *Kvinden og Hjemmet* (The Woman and the Home) crusaded for feminism with most notable success. As a monthly publication emanating from Cedar Rapids, Iowa, beginning in 1888, it was able to claim 34,000 subscribers by 1924. Its chief rival in the women's rights field was Waldemar Ager's *Reform*. Well ahead of his time, Ager declared that militant suffragists were within their rights in demanding equality with men, not only in the right to hold property but the right to vote.

Even the more staid Norwegians demonstrated a zeal for reform. Knute Nelson, who left the governor's office in Minnesota to serve in Washington from 1895 to 1923, never forsook the

Republican party. Yet he refused to go along with its protectionist tariff policy. For farmers of his constituency high prices on manufactured goods spelled doom. Senator Nelson favored popular election of senators, although he owed his senatorial seat initially to the state legislature rather than to the people directly. The Solon from Norway argued in favor of a federal income tax when many legislators were lethargic on that issue.

The list of forward-looking Norwegians in political office could well be extended. A few names will suffice.

Andrew E. Lee, born of peasant stock in Norway, emigrated with his parents to Wisconsin at the age of four. Eventually, as a Populist candidate, he became governor of South Dakota (1897–1901). In his campaign he advocated the initiative and the referendum, several years in advance of La Follette's "Wisconsin Idea." Sensing possible dangers in big business monopolies, he wrote to a friend: "We must get relief from this commercial despotism before it secures absolute control of every branch of government."[24]

James O. Davidson emigrated to Wisconsin in 1872. Beginning with six years of service in the state legislature in 1892, he became successively state treasurer, lieutenant governor, and governor (1906–1911). He succeeded La Follette when the young Progressive Republican was elevated to national prominence in the United States Senate. Davidson supported bills bringing public utilities under state regulation and a graduated federal income tax, in keeping with established Populist-Progressive objectives. Another La Follette Progressive was Peter Norbeck, elected governor of South Dakota in 1916. He is said to have moved far toward state socialism.[25]

Populism as a movement declined, but its spirit survived into the twentieth century. The Populist Grand Forks *Normanden* fell into independent Republican hands in 1893, but its lambasting of machine politics continued unabated. Fargo's *Fram* (Forward), published from 1898 to 1917, joined *Normanden* in demanding enforcement of prohibition legislation. The Norwegian press in North Dakota experienced a remarkable growth in circulation, reaching about 30,000 subscribers in 1910. A partial explanation for the quickening in reader interest lies in the acceptance of the Progressive challenge. Even a Scandinavian Republican League (1904) embraced reformist ideas.[26]

Nicolai Grevstad of Chicago's *Skandinaven*, the independent Republican newspaper, personified in high degree the trend toward progressivism, regardless of party, in the opening decades of the new century. His views on unfair practices and on shoddy law enforcement lack nothing in clarity. He challenged the "divine right" economic philosophy of coal operators and railroad managers during the anthracite strike of 1902 in Pennsylvania. He warned the operators that their stubbornness could only lead to a reaction in the form of state socialism. For Senator La Follette, as for Theodore Roosevelt before him, Grevstad had genuine admiration. Yet he emphasized that Norwegians already had adopted the Wisconsin senator's views before they had become widely accepted. In Grevstad's words, "The Norwegians did not march into the La Follette camp; he came into their camp."[27]

An analysis of Minnesota elections in the first decade of the twentieth century indicates that Norwegians and Swedes were overrepresented in the state government and legislature, as well as in Congress. But in Minnesota Republicans and Democrats vied for Scandinavian votes without significant interference by Progressives of either major party. Yet the La Follette spirit was there. Norwegians tended to associate the Democrats with reform, or at least with Scandinavian interests, and supported John Albert Johnson, a Swedish-American Democrat, in his successful race for the governorship in 1904. They were especially prone to vote Democratic when reminded that Yankee Republicans considered them "voting cattle." National origin was hardly a determining factor at the polls. Rather, party differences and prospects of reform weighed more heavily in Scandinavian thinking. This is not to say that sometimes the Republicans presented a more appealing program to the immigrants. Evidence points to the conclusion that, outside the Nordic countries themselves, Scandinavian activities affected social development in Minnesota more than in any other place in the world.[28]

There is justification for stressing the role of the press in reform. Editors and owners born on Norwegian soil, like many of their colleagues from other European lands, were often liberally educated and progressively inclined. Events falling within the new twentieth century lent themselves to a revival of admiration for new thought and to patriotic feeling, both Norwegian and American. Many harbingers of a new day in Norway, among whom were the literary geniuses, exerted their maximum influence before 1900. The deaths of the socially eruptive Henrik Ibsen in 1906 and the unconventional Bjørnstjerne Bjørnson in 1910 served to remind all Norwegians vividly of their place in the world of culture. Many recalled Ibsen's idealistic plea for fulfillment of personality: "A man is anyone who, whether in parliament or church, perceives the ideal behind his activities." More related to government was Bjørnson's slogan: "Politics is the highest form of neighborliness." By the time of the breakup in 1905 of the dual monarchy, sensitivity to political problems had increased due to the growing intensity of Norwegian national consciousness.

The centennial year of 1914 provided yet another outlet for appraising Norwegian progress on both sides of the Atlantic. Already the fervor of 1905 had inspired the organization of *Nordmanns-Forbundet*, an international league of Norwegians. Thousands of members of the Sons of Norway traveled in 1914 to Christiania to march under the Stars and Stripes in the colorful and stirring *syttende mai* (17th of May) parade up Karl Johans Gate to the royal palace. When they visited the emigrant exposition at Frogner Park in the capital city, they were proud of Norwegian achievements in the great American society. At the same time Norwegian veterans of the Civil War were meeting for their fiftieth encampment at the fair grounds in St. Paul, Minnesota. Little did either group, the representatives of the emigrated Norway in Frogner Park or the remnants of the Fifteenth Wisconsin Regiment in St. Paul, understand the ominous international rumblings that carried forebodings of a world catastrophe. Soon men would be catapulted into not merely a European war but into a conflict involving the new American homeland as well.

CHAPTER 8

The Life of the Spirit:
Norwegian Churches in America

IN COMMON WITH HER SCANDINAVIAN NEIGHBORS, NORWAY FIRST saw pagan myths and rites yield to Catholic Christianity after the year 1000. Then, in the early sixteenth century, the European Northland underwent a transformation to Lutheranism, as a part of the Reformation. As has been noted in the opening chapter, the Lutheran state church of Norway in its orthodox form was challenged by religious leaders both from within the organization and from without. The movement inspired by Hans Nielsen Hauge emphasized piety and lay participation in religious services. Hauge favored informal gatherings for purposes of spiritual edification. He defied the age-old laws forbidding conventicles, the practice of meeting secretly and without authorization. Gisle Johnson of the theological faculty of the University of Christiania accepted the personal holiness idea preached by Hauge but held out for guidance and control by the well educated clergy instead of by the lay folk. Thus Johnson combined piety with orthodoxy. A well qualified Norwegian church historian believes that "the Johnsonian revival ushered in a new relationship between the state church officials and the awakened groups throughout Norway" and "bridged the gap between social classes which had formerly given rise to the assumption that there was one religion for the cultured people and another for the masses."[1]

Between the positions of the Haugeans and the Johnsonians lay that of the Grundtvigians, a liberal and more rationalistic element within the church. Hans Nielsen Hauge died in 1824. He had never confronted either Bishop Nicolai F. S. Grundtvig of Denmark or Grundtvig's influential disciple in Norway, W. A.

Wexels, pastor for 47 years of Our Saviour's Church in Christiania, until his death in 1866. Gisle Johnson, on the other hand, belongs to a later era and, in his position as lecturer at the University of Christiania, he made direct assault on Wexels and the Grundtvigians. Among his charges was the failure of the popular Danish-inspired doctrine to teach "man's sinful depravity in all its depths." When Grundtvig died in 1872, Bjørnstjerne Bjørnson, Norway's literary genius and national hero, took up his cause, especially that aspect of it which pertained to liberal culture.[2]

Bishop Grundtvig's religious views were ahead of his time. His theology is suggestive of ecumenical thought of the twentieth century, in Europe and America. If one were to achieve personal completeness and satisfaction, he insisted, one must experience the reality of God's spirit. By a century he anticipated the emphasis upon literature, history, poetry, and ethics as an antidote to the inevitable mechanization of the age. Yet he distrusted intellectualism as the key to the fuller life. There must be no worship of Reason. His universality of thought and his love for the human race in its entirety brought upon him charges of infidelity to the spirit of the Reformation, possibly of a return to Rome. His broad-church Lutheranism might well be characterized as favoring ecumenism and a universal church, without the papal hierarchy.[3]

The various Lutheran factions, and non-Lutheran groups as well, were to find in America fertile soil for their growth. Perhaps the temptation toward divergence from the religious instruction of their childhood was even greater in the New World. At times it seems that the Song of Ruth was being negated into "Thy people shall not be my people, nor thy God my God." While one is constantly aware that social and economic factors played a more important role than religion in the decision to emigrate, it is proper for our present purposes to differentiate between the pioneer religious leaders in America, best represented, probably, in Elling Eielsen (Haugean), Claus Clausen (Grundtvigian), and Johannes W. C. Dietrichson (orthodox but with tendencies toward Grundtvigianism). Religious intolerance and persecution at home were but minor considerations in emigration, whatever significance they had in isolated instances.

Indeed, the Lutheran Church of Norway looked with dismay upon the vast exodus of its promising sons and daughters and consistently sought to discourage their departure. The dramatic appeal of Bishop Jacob Neumann of Bergen in 1837 serves as an illustration:[4]

Here in Norway rest the ashes of your forefathers; here you first saw the light of day; here you enjoyed many childhood pleasures; here you received your first impressions of God and His love; here you are still surrounded by relatives and friends who share your joy and your sorrow, while there, when you are far away from all that has been dear to you, who shall close your eyes in the last hour of life? A stranger's hand! And who shall weep at your grave? Perhaps— no one!

The Norwegian-American historian Laurence M. Larson did much to recapture the important role of the lay preacher in the Middle West. These hardy men, usually in their best years and of rough appearance, spoke with the unction of the Old Testament prophets at meetings in the settlements. With energy generated by the conviction of a personal call to preach, they "laid the sinner on the anvil and gave him blow after blow." Repentance was their theme, whatever the Scripture text that was chosen.[5]

Some lay preachers belonged to "the sects," which in the language of the day usually meant Baptists, Methodists, Adventists, or Quakers. With Bible in hand, they disputed with the Lutherans and with each other. Many professed to be Haugeans, puritans separated from the church of Norway. Those not separatists were aligned in spirit with Elling Eielsen and the Haugean tradition as it manifested itself within the old state church. One source lists seventeen preachers of the 1840s and 1850s, of which sixteen were or had been lay preachers.[6]

Eielsen and Clausen were ordained by German Lutheran pastors in America in 1843, there being no ordained Norwegians to perform that rite. Dietrichson arrived fully ordained from Norway in 1844. Officially the church of Norway withheld its support from the infant church in America, an attitude which annoyed Dietrichson. He returned to Norway in search of assistance in 1845. Once the initial Slooper settlement in upper New

York State had been completed, and the original company had for the most part found their way to the Fox River country of northern Illinois, the midwestern settlement attracted Ellingians (followers of Eielsen), Grundtvigians, orthodox Lutherans, Mormons, and the sectarians.

Elling Eielsen came to America in 1839 partly as the result of the encouragement of Tollef Bache, one of Hauge's more energetic lay followers in Norway. For two years, after extensive evangelistic efforts in his own country, Eielsen tried to awaken the peoples of Sweden and Denmark. Thrown into prison as a violator of the Danish conventicle act, he emerged to carry on his personal mission to the emigrants in America. His impact upon them in the Fox River settlement proved to be effective. He is credited with organizing in 1846 the Evangelical Lutheran Church in America, popularly known as Eielsen's Synod, lay-oriented and low-churchly. It continued as Hauge's Synod in 1875 and in 1914 claimed 350 congregations and about 40,000 communicants. A college and seminary at Red Wing, Minnesota (1879), were merged with St. Olaf College of Northfield, Minnesota, in 1917. Indicative of the foreign missions emphasis, Hauge's Synod opened its work in China in 1891. An author and editor of a later generation generously sums up Eielsen's contribution by saying, "Eielsen started more things in pioneer days than all the other pioneer ministers put together."[7]

Elling Eielsen's influence ran wide and deep. Alone he carried on the work in Illinois, Wisconsin, and Iowa. In 1854 he raised the question of assistance. The answer came during the years 1858–1876, when he and his associates ordained many men, some of whom may have been lacking in refinement, but they were not wanting in native intellectual capacity. So the man who had been ridiculed by adversaries for his opposition to chanting and robes, and for his encouragement to women to participate in public prayer and testimony, had made his mark in the settlements.

A second groundbreaker in the establishment of Norwegian Lutheranism in America was Claus L. Clausen. Like his contemporary, Eielsen, he began as a Haugean lay preacher. Of Danish birth, he became attracted to Grundtvigianism as a countermovement against rationalism among the Danish clergy.

Clausen came to Norway in 1841 to restore his health. He met many Haugeans there, among them Andreas Hauge, son of the deceased Hans Nielsen Hauge, and the Drammen layman and merchant, Tollef Bache. The Grundtvigianism influence was also present in the friendly person of Pastor W. A. Wexels of Christiania. In the company of Søren Bache, son of Tollef and already a pillar in the Muskego settlement of Wisconsin, Clausen sailed from Drammen in 1843. In Muskego he met Even Heg, the staunch Haugean layman who was to put his stamp upon many events and personalities in the formative years of the Norwegian community.[8]

Muskego settlers responded warmly to Clausen's ministry. Times were hard. Cholera was rampant. On New Year's Day in 1844 seventeen bodies were buried. But there were also pleasant experiences. Heg donated a site for a church building, the first Norwegian Lutheran structure in the New World. It was dedicated in 1845. Clausen's mission soon extended to neighboring counties. But trials came again. Clausen lost a son by death. Next his wife died. Relations with Eielsen deteriorated, as Eielsen made known his displeasure with the aristocratic pretensions of the state church of Norway, which in 1844 seemed to assert itself in the person of a recent arrival, Johannes W. C. Dietrichson, a graduate of the theological faculty of the University of Christiania.

Dietrichson's entrance upon the Wisconsin scene apparently caused no strain between him and Clausen, but between Dietrichson and Eielsen a cleavage of historical importance developed. Eielsen did not appreciate the ruff and the gown, symbols of the church of Norway. He may have wondered whether Dietrichson aspired to become a bishop in America. Dietrichson, on the other hand, looked askance at lay activities and expressed misgivings over the propriety of Eielsen's ordination. A schism in the church in America was in the offing, with high-church and low-church postures in rigid opposition, and with signs that officialdom, transported from Norway, resented and feared the self-assertiveness of the former peasantry, or *bondestand*, in America.

Clausen's Grundtvigianism had never been dominant in his thinking, nor was his Haugeanism as deep-seated as that of

Eielsen. Within two years he resigned from his Muskego appointment. Dietrichson had in the interval accepted a call to Koshkonong, farther to the west. Some speculate that Clausen felt incompetent in the company of the university-educated Dietrichson. If so, the feeling became accentuated when other graduates in theology came from abroad: Hans A. Stub in 1848, Herman Preus, Nils O. Brandt, and G. F. Dietrichson, cousin to Johannes Dietrichson, in 1851, and Jacob A. Ottesen in 1852. Most of the new arrivals spurned Grundtvigianism. They contributed personally to the founding of the Norwegian Synod in 1853. The official name was The Norwegian Evangelical Lutheran Church of America.

By 1850 Johannes Dietrichson departed from America permanently. His experience in the parish of Koshkonong had been hectic. One law suit and possibly several physical confrontations with drunken or violent members of his congregation demonstrated that his opposition came not only from rival Protestants and Ellingians. An examination of his church records reveals that he knew his flock well and did not hesitate to inscribe remarks about their character in the register. Of the more than one thousand, scarcely more than a hundred were mentioned favorably.[9]

Dietrichson's rough pioneering adventure was by no means an isolated one. A recent translation of the letters of Caja Munch, a woman of the parsonage, and of her husband's autobiography, throw considerable light upon Dietrichson's frustration among what he considered to be an uncultured and stubborn people. The same class feeling that hindered Dietrichson affected the progress of Johan Storm Munch's congregation in Wiota, Wisconsin. Munch and his wife waited in vain for properly educated and ordained ministers from Norway in the late 1850s to replace "itinerant bunglers." Prior to the delivery of his farewell sermon and departure for Norway Munch had declared that no true servant of the Lord could labor any longer in Wiota. His return to Norway was not without precedent. Of eleven ministers who came from the old country before 1856, seven returned, including the two Dietrichsons, Munch, and Adolph C. Preus, president of the Norwegian Synod from 1853 to 1862. Many who arrived after 1856 also returned.[10]

While the departure of well qualified pastors from Wisconsin denotes a measure of failure in their ministry, their contributions as trailblazers are noteworthy. Dietrichson in particular helped to build a solid foundation for a Norwegian church in America. He and Munch could not tolerate indefinitely "freedom" if it meant the legal right of hecklers to disturb religious services. Nor were they kindly disposed toward the public school, not simply because it neglected religious instruction but because of its superficial coverage of subject matter and, in many instances, its lax discipline. Dietrichson and Munch also preferred a separation from the German Missouri Synod. The clergy-supported *Emigranten* joined them in looking toward a church independent of the German Concordia Seminary in St. Louis, which offered its facilities to the Norwegians. But the Missouri Synod connection was to be continued in favor of the conservatives, not of Dietrichson and Munch, whose decision to return to Norway came after they had lost the argument.[11]

Claus Clausen's withdrawal from Muskego in 1853 did not terminate his close relationship with the Norwegian immigrant population. It opened up new vistas for him in Iowa and Minnesota. Until 1872 he resided in northern Iowa. With St. Ansgar as his center, he served a territory of vast dimensions, about 200 miles from east to west and 75 miles from north to south. His loyalty to the Norwegian Synod wavered in the late 1850s, at which time he sat in the Iowa state legislature. In 1861 he renounced his onetime Grundtvigian beliefs, publicly confessed his errors, and was readmitted to the Synod. But a second resignation came in 1868, when he could no longer subscribe to the proslavery stand of the Synod, a position made practically untenable by the outcome of the Civil War in any event.[12]

In 1870 Clausen became president of a newly organized Conference of the Norwegian-Danish Evangelical Lutheran Church of America. It was the result of a split between Swedes and Norwegians who had once formed themselves into a Scandinavian Augustana Synod in 1860. Ill health forced Clausen to resign as president in 1872. His effectiveness was sharply limited thereafter, although he lived another twenty years. By 1882 the Conference which he had helped to create numbered 360 congregations. Strokes and paralysis incapacitated Clausen in the 1880s. He retired in Austin, Minnesota. He lived to witness the formation of the United Norwegian Lutheran Church of America in 1890, when the Conference, his own organization, merged with the Norwegian-Danish Augustana Synod and a so-called Anti-Missourian Brotherhood, which had separated from the Norwegian Synod.

Clausen's funeral services in 1892 carried a suggestion of inter-denominational harmony. Since the Lutheran sanctuary in Austin was too small to accommodate the many who wished to pay their last respects to this popular veteran of both religious and civil warfare, the services were conducted in the local Methodist Episcopal Church. From the beginning this pioneer preacher and administrator had devoted himself to a far-flung Norwegian constituency as well as to the Danish.[13]

A substantial part of Norwegian-American church history, from an organizational standpoint, relates to the years 1890, 1917, 1946, and 1963. The trend was from fragmentation toward unification. The United Norwegian Lutheran Church, formed in 1890, brought together the Norwegian Augustana Synod (1870), the Conference of the Norwegian-Danish Evangelical Lutheran Church in America (1870), and the Anti-Missouri Brotherhood. The latter group had withdrawn from the Norwegian Synod in 1887 on the issue of predestination. Under the leadership of Gjermund Hoyme, president of the new organization until his death in 1902, the United Church claimed 830 congregations and 72,000 communicants in 1891. This figure increased by 1913 to 165,000.

The United Church suffered a loss in 1897 when a number of Free Church congregations withdrew. No constitution governed the actions of the Free Church. As intended by two of its leaders, Georg Sverdrup and Sven Oftedal, sovereignty lay in the local congregations. Theodore C. Blegen describes Sverdrup, of the Augsburg Seminary in Minneapolis, as one who "stood for a trained, democratic ministry functioning in a low-church atmosphere." Sverdrup's colleague Oftedal more dramatically declared his independence from the Norwegian Synod. The Free Church defection meant that St. Olaf College of Northfield, Minnesota, rather than the more religiously liberal Augsburg College of Minneapolis, would be recognized as the official institution of higher learning within the United Church. Augsburg continued as the college of the Free Church.[14]

The great majority of Norwegian Lutherans were merged in 1917 into the Norwegian Lutheran Church of America. The three components, representing various tendencies, were the United Lutheran Church (1890), Hauge's Synod (1876), and the traditionalist Norwegian Synod (1853). Hans A. Stub, president of the Norwegian Synod after 1912, served as president of the merged organizations from 1917 to 1925. Lay preaching and the congregational instead of the geographical emphasis, both important stones in the Haugean structure, ceased to be issues in the new body. In fact, they were incorporated into it.

From the Norwegian Lutheran Church of America emerged the Evangelical Lutheran Church (1946), which in 1950 entered into unity discussions with the United Evangelical Lutheran Church and the American Lutheran Conference. Led by President Fredrik A. Schiotz of the Evangelical Lutheran Church, the organization of the American Lutheran Church was consummated in 1963. In the process, the Evangelical Lutheran Church, the United Evangelical Lutheran Church, the American Lutheran Conference, and the Lutheran Free Church became one religious body, headquartered in Minneapolis and numbering about 5,000 congregations and 3,000,000 members.

The ecclesiastical story has been carried beyond the immigrant stage, and there are inevitably many omissions in the telling. Lacking are such names as Ulrik Vilhelm Koren and Olaus F. Duus. Koren, together with his cultured wife Elisabeth, arrived from Norway and the national university there in 1853. As a religious force in Decorah, Iowa, a center of Norwegianism down to the present day, and as President of the Norwegian Synod from 1894 to 1911, Koren bridged more than one transition. Olaus Duus represents the dozens of unsung clergymen in rural America. He left a wealth of America letters, recovered in Norway of course. They reveal him as pastor, teacher, farmer, land speculator, and, in a pinch, medical practitioner. He depicted immigrant life as he saw it from the vantage point of the Waupaca and Whitewater parsonages on the Wisconsin scene in the 1850s. The death of his wife in 1859 moved him to return to the homeland, where he completed his ministry.

His appreciation and love for her is aptly expressed in a single statement of tribute: "I am sure it was with good reason that Christ sent his disciples out two by two."[15]

Successive mergers may not have inspired greater loyalty from Norwegian Lutherans in pulpit and pew. Fidelity toward one's own branch of the church ran especially high in the nineteenth century. At one time or another Norwegian-Americans worshiped in fourteen different synods. By way of contrast, Swedish Lutherans found religious expression in only one synod, the Swedish Augustana. But Swedish Lutheranism never reached the strength of the Norwegian, although after 1880 the Swedes rapidly overtook the Norwegians numerically in America. Perhaps the organizational disunity among the immigrants from Norway was an advantage insofar as it offered many options and therefore could accommodate more minds and dispositions.

Norwegian national feeling may well have played a role in the movement toward church unity. As a church historian expresses it, the church, which once functioned within a "cultural ghetto," was almost catapulted out of its ethnic and spiritual isolation by the forces of Americanization during World War I. Regardless of synods and conferences, members from the same *bygdelags*, or social organizations comprised of members who had departed from the same communities in Norway, were attracted to one another. A common catechism and a common hymnal gave impetus to unification. And leaders in the various synods lent their support to the same end. Still another circumstance that characterized all segments of Norwegian-American Lutheranism was the shift from the use of the Norwegian language to the English. In 1917 about 75 percent of the services were conducted in the Norwegian tongue, in 1928 only about 40 percent. Norwegian and English services seem to have been evenly balanced around 1925.[16]

In the 1880s and 1890s missionaries and settlers carried the religious tensions of the Middle West to California, Oregon, and Washington. Yet the churches on the Pacific Coast were unique in some ways. Because of the limited Scandinavian population, successful church activity was usually possible only when Swedes, Danes, and Norwegians cooperated. Clerical control and social restraints were not as prevalent as in the Mississippi Valley. Religious indifference or its opposite, evangelistic emotionalism, were therefore more in evidence. The main centers of church life were so far removed from the parent institution that the Western communions functioned more independently.[17]

The first official attempt to minister to Norwegian religious needs in the Golden Gate region dates from 1870, when the Norwegian Lutheran Synod appointed Christian Hvistendahl to establish, if practicable, a congregation in San Francisco. On his way westward the young emissary of the church noted with regret the plight of Scandinavian Mormons in Utah. Transported on the newly constructed Central Pacific Railway, he reached San Francisco, where he found less than 4,000 Scandinavians, and over half of them Swedes. The religious apathy he observed was offset somewhat by the knowledge that some fifty congregations were engaged in a wide variety of denominational activity.

Following the formation of a committee of Scandinavians, the preparation of a constitution, and the signing of 56 charter members, Hvistendahl accepted the invitation to be their pastor. Failing health compelled him to resign in 1875. Surprisingly, he lived until 1913. His last twenty years were spent in the ministry in Norway. His name will survive in the religious annals of California. His mission was expanded by others into the Pacific Northwest.[18]

Taking advantage of the new transcontinental railways, large contingents of Norwegian emigrants of the 1880s proceeded directly from their homeland to the Pacific Coast. Their coming explains in part why ministerial gatherings were held in the West independent of control "back East." The contrast between the population figures over several decades is striking. In the eighty years from 1860 to 1940 the number of Norwegian-born residents in California, for example, rose from a mere 700 to over 15,000.

But population increase in the Far West failed of itself to bulge the rosters of the various branches of the Lutheran church. A substantial majority of Norwegian newcomers, and their children born in America, were urban dwellers employed in fishing, seafaring, lumbering, mechanical work, and merchandising. Observers noted a lamentable lack of interest in organized religion in cities and towns. Church leaders missed the steady support of a church-going rural people, such as they had enjoyed in the upper Midwest in earlier times. The anti-clericalism personified in Norway's nineteenth-century literary artists, Bjørnstjerne Bjørnson and Henrik Ibsen, and in men like Marcus Thrane in the socialist-labor field, bore fruit in the twentieth century. To illustrate the degree of religious luke-warmness in the West, in 1944 the Evangelical Lutheran Church had a nationwide membership of 600,000. Less than five percent resided in the Pacific Coast area, where over 15 percent of the Norwegian stock in America lived, counting first and second generations. Church membership in the West trailed far behind, relative to Norwegian population.

The Sunday morning ritual, sermon, and singing swung over to the English language by the time of World War II. A younger and more American-acclimated third generation had to be served. Less than five percent of the services on the Pacific Coast were in the original Norwegian tongue. In contrast, on the Atlantic Coast, where not more than one percent of the total E.L.C. membership could be found, 25 percent of the services were still conducted in the old language. Undoubtedly there was a larger first-born generation membership in the East.[19]

As on the Pacific Coast, so also along the Atlantic, and more specifically in the Greater New York area, Norwegians lived their lives somewhat independently. Lack of continuous com-munication with Illinois, Wisconsin, and Minnesota, as well as divergent interests and occupations, go far to explain the dis-tinctive Eastern experience. Maritime pursuits of easterners had no significant parallel in the Middle West, save for the activities of Norwegian seamen on the Great Lakes. Conversely, Mid-western agriculture could not be duplicated in the metropolitan centers of New York, Brooklyn, and Philadelphia. Yet there was an important tie between the two sections. The various church bodies, national in scope, came to be represented in the East by ministers educated in Midwestern seminaries. They grew considerably. In 1954 Greater New York had 35 Norwegian churches, of many denominations.[20]

While new arrivals found Norwegian-speaking congregations more accommodating to their social and linguistic needs in New York and Brooklyn, their numbers on the membership rolls were hardly impressive. In Norway membership was almost automatic, legally effective from baptism to death. In eastern America, where the Scandinavian element was never dominant in a sea of nationalities ranging from Yankee stock to the later Jewish, Italian, Polish, and Puerto Rican immigrants, Norwegian newcomers could make their own choice in the matter of church affiliation. It is estimated that on the threshold of World War II only 38 percent of the Norwegian folk in Brooklyn, where they were then concentrated, professed to be church members.[21]

Notwithstanding its shorthandedness, the church in the East was second to none in its outreach to its own ethnic community. In 1874 the Norwegian Synod employed Peder B. Larsen as a missionary to immigrants arriving at Castle Garden. Emil Petersen devoted himself to that service from 1889 until his death in 1919. A Bethesda Mission, after 1899, served Norwegian youth and later became a center for homeless men. Brooklyn provided a home and hospital (1883), a sailors' home (1887), a home for the aged (1902), and an orphanage (1914).[22]

Norwegian-American church bodies were engaged at home and abroad in missionary endeavors. In the spirit of nineteenth-century evangelism, which in cynical eyes appeared to represent a kind of religious imperialism, men and women of deep conviction volunteered for sacrificial service in foreign lands. Their faith was that "Jesus shall reign where'er the sun doth his successive journeys run." Literally, "from Greenland's icy mountains" to "India's coral strand" they preached the good news and made important strides in translating the Scriptures, in establishing educational institutions, in founding hospitals, and in introducing advanced medical, agricultural, and other scientific techniques. India, China, Japan, the Philippine Islands, Korea, Madagascar, the Congo, and Argentina, to mention a few, felt the impact of the missionaries, most of them well trained and fully committed to the coming of the Kingdom. In the course of time the overseas missions became self-sustaining, in whole or in part, as native Christians assumed positions of leadership. To the religious-minded the roll call of the saints who "brought in the sheaves" is impressive.

As indicated, the new Americans sometimes forsook their Norwegian traditions and joined various Protestant denominations, whether upon arrival or later. In comparison with their Lutheran countrymen, their numbers were rather small. The Baptist story revolves around Hans Valder, a Haugean layman and schoolteacher before his departure from Norway in 1837. In the following year he joined the colony of Norwegians in La Salle County, Illinois. As a Baptist minister after 1844, he was commissioned to work among his countrymen in the Fox River Valley. His ordination marked him as the first Norwegian Baptist minister in the world, since a Baptist mission was not opened in Norway until 1857.

Hans Valder forsook the ministry by 1856 and disappeared from Baptist annals. It is known that he became a part of the continuing westward migration and founded the Newburg community in Fillmore County Minnesota, an area made attractive through Clausen's reports. Was it the small salary and the large family that turned him from the religious profession? Or did he become more interested in politics than in religion? Twice he served in the Minnesota state legislature after 1871. He is said to have come under the influence of the writings of Robert G. Ingersoll, the great agnostic. He attended no church. Eventually, in 1879, he began to meet with the Norwegian-Danish Methodists in Newburg, probably in deference to his wife's wishes.[23]

Peder Stiansen, the historian of the Norwegian Baptist Church in America, joined the Baptist dissenters in Norway as a youth of eighteen. His book makes clear that Wisconsin was both source and center of pioneer Baptist efforts, often carried on in conjunction with Danish immigrants. In 1910 the Norwegian Baptist Conference came into being in the Middle West. The Norwegian Baptists had earlier separated from the Swedes. Stiansen exercised strong personal leadership in the twentieth century. He returned to Norway to engage in missionary work in the twelve-year interval from 1914 to 1926, then accepted the deanship of the Baptist Theological Seminary in Chicago. In 1939 he could report that since the inauguration of the Baptist ministry among Scandinavian immigrants in 1844 some ninety Norwegian congregations had been organized.[24]

In 1843 a handful of Fox River Valley Norwegians met together as a Methodist "class" as an indirect result of American influences upon the Stavanger Sloopers in New York State. Norwegians of the Middle West encountered Methodism in several ways. Christian B. Willerup, born in Denmark, yielded to the Methodist persuasion in Georgia in the late 1830s. In the 1850s he preached in the Norwegian settlements of Illinois and Wisconsin, before devoting himself for nineteen years to the Methodist mission in Denmark. He organized the first Norwegian-Danish Methodist congregation at Cambridge, Wisconsin, in 1851. His contemporary, Ole Peter Petersen, born in Norway, first chose the life of a seaman. He attended Methodist seamen's missions on the Atlantic seaboard where, among others, the Swedish Olof Gustav Hedström was serving as chaplain of the *Bethel Ship John Wesley* in New York harbor. Petersen, after beginning pastoral duties in Washington Prairie, Iowa, became the founder of Methodism in Norway.

In 1880 the Norwegian-Danish Conference of the Methodist Episcopal Church was recognized. Centered in Chicago, it expanded its activities northwesterly and eventually into the Far West and the East. Pastoral leaders like Andrew Haagensen and Christian Treider carried on a successful mission to the immigrants. John H. Johnson, a Union veteran, was instrumental in building several congregations. Asle Knudsen's long and hard ministry began as a convert to Methodism in Locust, Iowa, near Washington Prairie, where in 1852 the first Norwegian Methodist congregation west of the Mississippi River had been officially launched by O. P. Petersen. Hans Kristian Madsen and Carl W. Schevenius represent, with many others, the twentieth-century clerical leadership in Norwegian Methodism.[25]

In the Far West and the East the names of Carl J. Larsen and Albert Hansen shone brightly. Larsen, a pioneer administrator, preacher, and artist in wood carving single-handedly inaugurated Methodist work among Norwegians in California. The Eastern mission came late. Albert Hansen prompted the beginnings of a center of worship in Philadelphia in 1906 and remained with it for nine years. Andrew Hansen, not related to Albert, pastored the flock at Sunset Park, Brooklyn, for several years, beginning in 1910. But the church that best symbolizes Norwegian Methodism in the East is Brooklyn's Bethelship Church. Bethelship cut its moorings as a mission vessel for Scandinavian seamen and moved to the land in 1874. Its spiritual vitality and financial health were matched only by its distinguished pastors and loyal layfolk through the years.

Gradually, as in all non-English enterprises, the language question threatened Norwegian Methodism in America. For preachers born abroad the innovation of English services of worship for the benefit of the upcoming generation brought difficulties and often embarrassment, as when one struggling preacher dramatically declared, "And David picked up a stone, and he hit Goliath right in the pan!" (The Norwegian for forehead is *pande.*)

The Norwegian-Danish Methodist seminary in Evanston, Illinois, long under the superintendency of Wisconsin-born Nels E. Simonsen, ceased to meet the needs of the new constituency. It yielded to the English language, as well as to a declining demand for graduates in the Conference. The well educated Simonsen carries the distinction of introducing the works of Søren Kierkegaard, the Danish philosopher, to his classes from 1887 until his retirement in 1920. American seminaries were not yet considering the Danish thinker. In 1934 T. Otmann Firing, successor to Simonsen, guided the seminary in the transition to a junior college, now known as Kendall College. The new program in higher education was made possible by the merger of the former Swedish and Norwegian-Danish properties. Firing retired as president in 1954, leaving Wesley M. Westerberg, of Swedish descent, to fill the office, until his resignation in 1973. In 1932, well before the merger of Norwegian-Danish Methodism with the larger American church in 1943, the seminary had closed its doors. Seminarians would henceforth be served completely by Garrett Biblical Institute (now Garrett-Evangelical Theological Seminary), the American Methodist institution, located in Evanston.

The Moravian faith, which had deeply influenced the founder of Methodism, John Wesley, took root in Norway. A Pastor A. M. Iverson and his flock proceeded from Stavanger in 1849 to Milwaukee, where a congregation was quickly organized. In Iverson's party were eighteen Scandinavians, twelve of them Norwegians. The number grew, but prospects for making a good living in the city at mid-century were rather dim. Moreover,

Iverson wished to shield the Moravian community from the materialistic hubbub and diverse heresies among the restless urban population of Milwaukee. Farmland, wooded country, and the open water beckoned him and his company to the site where the city of Green Bay would one day stand.

Assisting Iverson in the move to northeastern Wisconsin in 1851 was the strong-willed and aristocratic Nils Otto Tank, scion of a wealthy family in Norway.[26] Destined, it was hoped, to high political office in the dual monarchy of Sweden-Norway by his father, who was influential at the court of Stockholm, young Tank was sent to the European continent for educational preparation. There fate stepped in to determine a totally different course for the Norwegian student. At Herrnhut in Saxony, where Count Zinzendorf had laid the groundwork for the Moravian belief, he met and married a Moravian girl. His father disowned him. After several years in missionary service in Dutch Guiana (now Surinam), the couple returned to Norway in 1850. There they learned that Iverson was shepherding a Moravian colony in Milwaukee, and they decided to join him. Nils Otto Tank was more than a follower, however. Upon arrival in the Wisconsin metropolis, he found that Iverson's congregation preferred a more sheltered location. Tank shortly acquired a thousand acres of land at the foot of Green Bay. Disregarding Iverson, he assigned lots paternalistically to the communitarians. But since Tank refused to grant legal title individually to the colonists, a transaction which in the aristocratic tradition he thought unbecoming, Iverson in 1853 led a major portion of his members farther northward into the Door County peninsula. Moravian authorities in Bethlehem, Pennsylvania, approved his action. The new settlement was named Ephraim.

From this point on, Tank's contribution to Moravian success in America declined. He lived elegantly, as befitted a prince, amidst beautiful imported furnishings. He prized his library of 5,000 volumes, which were donated by his widow to the state historical society in Madison.

Iverson is portrayed as a man of deep conviction and of strident voice in the pulpit, a description which matches many a contemporary in his profession. He guided the Ephraim flock until 1864, when he responded to a call from Leland and Mission

Point (later Norway) in La Salle County, Illinois, the cradle of many sectarian religious movements. Called to Green Bay in 1866, he remained until 1883. He had seen triumphs, but he had also suffered disappointments. Converts frequently forsook him in favor of the Lutheran church, their first love, or because they found more satisfaction among the ebullient Methodists. Trials and adversities aside, however, Moravianism survived in Wisconsin. By 1907, five of its congregations flourished in Ephraim and its vicinity.

Norwegian-Americans yielded in relatively small numbers to the gospel of Joseph Smith and the charisma of Brigham Young. Norwegian Mormons in the Fox River settlement of Illinois and the Koshkonong community in Wisconsin were among the earliest Scandinavian followers. Indeed, Mormonism gripped the immigrants before it reached the shores of Scandinavia. Mormon influence began in Illinois, when George P. Dykes, an itinerant elder, won a nucleus of devotees in 1842 in the Fox River settlement.[27]

Few Scandinavians accompanied the main body of Mormons on the trek westward after Joseph Smith's murder. Fox River converts were thrown into confusion by a controversial figure, James J. Strang, who announced himself to be the true successor to the Prophet. He vehemently opposed Brigham Young's plan to move to Utah. The result was a falling-off in enthusiasm and a tendency to remain as a unit in Illinois. Twenty-two who departed for the West were exceptions. Danish-born Canute Peterson, a convert of 1842 in Illinois, presided in the 1870s over the entire mission of the Saints in Scandinavia, with headquarters in Copenhagen. His first wife was Sarah Ann Nelson, daughter of one of the Norwegian Sloopers of 1825.

William Mulder's excellent chapter on "the ugly ducklings" describes the Mormon experience in Denmark, Sweden, and Norway as one of harvesting both wheat and tares. By 1905 there were over 46,000 professing Latter Day Saints. Approximately 30,000, including children, migrated to the American Zion, enough to give Utah's population an Anglo-Scandinavian complexion. From 1850 to 1905 Norway contributed only 14 percent of all Scandinavian converts to Mormonism. In the same half-century Sweden contributed 36 percent and Denmark 50 percent of the proselytes from Scandinavian Lutheranism.[28]

Mormon pilgrims from Scandinavia declined in numbers as the century progressed. Hardship in the old countries had eased a bit, with more industry and with greater recognition of the equality of all men before the law. Panic, strikes, and agrarian unrest prevailed in the United States and discouraged further emigration. In Norway the movement toward separation from Sweden also encouraged a firmer stand by the common citizen on behalf of national interests, including loyalty to the Norwegian church. Mormonism, by wooing its subjects away from European beliefs and traditions, affronted thousands of Norwegians who preferred to see their religious practices and their language undisturbed. Yet Scandinavian-American Mormonism turned out to be a hardy plant. As late as 1902, approximately 4,000 immigrants and descendants attended a reunion in Brigham City to honor one of the Scandinavian pioneers.

To complete this brief survey of non-Lutheran religious expression in the nineteenth century, the Seventh Day Adventists, the Protestant Episcopalians, and the Unitarians deserve mention. The first Scandinavian Adventists in America hailed from Norway. They arrived in Oakland, Wisconsin, in 1840. J. G. Matteson, of Danish descent, served as their pastor from 1866 to 1877. He was instrumental in spreading the second-coming doctrine beyond the borders of Wisconsin before leaving on a missionary assignment for Denmark.

A second Adventist pioneer, Lewis Johnson, returned to Norway in 1889 and presided over the conference there for a decade. His responsibilities extended also into Sweden and Denmark. Upon his return to the United States he was given supervision of all Scandinavian Adventist work until 1901. Scandinavian-American Adventists totaled 1,900 members in 1908. Norwegians were probably in a small minority among them. Over half of the pastors were Danish.[29]

The odyssey of Erik L. Petersen confirms the view that few Norwegians turned to the Protestant Episcopal Church in America. Petersen prepared for the Catholic priesthood in Europe, in France and Italy no less, but gave up the cloister to become a missionary to the Norwegians in America. He became disillusioned. Norwegian Lutherans were not as discontented with their church affiliations as he had been led to believe. Their organizational fragmentation, of which he had heard while in Europe, had deceived him. To cap it all, he himself was repelled by the doctrine of papal infallibility in matters of faith and morals, announced in Rome in 1870. He joined the Protestant Episcopal Church in 1873. In his own words, he hoped for a peaceful "union of the Lutheran and Episcopal Churches here in the West." During his fourteen years as an Episcopalian he contributed heavily to Norwegian-American newspapers in the form of scholarly book reviews and analytical commentaries on historical and literary themes. With his death in 1887 at the age of only 43 the Protestant Episcopal Church lost its liaison with the immigrants from Norway.[30]

Kristofer Nagel Janson proved to be an effective voice for Unitarianism among a limited following of Norwegians who questioned the doctrines of the Trinity and of the virgin birth. On his initial lecture tour in 1879 this grandson of Bishop Jacob Neumann, one who had implored his parishioners not to leave their beloved land, set out to "get to know the free religious thought in America," as he put it. Janson returned to Norway in the spring of 1880 imbued with the doctrines of Unitarianism through the writings of William Ellery Channing and Theodore Parker.

In 1881 Rasmus B. Anderson of the University of Wisconsin completed arrangements for Janson to lecture and to organize Unitarian congregations in the Minneapolis area. The American Unitarian Association accepted Janson into their ministry. His aim, it is said, was not to destroy the five rival Norwegian Lutheran synods in America but to promote religious toleration. During the next ten years as a priest he preferred to call his several congregations Free Christian rather than Unitarian. He had found his lifework. His interests in the Grundtvigian folk school idea and in reviving the Old Norse in the form of landsmål declined.[31]

This exponent of "happy" Christianity, in the Grundtvigian tradition, recognized the immigrants for what they were. Some he could not hope to reach. "There they come," he wrote, "the faithful, naïve Scandinavians, with the wife by the hand, and the bottle of brandy by the heart." It was not to the submissive folk that he appealed but rather to the liberally inclined. His possible lack of intellectual profundity was compensated for by his generosity, brotherly love, and exaltation of spiritual values. No permanent church resulted from his warm-hearted efforts in America. He returned to Christiania and founded a short-lived Unitarian congregation. In 1903 he published there an account of the experiences which had led him to Unitarianism. The title was *Ensom* (Alone).[32]

In matters of religion, the so-called emigrated Norway resembled the motherland in many respects. In both areas the Lutheran church prevailed. As a rule, from the 1840s on, Norwegian immigrants cherished their church life, for social and national reasons as well as religious. For the "sectarians," whether at home or abroad, separation from the main body of Norwegians due to doctrinal differences was the common lot. But their Norwegianness and their satisfaction in meeting with their countrymen in their own religious fellowships were equally pronounced. If some protested against the Lutheran church and aligned themselves with other Protestants, the same tendency was evident in Norway. If others revolted against formalism, they had company in the old country. And if American urban life tended to destroy the sense of religious community and to breed religious indifference, the same phenomena were not unknown in the Scandinavian homeland.

A shift toward Americanization is reflected in the successive name changes of the Norwegian Lutheran ecclesiastical organization. When Johan Arnd Aasgaard, born in Minnesota, was elected president of the Norwegian Lutheran Church of America in 1925, he succeeded Norway-born Hans Gerhard Stub. The immigrant identity of the church survived in the name. Its successors, the Evangelical Lutheran Church (1946) and the American Lutheran Church (1963), formed through various mergers, abandoned the Norwegian designation in their names, partly because fewer members were born in Norway and partly in recognition of mergers with German Lutheran congregations.

With the passage of the years Norwegian congregations in America underwent a metamorphosis from Norwegian-speaking to English-speaking, and organizationally from division toward unity. Faithful worshipers from the former congregations looked back nostalgically, especially after World War I and the onset of anti-foreignism. No longer did they hear the minister exclaim, "Og jeg siger eder!" (And I say unto you!) The choir no longer sang "Löft dit hoved, se det dages! (Lift your head, the day is breaking!) And fewer and fewer voices were able to join in the congregational singing, in the original tongue, of Luther's stirring "Vor Gud han er saa fast en borg" (A mighty fortress is our God). The stately melodies and noble lines of Brorson, Ingemann, and Landstad were lacking. The Scripture was read in what seemed to be an unelevating language. Even the church bells sounded discordant. The mission to the immigrants had practically terminated. The ministry to the American-born, many of mixed ancestry, was well under way.

CHAPTER 9

The Life of the Mind:
Public Education and the Church College

THE NEW AMERICANS FROM NORWAY GENERALLY CONSIDERED education to be vitally important, especially for their children. The American system of public education impressed them in various ways. Some looked askance at the "common school," because it failed to include religious instruction in its curriculum. The alternative, of course, was the Lutheran parochial school, which became established in many Norwegian communities. Older folk sometimes criticized the common school for its use of the English language, which seemed to make unwarranted and detrimental inroads upon Old World family life and culture. Still others literally rejoiced in the opportunity afforded by the public institution for free education and a minimum of churchly interference. Much of the complaint was not directed so much against the common school per se as against the content and spirit of instruction, and the lack of well qualified teachers.

Ole Rynning in *True Account of America* (1838) made mention of the fact that public education was "within the reach of all." He reported two schools "where the children learn English" in the Fox River settlement in Illinois. He admired the American institution. In much the same tone an immigrant wrote from Buffalo, New York, in 1844 to relatives in Stavanger, "I and my countrymen who came this year will now begin in an English school and attend free of charge." He and other adults quickly recognized the practical value of gaining facility in the English tongue, as well as the opportunity of general education for children of school age.[1]

One sometimes finds a cordial relationship between parochial and public school personnel. Johannes Dietrichson of Muskego was instrumental in organizing the district school at Rock

Prairie, Wisconsin. He anticipated that the parochial school teacher there, a Norwegian, would also be appointed to fill a vacancy in the public school, which was open only about three months during the year. But other spokesmen fell into bitter controversy over the ultimate effects of public education upon their religion and their national heritage. Such a one was the Reverend Hans A. Stub who, upon arriving from Norway, expressed his concern in *Nordlyset*, a Wisconsin newspaper, over the dangers of secular education.[2]

Perhaps the first plea on behalf of the public school in a Scandinavian-American newspaper came in 1850 when *Democraten*, under Knud Langeland's direction, published an editorial on the subject. In conclusion Langeland stated, "There is only one remedy for ignorance and that is the common school. ... Countrymen, fathers, mothers! Let me lay a serious word upon your hearts—education! Give your children a good education." His plea was only the first of many such utterances. During his editorship of *Skandinaven*, from 1866 to 1872, he consistently praised the public school. While he spared his readers a broadside attack upon the Norwegian Synod, he made clear his feeling against "the German-Missouri straitjacket, tyranny, and hierarchical domination." He questioned the patriotism of parochial school advocates. The city of Chicago honored him in 1884 by naming a new elementary school for him.[3]

John A. Johnson, successor to Langeland in the editorial chair of Chicago's *Skandinaven*, also favored public education. He sensed that not everyone agreed that it was performing a necessary and useful function. Pastors of the Norwegian Synod were protesting the "heathenish" character of the common school. Bernt J. Muus, whose name would be linked to the founding of St. Olaf College, was declaring that public elementary institutions "must, according to their principle, work against the Kingdom of God." Adolph C. Preus believed that the American schools were intended for those who scorned Christianity. Professor Friedrich A. Schmidt of Luther College called them "gates of hell."[4]

At this point Rasmus B. Anderson appeared as a defender of the common school and, at the same time, a champion of the Norwegian language. As one born in the United States, Anderson felt at home in the English language. But a major part of his professional career was spent as Professor of Scandinavian Languages in the University of Wisconsin, a rank he received in 1875. "Let us consolidate our influence and accept the American schools," he urged. "Let us labor to the end that our mother tongue may find a place in them." When a series of articles in *Kirketidende* (Church News), the official organ of the Norwegian Synod, condemned the public school, Anderson attacked its parochial counterpart. In 1877 he placed the following dictum on his letterhead: "Whosoever directly or indirectly opposes the American common school is an enemy of education, of liberty, and of progress. Opposition to the American common school is treason to our country."[5]

The school controversy extended into the 1890s. The distinguished novelist, Hjalmar Hjorth Boyesen, who became Americanized more rapidly than most immigrants, congratulated the public schools as "the most powerful agencies for assimilating the alien elements" and denounced the "bigoted Lutheran pastors from Norway," who used their authority to preserve a distinct Norwegian nationality, free from American contamination. Several years hence the persistent Boyesen, then serving as Professor of Germanic Languages and Literature at Cornell University, declared Scandinavian parochial schools to be "directly hostile to the settlers' best interests." It was not that he undervalued the Scandinavian contribution to America. On the contrary, he likened the assimilation of heterogeneous foreign stocks in America to that of England after the Viking invasions, "when Saxon, Norman, Dane, and Celt were gradually transformed into Englishmen."[6]

When the Wisconsin state legislature adopted the Bennett Law in 1889, requiring compulsory attendance of all children between the ages of seven and fourteen, and the teaching of certain courses in the English language in all schools, German resentment is said to have run higher than Scandinavian. In fact, it is possible that German-American opposition overthrew the Republican governor, William D. Hoard, and transformed the state legislature in the elections of 1890. The German element constituted 37 percent of the state's population, the combined Scandinavian only 11 percent. Eight of the nine Wisconsin Republican candidates for Congress suffered defeat by Democratic opponents in 1890. Of the Republican candidates for Congress, only Nils P. Haugen, a Norwegian who actually favored the Bennett Law, was reelected.

Had there been a noticeable change in the Norwegian-American climate of opinion recently? Apparently so. Some Norwegian parochial schools were already on the verge of changing to English. Many immigrants who recalled with mental anguish their own trials with the strange language in their younger days were now convinced of the practicality of the new legal measure enacted in Madison. And they may have become more certain that American citizenship demanded loyal support of the common school. In the case of German-Americans, in their very eagerness to prove that the Bennett Law was unnecessary, they seem to have begun to obey its behests. The same might also be said of the Norwegians. On the other hand, many Scandinavians voted Republican in opposition to German Catholics, who were thought to be reacting unpatriotically to the Bennett Law.[7]

Schools and churches coexisted in the Norwegian communities of the upper Mississippi Valley. It was deemed necessary to educate Norwegian-speaking teachers for the instruction of immigrant children. Public schools could not serve the purpose of preparing either ministers or teachers. Quite naturally, then, the churches began to concentrate upon building seminaries, colleges for teacher preparation, and academies corresponding in many respects to the public high schools of the twentieth century.

One of the earliest endeavors in theological education dates from 1860, when the Augustana Seminary was launched in Chicago, with Lars Esbjörn as president. It functioned as a joint Scandinavian venture until in 1870 the Norwegian-Danish Augustana Synod was formed, separate from the Swedish effort. Already the Norwegians had selected Marshall, Wisconsin, near Madison, as their site. In 1881 the seminary and academy were moved to Beloit, Wisconsin, and in 1884 to Canton, Dakota Territory. The academy division became Augustana College, in effect a teacher training school at that time. Following the church merger of 1917 into the Norwegian Lutheran Church of America, the Canton college was combined with a previously established normal school in Sioux Falls, South Dakota. Together they became a senior college in Sioux Falls in 1920.

Augustana College achieved distinction for its music and for its specialized curricula. Carl R. Youngdahl brought the college choir to national attention. In recent years programs designed for prospective teachers of the deaf, the mentally retarded, and the physically handicapped have been introduced. Since 1954 Augustana has produced 18 Woodrow Wilson teaching fellows, 25 Fulbright scholars, and 35 National Defense scholars.[8]

In 1869 Red Wing Seminary of Hauge's Synod, descended from the Eielsen group, had made an auspicious beginning in Minnesota. The story of the educational enterprise on the west bank of the Mississippi is captivatingly related by one who attended the institution for six years, beginning in 1907. Nostalgically Paul Knaplund, who arrived at the age of 21 from northern Norway, from the region of Bodö and the Lofoten Islands, recalls the experiences and impressions which determined his lifework. The path led from Red Wing to Madison, Wisconsin, where he spent the rest of his days, first as graduate student and later as professor of history. Knaplund won international recognition as a specialist in the history of the British Empire, more specifically on the foreign policy of William E. Gladstone, the eminent Liberal prime minister of the Victorian era.

When writing his autobiography, Knaplund could scarcely realize that Red Wing Seminary was no more. The church union of 1917 brought about an amalgamation of its theological branch with seminaries of other groups in St. Paul. St. Olaf College absorbed the college department. In the early 1930s Red Wing, then a junior college, finished its course.

If to others Red Wing Seminary was only a ghost, to Paul Knaplund it remained a living reality. He had first arrived by train from a relative's farm in Minnesota. Immediately he was ushered in to meet the president, a sympathetic and understanding servant of the Lord. Soon there was a dormitory roommate, whose bilingual ability would be helpful to Paul. Bells, spartan dining room furniture, grace recited in unison before meals, chapel services every forenoon, various classes, and the liberal use of two purchased dictionaries all come to mind in the immigrant lad's panoramic recollection. The seminary, the Hauge Synod, and the associations gave Paul rootage in a foreign land.

As years passed, college preparatory, college, and commercial departments were added to Red Wing's theological core. Graduates frequently transferred to the University of Minnesota for further liberal arts education. Sometimes they returned to Red Wing as teachers. Buildings and equipment left much to be desired. There was no playing field for sports. The faculty was understaffed and underpaid. Student turnover was heavy, because of the priority given to farm work during the planting and harvest seasons and the transient tendencies of Norway-born students who were literally on the move. Temperance advocates on the campus were disturbed over the "wetness" of Red Wing, a brewery town. There was music and debating, but dancing and card-playing were forbidden. Paul Knaplund survived these conditions, even thrived on them. He graduated with a B.A. and was valedictorian of his class. His experiences, save for his remarkable professional accomplishments, represent those of hundreds of young men and women of Norwegian descent who embarked upon the venture of higher education.[9]

Augsburg College originated in Chicago in 1860 as a seminary of the Scandinavian Evangelical Lutheran Augustana Synod. It was relocated in Paxton, Illinois, in 1863. August Weenaas, newly arrived from the University of Christiania, became dissatisfied with the Scandinavian aspect of the seminary. It was already noticeable that Swedish and Norwegian congregations were not in accord. Their disharmony was reflected in the theological school itself. On the other hand, Weenaas found cooperation with Danes to be feasible. The relatively small number of Danes in the Middle West and the similarity of the Danish and Norwegian languages brought the two nationalities together. So a break occurred with the Swedes in 1869. In the following year the Scandinavian Augustana Synod itself divided along national lines.

Minneapolis proved to be the permanent home of Augsburg Seminary after 1872. Weenaas participated in the rapid growth of the school until his return to Norway in 1876. His place was taken by Georg Sverdrup, fresh from the University of Christiania, and by Sven Oftedal, who arrived as a graduate of the same university.

Within the framework of the Conference of the Norwegian-Danish Evangelical Lutheran Church in America, founded in 1870, Augsburg College, as it came to be known, continued in the spirit of Claus L. Clausen's anti-rationalism and, in general, represented the low-church point of view. The study of Latin was frowned upon, as an insidious vestige from pagan Rome. Professors Sverdrup and Oftedal carried on as distinguished leaders not only in the classroom and on the campus but also in the Conference, as it was commonly called. Georg Sverdrup, nephew of the great Norwegian statesman and parliamentarian Johan Sverdrup, was devoted to the development of free congregations in a free church in a free country. Had he remained in Norway, he might have occupied a high office in the Lutheran state church. When the Conference merged with the United Lutheran Church in 1890, Augsburg's clientele was considerably expanded. In 1914 there were three programs of instruction: the theological, the collegiate, and the preparatory. In this respect Augsburg was not unique. And, like other church-related colleges, it would later offer courses leading to specialization in various fields.[10]

Luther College, founded near LaCrosse, Wisconsin, in 1861, and located after 1864 in Decorah, Iowa, became influential in the Norwegian Synod and remained so indefinitely. At the opening of the Civil War, when the slavery issue was uppermost, pressure from the Norwegian Lutheran laity, rather than from the proslavery clergy, resulted in a severing of ties with Concordia Seminary (Missouri Synod) of St. Louis. Not until 1876, however, did the Norwegian Synod establish its own seminary in Madison, Wisconsin. The dedication in 1864 of Luther's main educational building in the presence of 6,000 loyal Norwegian Lutherans was a remarkable event, especially when it is considered that a destructive war might have discouraged all cultural progress.

Peter Laurentius Larsen, who preferred his name to be spelled Laur. Larsen, occupied the presidential office of Luther College from its beginning until 1902, a total of over forty years. He had completed two years in St. Louis as professor in the Norwegian division of Concordia. Almost single-handedly he laid the groundwork and determined the policies for Luther College. Discipline was strict. The classics were stressed, perhaps to the detriment of the natural sciences.

Among the more prominent members of the faculty of Luther College was Andrew A. Veblen, brother of Thorstein Veblen, the radical economic theorist and social philosopher. A graduate, like his brother Thorstein, of liberal and Congregational Carleton College of Northfield, Minnesota, Andrew was surprised to be invited to join the staff in 1877. He remained for four years, teaching beginning Latin, English grammar, composition, and rhetoric. Olaf M. Norlie won distinction as the author of a two-volume work on the Norwegian Lutheran congregations in America (*Norsk-lutherske menigheter i Amerika, 1843–1916*), published in Minneapolis in 1918. In addition he published a *History of the Norwegian People in America* (Minneapolis, 1925), for which he is best remembered, and in mimeographed form *Norwegian-Americana Papers, 1847–1946* (Northfield, Minnesota, 1946). Over a span of years Knut Gjerset applied himself to several invaluable studies, including a *History of the Norwegian People* (Decorah, Iowa, 1915), a *History of Iceland* (New York, 1925), *Norwegian Sailors on the Great Lakes* (Northfield, 1928), and *Norwegian Sailors in American Waters* (Northfield, 1933).[11]

Both Augsburg and Luther were mainly preoccupied with providing pastoral leadership for their respective church bodies. Yet the various churches had their own seminaries. The Norwegian Synod moved its institution from Madison, Wisconsin, to St. Paul, Minnesota, in the 1890s. The United Church of 1890 succeeded in establishing in 1902 Luther Theological Seminary in St. Anthony Park, St. Paul. In 1917, another year of merger, Hauge's Synod closed its Red Wing seminary program and joined Luther Theological Seminary. The Lutheran Free Church remained separate, with its Augsburg Theological Seminary and College in Minneapolis.

St. Olaf College (originally St. Olaf's School) had no official synodical affiliation at the beginning. It differed from Augsburg and Luther also in that it emphasized the liberal arts rather than theological preparation for ministers. At first intended as an academy for girls and boys, the school, unlike others, was co-educational. It had its inception in the mind of Bernt J. Muus while he was serving the Holden, Minnesota, congregation in 1869. He became president of the board of trustees in 1874 and exerted a dominant influence in determining the policies of the school. While Muus is regarded as one of the pillars of the Norwegian Synod, he was associated for 35 years with leaders outside the denomination as well, testifying to a breadth of sympathy and appreciation not commonly displayed at that time among churchmen. Muus was born in Norway in 1832, not far from Stiklestad (near Trondhjem), where the Christian king, Olaf Haraldsson, fell in battle in the year 1030. St. Olaf College was named after this king. His battle cry became their motto: "Onward, Onward, Christ Men, Cross Men."

The school grew into a college. The issue of predestination had split the seminarians and pastors of the Missouri Synod. A so-called Anti-Missourian faction withdrew and made overtures to St. Olaf School for a single institution of higher learning. A joint college department resulted in the Northfield institution in 1886. With the successive church mergers of 1890 and 1917 the base of the college was academically and jurisdictionally broadened.

Thorbjörn N. Mohn, a graduate of Luther College, served as president of St. Olaf from 1875 to 1899. He was followed by Johan N. Kildahl, also a Luther College graduate. Then came Lars W. Boe, during whose administration the names of Ole E. Rölvaag, F. Melius Christiansen, Nils Flaten, Theodore Jorgenson, Karen Larsen, and others reflected to great advantage upon the college and upon Norwegians everywhere.[12]

One of St. Olaf's alumnae, Leola Nelson Bergmann, bespeaks the academic prestige of the school on historic Manitou Heights in Northfield. She gives much credit to President Boe and to Professors Rölvaag and Christiansen. Rölvaag not only headed the Norwegian department but won renown with his immigrant novel *Giants in the Earth,* and its sequels. Leipzig-trained Christiansen's contribution in the field of choral music is appraised in Mrs. Bergmann's words:

> The big cities of America listened in amazement to choristers from the little midwestern college they had never heard of. Christiansen's exacting standards, his unflagging patience with untrained voices . . .

molded choirs of students that sang with a technical precision and a freshness of spirit which baffled and stirred to paeans of praise . . . the most jaded of critics in metropolitan centers.

Nils Flaten, whose parents brought him from Norway in 1868 at the age of one year, deeply impressed Ole Rölvaag, then a freshman, at the turn of the century. Flaten at the time was headmaster in Latin. Rölvaag borrowed books from his professor, who had himself been a student at St. Olaf. Flaten later gave up Latin for Romance languages. He contributed numerous articles to philological journals.

Theodore Jorgenson, an able teacher and scholar in Norwegian language and literature, arrived later at St. Olaf. He too was born in Norway. As a student he lived in the home of the Rölvaags and came to know the distinguished novelist intimately. Jorgenson headed the department of Norwegian after Rölvaag, from 1934 until his retirement in 1965. This writer remembers Jorgenson as a sturdy, friendly, and stimulating personality who made a younger member of a seminar feel worthy. He produced several outstanding volumes, among them a *History of Norwegian Literature* (New York, 1933), *Norway's Relation to Scandinavian Unionism, 1815–1871* (Northfield, 1935), *Henrik Ibsen: A Study in Art and Personality* (Northfield, 1945), and, together with Nora O. Solum, *Ole Edvart Rölvaag: A Biography* (New York, 1939).

Karen Larsen's effectiveness as a teacher at St. Olaf College lacked nothing because of her scholarly interests. Her *Laur. Larsen: Pioneer College President* (Northfield, 1936) paid a deserving tribute to her father, first president of Luther College. A *History of Norway* (Princeton, New Jersey, 1948) expressed her desire for knowledge of her ancestral homeland. The publications of Kenneth O. Bjork and Lloyd Hustvedt, both associated with St. Olaf for a lifetime, are frequently cited in these pages. They stand as unique contributions in the fields of Norwegian-American history and letters.

In 1950 the students of St. Olaf, Luther, and similar colleges were still predominantly Lutheran. President Boe of St. Olaf was well aware of a transition, however, through which the church-related college was passing, as it ceased to meet the needs of immigrant children and ministered to a more Americanized generation:[13]

> Ours is the riches of two cultures, and often the poverty of the desert wanderer. . . . Like Moses of old, we seek the new but cannot fully enter in. To us has been given the task of mediating a culture, of preserving and transferring to our children in a new land the cultural and spiritual values bound up in the character, art, music, literature, and Christian faith of a generation no longer found even in the land from which the fathers came.

The aforementioned colleges may be the most conspicuous. Many others might be warmly commended for their achievements. Concordia College of Moorhead, Minnesota, and Pacific Lutheran University of Tacoma, Washington, belong in this category. Organized in 1891, Concordia was guided by Presidents R. R. Bogstad and Johan A. Aasgaard during the many years when the sons and daughters of the immigrants frequented its halls. That the clergy were often intellectual leaders of their people is shown in the life of Aasgaard. Born in 1876 in Albert Lea, Minnesota, the home of one of many Norwegian Lutheran academies, he was named president of Concordia in 1911. There he served with distinction until his election in 1925 to the presidency of the Norwegian Lutheran Church of America. Like other educational establishments of its kind, Concordia was at once a college, an academy, a normal school, and a ladies' seminary until well into the present century.

Pacific Lutheran University began in 1894 as an academy, under the direction of a private corporation composed of members of Pacific Coast Lutheran parishes. In the case of the Norwegian-American church-related colleges, enrollments as of today are not as relevant to the immigration theme as formerly. Ethnic and denominational homogeneity no longer prevail in the student bodies and faculties.

Non-Lutheran Norwegian immigrants established their own seminaries and colleges or supported Norwegian divisions within American institutions. Baptists had their Morgan Park Seminary, affiliated with the University of Chicago. Seventh Day Adventists utilized, after 1891, Union College of College View, Nebraska, and after 1908 Walla Walla College of College Place, Washington. Mormons could attend Brigham Young University in Salt Lake City, Utah, for their advanced education. Norwegian-Danish Methodists supported a theological school in Evanston, Illinois, beginning in 1890. From the outset the American Methodist Garrett Biblical Institute, located in the same city, was open to the seminarians for certain required courses, and their degrees were granted by Garrett.

When it is recalled that public high schools were few in number in the nineteenth century, and that private and denominational academies offered the best in secondary education, it is not surprising that the academy idea took hold among the religiously inclined Norwegians. As with seminaries and colleges, entrance requirements for the academies were flexible. Students were enrolled, as a rule, not so much on the strength of their previous academic accomplishments as on the basis of moral character and Christian purpose.

Educators of today are often disposed to design programs of study that take into account the individual differences and specific needs of their student clienteles. The idea is not new. In the denominational academies of a century ago, young immigrants of varied educational backgrounds attended classes of direct vocational value. As workers on Midwestern farms or in the lumber camps of the Northwest, they studied during the off-seasons. Usually older than the average student, and less proficient in the English language, they were often embarrassed in classroom situations. Yet they made the best of their opportunities within the friendly and understanding confines of the church school. While not many gained wide prominence in the great American society, their achievements should not go unheralded.

Although Lutheran-sponsored academies were hardly on the scene before the decade of the 1880s, a meeting in Madison, Wisconsin, in 1869 appears to have inspired their beginning. On that occasion overwhelming opposition was expressed to a plan proposed by Knud Langeland, editor of *Skandinaven*, Rasmus B. Anderson, then on the threshold of a career as professor of Scandinavian languages and literature at the University of Wisconsin, and Claus L. Clausen, veteran pastor and organizer. The stated purpose of the three gentlemen was "to pledge support to genuine public education among the Scandinavian people and especially to bring about the establishment of Scandinavian professorships in American higher schools." Most of the three hundred in attendance objected and withdrew to formulate their own educational plan. With Hans A. Preus leading the way, they designed an academy program within the jurisdiction of the Norwegian Synod.

There were, at one time or another, some 75 academies, varying in size of student body and in length of operation. In general, the institutions of longest duration also accommodated the largest number of students. Not always did the schools carry the name "academy." A listing of those that remained active the longest and saw the most students come and go would include the following: Luther College Preparatory, Decorah, Iowa (1861–1928), with a total of 5,700 students; Red Wing Seminary, Red Wing, Minnesota (1879–1932), with 5,025; Pacific Lutheran Academy, Parkland, Washington (1894–1944), with 4,950; and, St. Olaf Academy, Northfield, Minnesota (1874–1917), with 6,592. Several academies were in existence for forty years and enjoyed substantial enrollments.[14]

The rise of the American public high school after 1890 hastened the decline of the private and church-related academy. The climate of opinion in the nation during World War I, when superpatriotism prevailed, did nothing to alleviate the condition for institutions employing foreign languages, although nearly all Norwegian academies had made the transition to English before the war. Postwar secularism, accentuated in law-breaking and in a general lapse in morals, adversely affected not only church attendance but the support of religious institutions as well. Moreover, isolationism had determined through the medium of quota legislation that immigrants would henceforth be allowed to enter the country only on a restrictive basis. And the church school, on all levels of instruction, had frequently suffered criticism, even from persons within the denomination, who insisted upon experimentation with newer teaching techniques, a broader and more practical curriculum, and a more cosmopolitan approach.

The number of Norwegian-American academies dropped sharply during and after World War I. Thirty-seven of the 75 had already closed, many before 1900. Undoubtedly the rise of the public high school offers one explanation for the sudden weakening of the academy program, whether private or denominational. Long before the middle of the twentieth century neither the teaching staffs nor the student bodies bore much resemblance to the immigrants.

The solidarity of Norwegians in nineteenth-century America is demonstrated in several ways. The new Americans from Norway established, as we have seen, their own newspaper press. Given a choice, they preferred to fight as Norwegian units in the Union Army. They organized distinctively Norwegian churches and regarded the education of their children and young people as a responsibility of the church.

Whether the decision to inaugurate Lutheran-sponsored education was predicated mainly upon the fear of materialistic and agnostic forces in American society is difficult to determine. On the one hand, the founders were motivated positively to create and to nourish educational establishments solely for the glory of God. To that extent, their actions were not simply responses to undesirable or threatening conditions around them. Still, the clergy were apprehensive of the nonreligious aspects in a society which was bent, Horatio Alger style, upon rapid accumulation of wealth. Possibly also the Norwegian Synod leaders were repelled rather than persuaded by the eloquent espousal of public education by prominent Norwegian intellectuals, whom they did not wholly trust. Knud Langeland, Rasmus B. Anderson, and Hjalmar Hjorth Boyesen, all strong advocates of the public institution, were not good churchmen in the estimation of their Lutheran contemporaries. As a man of politics, Langeland had become a political figure, and Anderson and Boyesen occupied chairs in large American universities. These men were seeking to blend two cultures, American and Norwegian, with no apologies for either.[15]

Yet another factor may have operated in the decision to establish and maintain parochial schools and church-connected seminaries, colleges, and academies. In the decade of the 1880s, when Norwegian Lutherans were witnessing a flourishing of their educational enterprises, Norway was at odds with Sweden over the powers of the Norwegian parliament within the Union. The two Scandinavian states were drawing apart. Simultaneously, the tide of Swedish immigration threatened to inundate Norwegians in America. The mere anticipation of becoming outnumbered and outweighed in the life of the new transatlantic world may have turned Norwegians in on themselves. It was not that they were unappreciated by their neighbors. In the 1850s they had had little reason for alarm when nativists were decrying the danger of alien German and Irish elements to American institutions. In the half-century down to 1914 they had engaged in politics and had, in numerous instances, won a place for themselves in American hearts. And during the holocaust of 1914–1918, when German-Americans unfortunately suffered the stigma of their national origin, Norwegian-Americans came under much less suspicion of disloyalty than many other foreign groups. Norwegians were anxious to insure that Yankees, Swedes, or others would not destroy their ethnic identity. They celebrated without hypocrisy both the Fourth of July and the Seventeenth of May.

Norwegian Lutheranism surrended its distinctive educational mission. American Lutheranism assumed responsibility for theological training. In time the sons and grandsons of the pioneers found themselves in Lutheran and other private colleges that yielded to the needs of the American-born, or in state universities where courses in Norwegian language, literature, and history were offered, if at all, as electives. Those who are capable of attuning their ears to the voices of past generations of students will recognize the founders and supporters for their faithful role in cultivating the talents of countless young folk who later excelled in the various professions and in many other worthy fields of endeavor.

CHAPTER 10

Social and Cultural Organizations

AMERICANS BEFORE AND AFTER 1900 ACQUIRED A REPUTATION FOR joining a mystifying variety of social and cultural organizations, of which some were secret societies. Lodge night came with weekly regularity in town and country, offering release from the tedium of the farm, the factory, and the office. Millions found satisfaction in ancient and exotic rituals of numerous fraternal orders and in combining their efforts in good works not only in the lodges but also in societies for the advancement of this, or the prevention of the other. But even without passwords, plumes, scimitars, and rites, there was ample reason for committing oneself to one or another societal organization. At the basis was the innate human yearning for belonging, for mingling with one's neighbors, one's peers, or with people of one's own ethnic origin.

Granted that native Americans demonstrated a sort of gregariousness in maintaining numerous societies, secret or open, the question remains as to why the Norwegians chose to emulate their Yankee neighbors. While a degree of clannishness may be detected among all national groups on American soil, for the Norwegians this characteristic had its roots in circumstances similar, in part, to those of other nationalities, and partially in circumstances peculiar to their history. Norway's status after 1814, within the dual monarchy of Sweden-Norway, may have engendered greater national sensitivity among her people. Swedish incursions, whether real or imagined, upon Norwegian prerogatives produced a defensive attitude not prevalent among all peoples. Perhaps an unacknowledged feeling of being overshadowed by her larger Scandinavian neighbor manifested itself outwardly in a growing national assertiveness.

In the case of the Norwegian immigrants, they did not ordinarily leave the homeland with harsh feelings. On the contrary, they loved Norway. Unfavorable economic conditions drove them to emigrate. Years of loneliness and hard work in America deepened their love for the land of their birth. As happens so often, childhood memories took on new glamor. The generation of pioneers, and to a lesser extent their descendants in the new land, were loath to surrender the language which identified them with the treasured past. At Yuletide and on other occasions the old songs came to life, and Norwegian delicacies appeared on the table. Even when horse and buggy yielded to the automobile, national customs were not forgotten. Moreover, American society provided no serious deterrent to Norwegian organizations. And by the late 1920s American historians were beginning to show appreciation of immigrant contributions to America. Why, then, should not Norwegian-Americans remain interested in their heritage, while at the same time broadening their interests in things American?

For the Americans from Norway the desire to meet socially at stated intervals gave impetus to the formation of musical organizations and athletic clubs, to *bygdelags* (social units comprised of folk who had been born in or traced their lineage from a particular valley or community in Norway), and to other means of promoting a feeling of togetherness. All such associations were imbued in some degree with patriotic fervor, for the old country and the new. Yet the mere desire to convene regularly did not of itself guarantee success in organizing. Leadership was required, and persons possessing this quality rose to the occasion.

Perhaps no one has depicted Norwegian-American social and cultural organizational beginnings more graphically than the onetime Chicago investment broker, Birger Osland. Born in Stavanger, he emigrated as a young man in 1888. Almost immediately he assisted in the organization of the Norröna Literary Society, in which the members delivered prepared lectures to their fellows on both academic and practical themes. After a year "a much breezier and more modern flock of young intellectuals" pressed for a merger, which resulted in the name being changed to the Arne Garborg Club. Osland was elected president.[1]

Osland speaks with unconcealed pride of his colleagues. One, Haakon Nyhuus, returned to Norway to introduce the American library system. He became head of the famed Deichmann public library in Christiania (Oslo). Jon Olafsson, once a member of the Icelandic parliament, was banished from the island for political reasons. Eventually he returned to assume leadership. Juul Dieserud was to hold an important post in the Library of Congress for the balance of his long life. Andreas Nilssen Rygg, later part owner of Brooklyn's *Nordisk Tidende,* became influential in the Norwegian colony in the East. Sigvald Asbjörnsen distinguished himself as a sculptor. The Edvard Grieg statue in Brooklyn and the Leif Erikson monument in Chicago are among his creations.

Dependent upon the inflow of a better educated element from Norway, the Arne Garborg Club encountered difficulty in continuing. By 1896 it had ceased to exist. Scarcely two percent of Chicago's growing population were Norwegians, and relatively few of them had had university training. At age 26 Osland formed a select "Quartet Club" of twelve men. Their second director, Alfred Paulsen, achieved recognition among Norwegians everywhere for his composition of "Naar Fjordene Blaaner" (When the blue of the fjords deepens), a song beloved of all Norwegians.

In 1911 the Quartet Club, having lost momentum, merged with Den Norske Klub, soon to become the Chicago Norske Klub, which was honored with the presence of many lecturers of stature. Singing played only a minor part. Jane Addams of Hull House and Charles Wacker, champion of many civic causes in Chicago, and Osland's onetime employer, appeared before the club. Osland's experiences as a joiner portray, in microcosm, the history of immigrant social and cultural efforts, particularly on the urban scene.

What Birger Osland was culturally to the Chicago Norwegians, Carl G. O. Hansen was to the Minneapolis-St. Paul (Twin Cities) colony. Hansen was brought in 1881 as a child to the United States. By the turn of the century he was pursuing a career in music and journalism. *Minneapolis Tidende,* successor to *Fædrelandet og Emigranten,* engaged his skill, first as a music columnist and later as editor in chief, until the paper ceased publication in 1935. Hansen organized the Norwegian Glee Club of Minneapolis in 1914 and directed it with inspiration for forty years.

His interests were boundless, ranging into history, literature, and theology. His column in the *Minneapolis Sunday Journal,* entitled "Sagas of Today," told of Norwegians on both sides of the Atlantic. As one of the more scintillating personalities among Norwegians in America, he demonstrated in his life and behavior the feasibility of loyalty to America and to Norwegian traditions and values alike. None knew the story of Norwegian music in America better than he.[2]

Many factors pointed to the eventual prominence of Minneapolis as the mecca of Norwegian newcomers. There the flour mills offered adequate employment. In the vicinity of "the city of waters" lay the most fruitful farmlands. In Minneapolis too the Great Northern Railway and other lines provided shipping facilities for the burgeoning Northwest. The Norwegian Lutheran Church of America established its headquarters in Minneapolis and seemed to regulate the day-to-day activities of its parishioners in the mill city. The church did not condone membership in secret societies, which often propagated deistic beliefs in their induction ceremonies, their rituals, and their funeral routines. With the passage of time, however, such organizations would flourish among the Norwegian element.

Madison, Wisconsin, also proved to be a lively center of Norwegian cultural activity. There, for example, the Ygdrasil Literary Society was founded in 1896, mainly through the inspiration of Rasmus B. Anderson of the University of Wisconsin. It took its name from Norse mythology, in which Ygdrasil, "the tree of life," extended its branches heavenward and outward over all the earth. Membership was restricted to men of academic background. Many achieved distinction, among them J. C. M. Hanson and George T. Flom. As chief cataloger of the Library of Congress, Hanson originated the now widely accepted LC system. Flom became eminent in the field of Germanic philology, as editor of *Scandinavian Studies* (1911 to 1921) and of *The Journal of English and Germanic Philology* (1911–1940). While Ygdrasil members themselves presented the monthly programs, distinguished visitors from Norway sometimes occupied the podium. Ties with the old country were always close. A women's counterpart, the Gudrid Reading Circle, was organized in 1897. Only wives of Ygdrasil members were eligible to join until 1947.

The women studied Norse literature and engaged in charitable work.[3]

In his article of 1914 Carl G. O. Hansen surveyed Norwegian societies of various kinds not only in the Twin City area of Minneapolis-St. Paul but from the East Coast to the West Coast. The numerous clubs, lodges, and *bygdelags* differed in their specific objectives and were sporadic in their activities. Younger members moved about the country freely, and older people lost interest. There was little historical continuity. Hansen found that the use of English proved to be advantageous in the conduct of meetings of Norwegian groups. It was not to lodges operating along American lines, however, that Hansen addressed himself. Norwegians, he declared, felt more at ease with a minimum of fanfare and ceremony.

In the Greater New York area there were some forty Norwegian societies by 1914. They represented the diverse interests of over 35,000 people, most of them born in Norway. One of the more successful, and the most permanent, was the Norwegian Club (*Det Norske Selskab*), organized in 1904. When a brief history was published on the occasion of its sixtieth anniversary, the author explained that the Club had greeted many prominent men and women, both American and Norwegian-American, and had thus provided a forum for visiting statesmen, scientists, artists, and lecturers of various kinds. They had remained true to their mandate "to advance Norwegian cultural interests," as stated in their by-laws. In 1905 a Norwegian National Federation (*Det Norske Nationalforbund*) united all Norwegian societies in the New York and Brooklyn area.[4]

From the reminiscences of Karsten Roedder, editor of Brooklyn's *Nordisk Tidende*, and his successor Carl Söyland, it is clear that this metropolitan newspaper exercised notable leadership of the entire Norwegian community of Greater New York and was widely read through Norwegian America. After its founding in 1891 *Nordisk Tidende* promoted the idea of a united 17th of May festival. Andreas Nilssen Rygg, editor from 1912 to 1929, identified himself with several Norwegian charities. He had left his native Stavanger in the company of his friend and fellow citizen Birger Osland. After 1905 Brooklyn, rather than

Chicago, was his home. By then most Manhattan Norwegians had accomplished the short migration over to Brooklyn.[5]

Meanwhile, Rygg witnessed the growth of the Norwegian population in the New York area from more than 33,000 in 1910 (over 22,000 born in Norway) to nearly 63,000 in 1930 (over 38,000 born in Norway). It was a far cry from 1870, when less than a thousand Norwegians resided in or near the great seaport city. Now the Bay Ridge area of Brooklyn had the largest concentration of Norwegians of foreign and American birth outside of Norway. By 1940 the figure reached 109,000, including 55,000 foreign-born. Because of personal ties with seamen's missions, with fresh arrivals from abroad, and with visiting celebrities, the relations of the Norwegian colony in the East with the European homeland were deep and continuous. However, contacts with Norway did not prevent, but rather stimulated, an ethnic camaraderie in the metropolitan area in the form of societies.

Among the "firsts" west of the Mississippi Valley was a Scandinavian society in San Francisco, dating from 1869, when gold fever was rampant. Its humanitarian purpose is revealed in a report of 1909, the fiftieth anniversary, that an aggregate of $225,000 had been donated during the half-century for sick relief. West Coast federation was realized in 1910 when 45 delegates, meeting in Seattle, effected a union of fourteen organizations. A probable reason for the interest in fraternal associations, apart from church membership, is that many of the recent arrivals from Norway were religiously indifferent, sharing the skepticism of Ibsen and Björnson. The Lutheran hold upon the baptized immigrants was tenuous. In the state of Washington in 1910, for example, there were scarcely 6,000 registered Lutherans in a Norwegian population of 40,000.[6]

A closer look at the activities of Norwegian-American joiners reveals that from the original singing and athletic societies the way led to well patronized lodges, *bygdelags*, and to more intellectual outlets for the expression of things Norwegian. A detailed coverage of all organizations providing sociability and opportunity for creativity is impractical here. Carl G. O. Hansen's article of 1914 acknowledged some 650 separate Norwegian endeavors. The vast majority can only be recognized in a general way. Hansen estimated that lodges carried on their rolls 30,000 names, and *bygdelags* the same number. He did not presume to know the numerical strength of all types of organizations.[7]

The field of drama never seems to have been usurped by Norwegian immigrant leadership. Perhaps its image of worldliness and its controversial themes rendered its acceptance dubious. Marcus Thrane, a self-exiled labor leader and socialist, inspired a handful of amateur players in Chicago after 1866. Of the 32 plays presented or produced, Thrane wrote five, all of them grounded in Scandinavian or European literature. By 1870, dramatic societies had been formed in Chicago and Minneapolis. But the predominance of Scandinavian themes failed to disarm critics. Ibsen and Björnson were then riding crests of popularity as playwrights, yet they were scathingly denounced by defenders of the status quo in social relations. Ibsen was charged with portraying a "godless life" in *A Doll's House.* Björnson, who during his America tour in 1880–1881 lectured in immigrant communities, lost ground with church folk by ridiculing belief in the supernatural and heralding the day of "free thought."[8]

The controversy engendered by cosmopolitan and libertarian drama did not plague the field of music. Most commonly, Norwegian *a capella* male choruses in cities and towns, often beginning with Swedish and Danish voices as well, entertained themselves and their friendly concert audiences with stately hymns of Scandinavia in four-part arrangements for men, with Norwegian folk melodies, and with modern Norwegian compositions. From the inauguration of the Normanna Singing Society in La Crosse, Wisconsin, in 1869 until the present day this form of artistic expression has never ceased. Nor were the ladies excluded. As an example, Signe Lillejord of Minneapolis conducted the Olive Fremstad Singers for eighteen years and the Nina Grieg Chorus for twenty-four years prior to her retirement in 1973.[9]

The bonds of fellowship which brought together men of a single community to lift their voices in song can be seen in regional and national organizations as well. A Scandinavian federation of 1886 met biennially in Philadelphia, Chicago, Minneapolis, and other cities. Carl Hansen himself participated in it actively almost from the start. In 1891 there were fifty societies with a total of 1,800 members, about two-thirds of them Norwegian voices. In 1893 the united singers (the Swedes had broken away in 1892) sang at the Columbian Exposition in Chicago.[10]

Now that the nationwide federation was almost wholly Norwegian, societies in the Northwest and the East began to join. The singing society of Brooklyn replaced in 1890 the declining organization in New York. Ole Windingstad, an emigrant of 1907, occupied the podium from 1911 to 1939, whether he conducted the singers or directed an orchestra. From New York and Brooklyn he proceeded to the directorship of the New Orleans Symphony Orchestra. His career paralleled that of Carlo A. Sperati, son of a chapel choir leader in Christiania. Although the younger Sperati was educated in America for the Lutheran ministry, he became director of the combined male choruses on the Pacific Coast in 1903. Luther College, his alma mater, called him in 1905 as professor of music and religion. There he brought the concert band to new heights of performance.

Sangerfests played an important role in preserving the Norwegian tradition in America well into the present century Sons and grandsons of the immigrants continued to be active. Seven hundred musicians gathered in Chicago in 1950 to present a concert, accompanied by the Chicago Symphony Orchestra. Before an audience of five thousand, they first sang the national anthems of the United States and Norway. With the famed Danish soloist Lauritz Melchior, they presented "Den Store Hvite Flokk" (The Great White Host), the lines of which had been composed by Hans Adolph Brorson, Danish hymn writer and bishop. Carl Söyland speaks of this number as a "melody that first was softly sung in a Norwegian valley centuries ago, and then began to move as a stream through the generations." It belonged to the cultural baggage of the immigrants, and it remains in the possession of their children.[11]

Skiing and ice-skating were more universally adopted in Scandinavian-American communities. Of the two, skiing was most popular. Norwegians took the lead in introducing skiing to America. Cross-country travel on wooden runners was, as in Norway, a practical means of transportation. Not until the 1880s did skiing become a well organized sport. Clubs were formed from New Hampshire to Minnesota. Eventually skiing was popularized, in the early 1900s, in the Far Northwest. For the next thirty or forty years Norwegians dominated the annual American tournaments. In 1904 they organized the National Ski Association and went on to construct ski jumping hills, supported in many instances by steel scaffolding, on the peripheries of many northern cities. By the 1930s Austrian influence in skiing began to be felt.[12]

Ice-skating ranked second to skiing. The Sleipner Athletic Club of Chicago, organized in 1893, inaugurated the annual ice-skating races in the city. Athletic clubs in other cities followed Sleipner's example. Norwegian champions came from abroad to add zest to the contests.

Another type of group activity, devoted to temperance, appealed to Norwegians for reasons of sociability as well as for improvement of private and public morals. In 1885 a Minnesota Total Abstinence Society was formed. By 1914 it consisted of 125 local chapters, with a total of 8,000 members. Norwegians in Wisconsin and the two Dakotas followed Minnesota's lead between 1888 and 1898, and a Pacific Coast branch began in 1904. Consumption of alcoholic beverages was at an all-time high in the last quarter of the century. This situation, deplorable to many, is reflected in the growth of the temperance movement throughout the nation. Waldemar Ager, publisher and editor of *Reform* of Eau Claire, Wisconsin, came to be recognized as the temperance leader among his countrymen in America.[13]

A secret temperance fraternity, the Independent Order of Good Templars, enjoyed popularity with a considerable segment of the Norwegian-Americans. It began in 1879 with a lodge in Brooklyn. A Scandinavian grand lodge was organized in Minnesota in 1891. By 1913 there were 81 Scandinavian I.O.G.T. units, with a total of over 3,500 members, about half of them Norwegian. The lodges spanned the continent, from Greater New York to the State of Washington. Many members, especially in the East, had been Good Templars in Norway.[14]

The largest and most active of Norwegian secular organizations in America is the Sons of Norway. Its purpose is not only to provide insurance benefits for its members but "to create and preserve among its members interest in the Norwegian language, in so far as compatible with the loyalty which they owe to their adopted country' 'and "to educate its members socially, morally, and intellectually."

Whether the times were propitious for the success of the first Sons of Norway lodges in the 1890s is debatable. On the one hand, Norwegians were becoming more numerous in America through immigration and through natural increase but, on the other hand, the "gay nineties" were somewhat cheerless. Panic and depression cast a somber spell over the entire nation. The Pullman strike of 1894 testified to deplorable conditions for urban labor. Midwestern farmers complained constantly of poor crops, of low prices on their produce, of scarcity of money, and underrepresentation of the agricultural segment of society in the state legislatures. Hard times drove the miserable to seek the company of others like themselves. There was yet another factor. As Swedish-Norwegian relations deteriorated abroad before 1905, and as the constitutional centennial of 1914 approached, the feeling of Norwegianism became more pronounced in immigrant communities and reflected itself in a phenomenal growth of fraternalism, as in the Sons of Norway.

The geographical spread of the new order and the rapid increase in its membership are clearly traceable. From Minneapolis, still the headquarters, the way led westward to Seattle (1904), then eastward to Chicago (1909), and Brooklyn (1910). Since the metropolitan areas were the first to embrace the new fraternal idea, it appears that farmers played a lesser role in the beginning years. Unquestionably the Sons of Norway owed its rise largely to its insurance program. In 1901 the State of Minnesota recognized it as a mutual benefit insurance organization. Already by 1914 the amount of insurance in force reached $2,246,000. In the same year it was decided that two classes of membership should henceforth be recognized, insured and non-insured. The insurance feature, however, has become increasingly attractive. In 1972 the amount in force surpassed the $100,-000,000 mark.[15]

Sons of Norway rosters varied with the times, but the numbers generally increased. The wave of Norwegian immigration from 1900 to 1913, with over 25,000 arriving in 1905 alone, further stimulated the national feeling, a factor reflected in the growth of social and cultural institutions. The number of lodges rose from about two hundred in 1924 to about three hundred in 1973. Meanwhile, total membership increased phenomenally, from 16,488 (1924) to about 90,000 (1973).[16]

Prior to 1914 all reports in Sons of Norway meetings were in the Norwegian language. By 1942 all were in English. In 1943 the official monthly magazine, *Sons of Norway* (now *Sons of Norway Viking*) also switched to English. With the declining use of the mother tongue, individual lodges devoted themselves more to social life and to charitable work in hospitals and homes. As auxiliaries to the Sons of Norway there developed women's societies, notably the Daughters of Norway, organized in 1897, and later merged with the Sons of Norway. The Sons of Norway did not depend for its existence upon the preservation of the Norwegian language. The order has expanded without the loss of unity. It is estimated that as many as 200,000 men and women of Norwegian descent have at one time or another been active in the Sons of Norway movement.[17]

Concurrent with the Sons of Norway since 1907 has been *Nordmanns-Forbundet* (The League of Norwegians). This organization seeks to strengthen the ties between emigrants and their progeny all over the world with their compatriots in Norway. When the union with Sweden was dissolved, countless expressions of sympathy and offers of contributions came from Norwegians in the United States and elsewhere. So impressed were leaders in Norway that they decided to issue an appeal for a worldwide organization.

The League of Norwegians has been tremendously effective. Through *Nordmanns-Forbundet*, the monthly magazine published at the headquarters in Oslo, former countrymen are kept abreast of events and trends of thought in Norway and of activities of Norwegians from Canada to Hong Kong, from Madagascar to the Galapagos Islands, but with major attention given to Norwegians in America. The services of the League are many and varied. Norwegian literature of all kinds is distributed, and special Norwegian foods are sent upon request to distant places. Books, films, lectures, and exhibits are offered for use or display to chapters all over the globe. Since World War II a legal consultant has been available to members living abroad who may be confronted with citizenship problems, taxation difficulties, and the like. In 1956 a free travel service was inaugurated for those contemplating tours of Scandinavia or Europe.

Nordmanns-Forbundet has been fortunate in its leadership. Carl Berner, president of the Norwegian parliament, functioned as the first chairman of the board of directors. The present chairman is Torolv Kandahl, the former editor-in-chief of Oslo's *Aftenposten*, considered by many to be Norway's leading newspaper. Arne Kildal, once head of the Deichman Public Library in Oslo, and a loyal and well informed friend of America, held the office of general secretary from the beginning. In recent years Johan Hambro, son of the late Carl J. Hambro who at one time presided over the parliament, has performed that function. He also edits the bimonthly magazines, *Nordmanns-Forbundet* and *The Norseman*.[18]

In the twentieth century a *bygdelag* movement has accentuated and in large measure satisfied the urge for meeting socially. Andrew A. Veblen, himself instrumental in founding a *bygdelag* of folk from the Valdres district of Norway in 1901, defined it as a "society composed of natives of some particular settlement or group of settlements in Norway and of their descendants in this country." Another source adds that "the bonds of union were dialect, common customs, songs and music, acquaintanceship, and shared traditions." Meetings resemble family reunions, but on a larger scale. The Valdres *Samband* (Union) was the first successful effort to promote togetherness of folk originating from a particular region in Norway. While the *bygdelags* drew their strength mainly from the rural areas in America, their rise was nevertheless rapid. After Telelaget (1907) and Hallinglaget (1908), many others were to follow.[19]

Lag objectives are variously stated in their constitutions. Hallinglaget emphasizes, among other things, the writing and preservation of stories concerning the Hallings in Norway and in America. Landingslaget aims to foster the understanding of the Norwegian language. Modum Eiker Laget proposed to support all undertakings that would honor the race and things Norwegian in America. Nordhordlandslaget sets as its goal "to work for all that is noble and good which, founded upon Christian principles, has unfolded itself in the life of the Norwegian people." Here is a reminder of the common Lutheran tradition, an important bond in itself.

The year 1914, which marked the centennial of the Eidsvoll Constitution and of Norwegian independence, gave special impetus to the *bygdelag* movement. The 1925 centennial of *Restauration's* epochal voyage, commemorating the beginning of mass migration from Norway to America, gave further inspiration. On both occasions members, whether singly or in groups, attended the ceremonies in Norway and America. It is estimated that when President Calvin Coolidge spoke in St. Paul on June 8, 1925, he drew an audience of 200,000 people of Norwegian descent. For that observance the *bygdelags* did most of the planning and covered most of the expense. They revived the memory of Cleng Peerson, the pathfinder of the 1820s. Colonel Hans C. Heg, who laid down his life for the cause of the Union, was feted in a pageant. The city of Oslo (Christiania before 1925) celebrated the initial group landing with a week of festivities, and Stavanger, from which the Sloopers had sailed a hundred years earlier, made July 4 more meaningful to the citizens of Norway with appropriate observances.[20]

The *bygdelag* movement is mainly a twentieth-century phenomenon. One of the growth-encouraging factors was the greater interest on the part of older immigrants, who had survived the busy and trying years of the struggling newcomer and now had more opportunity for life's amenities. Increased mobility of the population has also been responsible. At one time the church was the only social center. After Sunday services there was opportunity to mingle, and sometimes during the week a wedding, a funeral, a picnic, or a convention broke the monotony of everyday life. Without parent-teacher associations, at the beginning of the century, the schools had little sociability to offer. The railroad and soon the automobile broadened the chances for social life, while the church lost some of its social importance in competition with secular developments and with technological advances.

Bygdelags have gained in popularity, despite a definite decline in the number of Norwegian-speaking members. English is now the official language in meetings and publications. In 1970 some 24 *lags* were represented in a council, which dates back to 1916.

An extensive *bygdelag* history is scheduled for publication in 1975. The third and fourth generations, wishing to build upon the cultural legacy of their forefathers, are looking optimistically ahead.[21]

The American-Scandinavian Foundation, organized in New York in 1910, represents a successful effort to promote cultural exchange between the peoples of the Scandinavian lands and the American people, and to foster good relations between Scandinavian-Americans everywhere. Consequently, as "a new departure in non-governmental international relations," the Foundation has at once made Norwegians more conscious of their heritage and, at the same time, quickened their awareness of the Norwegian, and Scandinavian, role in American life. In 1972 the Foundation had a membership organized by chapters in 22 cities throughout America.[22]

The American-Scandinavian Review, begun in 1913 as a bimonthly magazine but issued quarterly since 1933, performs a function of inestimable value in fulfilling the Foundation's purposes. Under the consecutive editorships of Henry Goddard Leach, Hanna Astrup Larsen, and Erik J. Friis the periodical has set a worthy pattern for ethnic groups in America.

Erik J. Friis, an immigrant of 1929 while still in his teens, was honored in 1971 on completion of 25 years of service. During most of that period he has borne the responsibility for the publications program, including the *Review* and all new books and reprints. He has translated a number of books from the Scandinavian languages to English. He also serves as general editor of the Library of Scandinavian Literature, co-published by Twayne Publishers and The American-Scandinavian Foundation. He is also the editor and publisher of *The Scandinavian-American Bulletin*.

The Foundation has provided financial support for a large number of students, fellows, and trainees. In 1908 Niels Poulson, a Danish-American industrialist, established a trust fund of $100,000 for student scholarships and fellowships. The Foundation has entered into cooperative relationships with the Norway-America Association in Norway and similar organizations in the other Scandinavian countries.

The universities, and more recently American businessmen,

have been impressed with the services of The American-Scandinavian Foundation to scholars on both sides of the Atlantic. A record for the number of traveling fellows was set in 1939, when 95 students were awarded stipends, averaging a thousand dollars each. Their studies and researches touched many fields of knowledge. A trainee program, approved by the Department of State in 1946, offers practical experience, usually for one year, to Scandinavian young men and women seeking development of their skills with American firms and laboratories. Interrupted by World War II, student interchange was resumed in 1945, when the Foundation accommodated 52 fellows from Sweden, 41 from Norway, and 33 from Denmark. The program expanded rapidly in the following years. In the trainee development the name of Lithgow Osborne, once United States Ambassador to Norway, stands preeminent. Osborne retired from the Foundation in 1973 after serving as president or board chairman for twenty-six years.

Among the many Foundation fellows who were assisted in their researches in Norway were Oscar J. Falnes, Hanna Astrup Larsen, Karl Fritjof Rölvaag, and Martin B. Ruud. Falnes is perhaps best known for his publication of *National Romanticism in Norway* (New York, 1933). As mentioned above, Hanna Astrup Larsen, daughter of Laur. Larsen, first president of Luther College, served as editor of the *American-Scandinavian Review* for many years. Karl Rölvaag, son of Ole E. Rölvaag of literary fame, became governor of Minnesota. Martin Ruud served as a professor of literature in the University of Minnesota. Franklin D. Scott, formerly professor of history at Northwestern University, did his research as a Foundation fellow in Sweden. Among his published works are *Bernadotte and the Fall of Napoleon* (Cambridge, Massachusetts, 1935) and *The United States and Scandinavia* (Cambridge, 1950). Scott remains active in the fields of Scandinavian and immigrant history.

A second organization not limited to the study of Norway alone, and definitely not designed to meet the needs of the average immigrant, is the Society for the Advancement of Scandinavian Study, founded in 1911. Its stated objectives are to promote Scandinavian study and instruction in America, to encourage original research in Scandinavian languages, literatures, history, culture, and society, to provide an outlet for publication of researched material, and to foster closer relations between scholars everywhere in the field of Scandinavian studies.

The Society for the Advancement of Scandinavian Study publishes a quarterly magazine, *Scandinavian Studies*, edited in turn by George T. Flom of the University of Iowa, Albert Morey Sturtevant of the University of Kansas, Walter Johnson of the University of Washington, George C. Schoolfield of Yale University, and presently Harald S. Naess of the University of Wisconsin at Madison. The Scandinavianists meet annually at various colleges and universities. Their success in introducing and maintaining programs in Scandinavian studies in American institutions has fluctuated with the times. During World War I American popular sentiment precluded the pursuit of foreign-language study, except French. The isolationist 1920s and the depression-plagued 1930s hardly improved the chances for implementation of new courses. Today, however, several Scandinavian area studies programs are in operation in American institutions of higher learning.[23]

Historical interests of Norwegians in America may be traced to a combination of filiopietistic and professional motives. This is the view of Lloyd Hustvedt, the present secretary of the Norwegian-American Historical Association.[24] From the time when ethnic writers responded with a "who's who" approach to the obvious neglect by American historians of immigrant achievement and significance, concern was expressed for the establishment of a permanent historical society.

Hustvedt's essay, a forerunner to what hopefully will be a fiftieth anniversay history in 1975, brings to light earlier historical efforts. Knud Langeland's *Normændene i Amerika* (Chicago, 1888) was the first book of its kind. *Symra*, a literary periodical circulating from Decorah, Iowa, after 1905, carried many articles pertaining to immigrant experiences. Hjalmar Rued Holand made a significant contribution with his *De Norske Settlementers Historie* (Ephraim, Wisconsin, 1908).

Following a preliminary meeting in the summer of 1925 in Decorah, Knut Gjerset and others pledged their financial support and completed the plans for an organizing meeting at St. Olaf College, Northfield, Minnesota, on October 6. As a concession to the Luther College contingent, the new Norwegian-American Historical Association promised to assist in maintaining an already functioning museum in Decorah.

The Norwegian-American Historical Association launched upon an unusually productive career in publication with certain advantages. Enthusiasm engendered by the centennial celebration commemorating the arrival of the Sloopers was one asset. Secondly, prominent American historians like John B. McMaster and Frederick Jackson Turner had come to appreciate the role of immigrants in the American pageant. Finally, the invaluable editorial leadership and personal inspiration of Theodore C. Blegen, professor of history and subsequently dean of the graduate school of the University of Minnesota, proved to be a great boon to success. Kenneth O. Bjork succeeded Blegen in 1960 in the important editorial chair.

Among the now 55 books published by the Norwegian-American Historical Association are 26 volumes of *Studies* (*Studies and Records* before 1962), eight volumes in a series devoted to travel and description, eighteen special publications, two in a recently inaugurated authors series, and one in a new series of topical studies. Recognition should be given to two diligent secretaries, J. Jörgen Thompson and Lloyd Hustvedt, and two competent archivists and bibliographers, Jacob Hodnefield and Beulah Folkedahl.

The Association has frequently received favorable comment from American historians and Norwegian officials. The role of emigration in Norway's history was little appreciated before the turn of the century. But the political crisis of 1905 and the founding of the League of Norsemen two years later did much to promote mutual understanding between Norwegians at home and overseas. To this new comprehension the historical society contributed notably through systematic research and publication, making emigrant history a vital part of Norway's history also.

The above-mentioned Norwegian-American Historical Museum, now known as Vesterheim, has deeper roots than the historical society of 1925. In 1877 certain folk in Decorah and at Luther College began the somewhat pleasant task of collecting spinning wheels, decorative chests, tapestries, household utensils, and even pioneer log cabins. Eventually displays of

Bibles and hymnals, of *rosemaling* (rose painting), wood carvings, sculptures, portraits, and group pictures would be offered to twentieth-century viewers. Under Haldor J. Hanson's initial direction, the museum acquired thousands of items. In 1933 the collection was moved from the Luther College campus to downtown Decorah, where it now flourishes.[25]

The museum's purpose and justification were stated by Knut Gjerset, historian and author, when he declared that "a collection of material which throws light upon the life and history of some individual group becomes a valuable source for the larger history of our whole American people." Gjerset was followed as director by Inga Bredesen Norstog, widow of the dramatist and poet Jon Norstog, in 1947, and by Marion John Nelson in 1964.

Under Marion John Nelson, Vesterheim, a term used by the immigrants when referring to their home in the New World, has embarked upon new projects. A report of 1970 notes a substantial increase in membership, a *rosemaling* tour of Norway, and what may become a permanent Nordic Fest in association with the city of Decorah. Craft, painting, and drawing classes are held regularly. Lectures, concerts, and tours of the Decorah area are sponsored.

Immigrants from the northern climes of Europe joined, in addition to their church congregations, a wide diversity of more or less secular clubs, choirs, lodges, sporting groups, charitable enterprises, and historical and literary societies. Once the adjustment to life in the New World was at least partially completed, the opportunity and desire for association with their kinsmen increased. What followed was more than a carnival of spectacle and sound. Besides entertainment, there were the intangible rewards of good fellowship and often solid achievement along religious, humanitarian, and cultural lines.

On occasion there were outlets for spontaneous outpourings of goodwill and rejoicing, as during the Norway Relief drive in the wartime 1940s and the annual 17th of May Constitution Day festivities in Brooklyn, Chicago, Minneapolis, and Seattle, and smaller but predominantly Norwegian communities like Stoughton, Wisconsin. On the national holiday for Norwegiandom all organizations still tend to combine as one, with church congregations, army bands, and fraternal organizations participating in the parades. The Brooklyn celebration, which had its inception in 1952, has become a forum for all participating units. The enthusiasm and success of the occasion, with cadence suggesting harmony of purpose and singleness of goal, is in no way lessened by the circumstance that Brooklyn, sometimes called a second Oslo, is the home of numerous recent immigrants from Norway, the most popular calling port in America for Norwegian seamen, and a stopping-off place for distinguished visitors.

But the high points in Norwegian-American experience nationwide came in the red-letter years of 1905, 1914, and 1925. It was then that the Norwegian people demonstrated their gregariousness most conspicuously. Respect for the Old World and loyalty to the New characterized their celebrations. In a spirit of ethnic consciousness Norwegians in America also turned creatively to the writing of their history and to fictional, yet realistic, immigrant sagas.

CHAPTER 11

Literature in the Making:
From Boyesen to Rölvaag

SINCE WALDEMAR AGER'S SURVEY OF NORWEGIAN-AMERICAN *belles lettres* several writers of Norwegian descent, lovers of fiction for the most part, have made valuable contributions to his pioneering effort. But perhaps there is no better point of departure for a journey into the world of the immigrant novel than Ager's perceptive essay, which commemorated Norway's hundredth anniversary as a modern constitutional monarchy in 1914. Ager's skillful presentation, however, was inspired not so much by thoughts of the Old World as by literary progress in the New, among countrymen of his own ethnic origin.[1]

Ager modestly omits his own creations from his helpful commentary. As an author and an editor of no mean ability he worked in his home in Eau Claire, Wisconsin, and often rose from his chair to consult one or another volume in his private library. There was room for soliloquy also. He speculated, not without reason, that a more impressive body of Norwegian-American literature would depend upon the ideals and the interests of the second generation. Immigrants, after all, were practical folk, having come as a rule from humble circumstances in Norway. They were compelled to move from place to place, generally in the American Middle West, in the serious search for more fertile soil. Loneliness sharpened their religious sensitivity. Pastors and churches made their appearance as settlements grew. The earth's increase freed the struggling farmers from the threat of poverty. They began to read religious and political tracts and newspapers. Ager regretted that the first attempts at creative writing should be smothered by a people living in a restrictive intellectual environment, where sectarian beliefs were the sole concern of the mind, apart from such mundane affairs as narrow-minded politics.

Ager noted that his shelves contained a fair number of works. He owned 34 bound volumes of Norwegian-American poetry, and apparently many fictional productions as well. He complained of too much diversity in content and style. Here one found grief, feverish fantasy, pleas to heaven, and curious phraseology, but poetic strength was lacking. Authors gasped rather than breathed. And no wonder. Poetry could not raise land prices or lower taxes. So the poetic child remained, for the time being, an infant. Yet the more talented bards, with no promise of an audience, penned their beautiful lines out of sheer love of creativeness. Only the temperance writers had an assured public. Hence, prohibition literature was conspicuous in immigrant homes.

A quarter-century after Ager's literary assessment Theodore C. Blegen, in the second volume of his ground-breaking history of Norwegian immigration, devoted a chapter to frontiers of culture. Since the Civil War a hundred novels, most of them available only in the original Norwegian, had been published. Much had been achieved in the writing of immigrant history, poetry, religious works, reminiscences, and biographies. Ole Edvart Rölvaag displayed the greatest artistry in his *Giants in the Earth* and other novels. Otherwise, Norwegian-American fiction tended toward social documentation, as it focussed upon immigrants, without the esthetic appeal of a Rölvaag.[2]

Prior to the Civil War there were ballads, both oral and written. Travel accounts appeared early. Often these reflected not only true descriptions but also stylistic refinement. As the common man came to be exalted in the more widely known works of Mark Twain and Bret Harte, so in the lesser known Norwegian efforts the lowly immigrants merited the attention of the literary coterie.

As competent appraisers of immigrant sagas have more than once observed, newspapers published in the mother tongue gave impetus in the 1870s to an outpouring of fiction and poetry. *Skandinaven* of Chicago carried a literary supplement, *Hus-bibliothek* (Home Library); *Decorah-Posten* did the same with *Ved Arnen* (By the Fireside). Literary beginnings are best traced in the daily columns of *Skandinaven,* where Hjalmar Hjorth Boyesen and Bernt Askevold were personally identified with the immigrant world. However, the two authors did not ordinarily choose immigrant themes for their literary creations. They were in, but not of, the immigrant milieu. Yet as forerunners they in no way discouraged the preparation of immigrant novels by their contemporaries and successors.

The year 1874 proved to be a red-letter year for Norwegian-American literature. Boyesen's *Gunnar* appeared in book form, after being serialized in the *Atlantic Monthly.* Nicolai Severin Hassel came forth with two immigrant novels, *Alf Brage, eller Skolelæreren i Minnesota* (Alf Brage, or the Schoolteacher in Minnesota) and *Rædselsdagene: Et norsk Billede fra Indianer-krigen i Minnesota* (Days of Terror: A Norwegian Portrayal from the Indian War in Minnesota). Both appeared in *For Hjemmet* (For the Home), a weekly journal of literary sketches and practical information.

In 1876, a time of economic trials, two little known novelists rose above the dismal scene. Bernt Askevold published *Hun Ragnhild, eller Billeder fra Söndfjord* (Ragnhild, or Pictures from Söndfjord), with its setting in the Norwegian countryside, while Tellef Grundysen made his debut with *Fra Begge Sider af ,Havet* (From Both Sides of the Ocean), relating his family's experiences in Norway and in southern Minnesota.[3]

Some who produced dramas, poems, and novels were not immigrants in the technical sense, yet their writings encompassed the immigrant scene. Men like Kristofer Janson and Knut Hamsun sojourned in the New World only a few years, Janson from 1881 to 1893 and Hamsun from 1882 to 1884, and again from 1886 to 1888. In their later years on Norwegian soil both continued to reflect their American experiences and their interest in Norwegian-American life. In that context, perhaps, they merit inclusion in our literary survey.

Kristofer Janson holds the distinction of being the first Norwegian writer to have his work published in America. It was a three-act drama, *Amerikanske Fantasier,* which appeared in 1876 in *Skandinaven,* before he came to America. In *Vildrose* (Wild Rose) of 1887 Janson relates with real artistry the adventures of Gunhild, a girl who made friends with the Sioux Indians of

Minnesota at the time of the uprising of 1862. Pioneer life is made vivid in his *Præriens Saga* (1885). His wife, Drude Krog Janson, supported her ministerial husband's endeavors with *En Ung Pige* (A Young Girl), *Ensomhed* (Loneliness), and *En Saloonkeepers Datter* (A Saloonkeeper's Daughter), all between 1887 and 1894. Mrs. Janson found a kindred soul in the temperance field in Ulrikka Bruun, who contributed *Menneskets Största Fiende* (Mankind's Greatest Enemy) in 1877. Those familiar with American history are aware that the final quarter of the nineteenth century was the heyday of the brewing industry, with record-breaking consumption of beer and whiskey.[4]

Ager, himself an avid temperance man, and editor of *Reform* for many years, cites the saloon and the church as major forces, however incompatible, in Norwegian-American social life. Peer Strömme in his autobiographical *Hvorledes Halvor Blev Prest* (How Halvor Became a Minister) had a chapter on the saloon. Simon Johnson's first and best novel is of that genre. Julius Baumann made his entry into literature as a temperance poet. Kristofer Janson's *Bag Gardinet* (Behind the Curtain) is tinged with hatred for alcoholic beverages. And Ole Amundsen Buslett's and Jon Norstog's works frequently direct a kick toward John Barleycorn.[5]

Despite Hamsun's Norwegian moorings, it is appropriate to sketch his literary career in the context of Norwegian-American literature. One must recognize the influence of others upon his life and thought. August Strindberg, the Swedish playwright, Feodor Dostoevski, the Russian novelist, and the American Mark Twain all left their mark upon him. But Hamsun admired Bjørnstjerne Bjørnson most of all, not alone for his specific talents but for his total outlook and scope of production. Hamsun's personal reminiscences and short stories fall partially within the framework of regional Middle West literature, which constitutes the bulk of Norwegian-American *skjönliteratur*.[6] Hamsun's youthful impressions, as set forth in *Det moderne Amerikas Aandsliv* (The Cultural Life of Modern America), reveal a definite repugnance for American society, where people were basically creatures of the prairie, and all Scandinavians were called Swedes by the undiscriminating Yankees.

Much of Hamsun's later writing lends credence to the argument that America influenced him strongly in his maturer years. His vagabond life in the Middle West turned his sympathies toward the rootless hero. He had traced the imperfections not of American society alone but of Western civilization as a whole. His son's biography of Hamsun expressed the view that his father valued his New World experiences. In fact, the elder Hamsun had said as much both privately and publicly. He proceeded from severe criticism, as in *The Cultural Life of Modern America,* to creative writing in his short stories drawn from his wanderings abroad.[7]

Waldemar Ager characterizes Hans A. Foss as the Björnson of the immigrants. In *Husmands-Gutten: en Fortælling fra Sigdal* (The Cotter's Boy: A Tale from Sigdal) Foss traces with intimate knowledge of the immigrant mind the fortunes of Marie and Ole, a married couple of different social backgrounds. This novel of 1889 fulfills the universal dream of emigrants. Ole returns to Norway to buy the whole estate. To settle an old score he holds two revolvers, one in each hand, under the nose of a onetime rival at home. The book won so much acclaim as a serial in *Decorah-Posten* that the newspaper gained 6,000 new subscribers in a single year. If Norwegian-Americans are criticized for eagerly accepting its violence, Norwegians at home were no less attracted to the story. By 1921 at least eleven editions had been published in Norway. Other books by Foss were to follow.[8]

Foss's *The Cotter's Boy* stimulated, among others, Peer Olson Strömme. In his home in the Red River Valley of the North, where he served briefly as pastor of a Lutheran congregation, Strömme was challenged to improve upon Foss's effort. The result was the novel that made Strömme famous, *Hvorledes Halvor Blev Prest.* The story first came to light in *Superior Posten* in 1892, by which time its restless author had forsaken the pulpit. What *The Cotter's Boy* had done for *Decorah-Posten,* Strömme's *How Halvor Became a Minister* did for *Posten* of Superior, in northwestern Wisconsin. Whereas Foss was intrigued by the peasant novels of Björnson, Strömme was swayed by Mark Twain and Charles Dickens. Some refer to him as the Twain among Norwegian-American literati. He dispensed humor freely and, like Twain, traveled and lectured extensively, partly in the cause of the Democratic party, which enjoyed little popularity in predominantly Republican Norwegian communities. Indeed, his humor stood him in good stead before politically hostile audiences. Strömme's written contributions were many and various. He edited *Norden* (The North) of Chicago from 1888 to 1892, *Amerika* of Chicago from 1895 to 1898, and *Normanden* (The Norwegian) of Grand Forks from 1911 to 1918. For *Symra*, a literary magazine of Decorah, Iowa, he wrote short stories, poems, and book reviews. An account of his world travels in 1911–1914 was presented in his usual illuminating style in *Normanden.*[9]

In *Halvor* even the uninitiated could detect Strömme's own life story, from his birth in the immigrant settlement of Winchester, Wisconsin, in 1856, to his epochal trip by rail (his first train ride) to Luther Academy in Decorah. There he continued through college and seminary. *Unge Helgeson* (Young Helgeson) furnishes a sequel, in which a Dakota blizzard, local politics, and endless church strife over the doctrine of predestination combined to make his pastorate exciting. In 1910 Strömme wrote his third and last novel, *Den Vonde Ivold* (In the Clutches of the Devil), concerning the Norwegian colony in Chicago. Decadence is the dominant note as two young men, recent graduates of the University of Christiania, discuss free love and suicide. Driven in hard times to translating cheap dime novels and detective stories, their steps, often as not, led them to the saloons. Both met with sad ends. Yet Strömme's realistic pictures of Norwegians in America are ordinarily buoyant and optimistic. His principal weakness was his restlessness. As Ole Rölvaag was later to say, "Strömme was a man of great talents. The vital error of his life, or perhaps the fatal flaw in his character, was this, that he never surrendered his being fully and single-mindedly to a ruling life task."[10] Waldemar Ager sums up the carefree Strömme as a gifted man, but lacking in imagination.

In 1924, a year after the death of the beloved poet Julius B. Baumann, there appeared a 250-page collection of his lyrics, entitled *Samlede Digte* (Collected Poems). Born in 1870 on Christmas day (hence the name Julius, from the Norwegian *jul*, or Christmas) in the northernmost Norwegian province of

Finnmark, he emigrated in 1891. As a lumberjack in Drummond, Wisconsin, his poetic talent found an outlet in the Norwegian-American press. In 1909 Baumann produced a poetic collection entitled *Digte,* and in 1915 a second volume, *Fra Vidderne* (From the Wide Expanses). In 1970, the centennial of his birth, there were no special observances. Yet in his time Baumann's name met with warm reception not only in the immigrant settlements but among native Americans as well. Ager calls him the greatest lyricist among his countrymen in America.

Baumann's intimate friend, John Heitmann, has sketched a deserved tribute to "an outspoken American patriot" who became "an intellectual guide and moral and spiritual leader among his people."[11] In the medium of the Norwegian language Baumann wrote of love, faith, and beauty. He was a man of peace, not of contention. Far removed personally from the scramble for material gain, he penned lines that suggest spiritual kinship with John Greenleaf Whittier, the Quaker. Freely translated, they would read,

> I ask no riches with red lurid light.
> They are but tinseled joys with transient splendor.
> But give me, Lord, the will and wondrous might
> To be my brother's guide and staunch defender.

In Heitmann's view, his friend was the most beloved and appreciated Norwegian writer in America prior to the appearance of Rölvaag and *Giants in the Earth.* Born where the sun shone not at all in late December, Baumann became a worshiper of light. He stood in awe of nature. The sight of a pine forest in northern Wisconsin moved him to write,

> Give me your hand, child, as humbly we wander
> Into the forest's magnificent hall,
> List to its voices with reverent wonder,
> Our footsteps on thousand years' mosses will fall.

Baumann was well acquainted with the principal Norwegian-American authors. He was a personal friend of both Waldemar Ager and Ole Rölvaag, although he disagreed sharply with them in their intense Norwegianness. How much influence he exerted on them is difficult to say, but Heitmann believes that it was determinative. He quotes Baumann as prompting Rölvaag to "write a book about the salty old giants." Leave the lumberjacks to Ager, he suggested, and tell about the struggles, dreams, and achievements of the fishermen and the farmers whom Rölvaag knew so well. Rölvaag did go on to write *Giants in the Earth*. Heitmann's evaluation of Baumann's influence upon Rölvaag, if correct, deserves wider publicity.

In 1876 Bernt Askevold published in *Budstikken* (literally Message Stick or Arrow) of Minneapolis an appeal for a distinctive Norwegian-American literature. He suggested the need of a good literary periodical. In so doing he pricked the imagination of numerous compatriots and inspired the production of fine writing. Between 1875 and 1885 a number of Norwegian-Americans stepped upon the stage as novelists. Among those who contributed to the tradition of creative writing was Ole A. Buslett, who as novelist, editor, and reformer was once described by Ager as the first poet worthy of the name among Norwegians in America. According to Ager, Buslett played around with social problems and stormed ahead with a lyre in one hand and a dissecting knife in the other. His last venture in journalism was in the late 1890s, as editor of *Normannen* of Stoughton and later Madison, Wisconsin.

Buslett's *Sagastolen* (The Seat of the Saga) of 1908 told not only of life in a lumbering town but dealt with socialism, communism, and free love. In the same year he described lumbering further in *Fra Min Ungdoms Nabolag* (From the Neighborhood of My Youth). *Veien til Golden Gate* (The Road to Golden Gate), a romantic tale of a Midwestern community and an excellent study in immigrant psychology as well, came in 1916.[12]

Joining Buslett after 1900 were N. N. Rönning, M. Falk Gjertsen, and others. Rönning's humor sparkled in *Bare for Moro* (Just for Fun), a volume of sketches produced in 1913. In 1928 his *Gutten fra Norge* (The Boy from Norway) depicted religious life in a section of the old country where *læsere* (readers) were the bane of some adolescents. These readers descended spiritually from Hans Nielsen Hauge and other pietists who expounded the Word of God, generally as self-educated laymen carrying the salvation of souls upon their hearts. Lars Lee rebelled against them and fled to America. Like others, Rönning published a collection of short stories, entitled *Da Stjernene Sang* (When the Stars Sang). M. Falk Gjertsen's *Harald Hegg: Billeder fra Prærien med Skildringer af Norsk-Amerikansk Folkeliv* (Harold Hegg: Pictures from the Prairie with Accounts of Norwegian-American Folk Life, 1914) featured once again life in the open spaces. As one who as a young pastor in the 1870s had defended the American public school, his association with the American scene was of long standing.[13]

More outstanding among the early twentieth-century writers were Waldemar Ager, Simon Johnson, Jon Norstog, and Johannes B. Wist. Ager arrived with his mother, brothers, and sisters, in Chicago in 1885. His father had emigrated earlier. Young Waldemar learned the typographical trade from *Norden,* then moved on to *Reform* in Eau Claire, Wisconsin, in 1892. There he remained until his death in 1941. For almost a lifetime he served as secretary of *Det Norske Selskap* (The Norwegian Society) and as editor of its quarterly publication, *Kvartalsskrift* from 1905 to 1918. More important, as manager and editor of *Reform* for half a century, Ager encouraged the growth of a Norwegian-American consciousness that would result in almost countless literary and historical contributions by himself and others. His publications are too numerous to be mentioned here. They ran the gamut from temperance works, as in *Paa Drikkeondets Konto* (To the Account of the Liquor Evil) of 1894 to social and religious themes. *I Strömmen* (In the Crowd) came in 1899 as a moral tract. *Fortællinger for Eyvind* (Tales for Eyvind) of 1906, a collection of delightful stories, was intended for his son. The stories were related in the first person and were pointed against the liquor traffic. *Hverdagsfolk* (Everyday People) appeared in 1908 as sketches of town and country. Ager criticized the hastiness of the Americanization process in *Paa Veien til Smeltepotten* (On the Way to the Melting Pot) in 1917, a critical year as far as immigrants and their children were concerned.

In the wartime hysteria the cry was for 100 percent American-ism, but Ager argued that the immigrant heritage might well contribute more to American culture if allowed to develop naturally rather than under the dicta of so-called pure Americans or of the government. In 1926 he produced *Gamlelandets Sönner* (The Sons of the Old Country), which took readers back to the Civil War, to the exploits of the Norwegian Fifteenth Wisconsin Regiment, which distinguished itself at Chickamauga, and to the Andersonville prison camp.

Ager's last book, *Hundeöine* (Dog Eyes) appeared in 1929 as a psychological study. It told of the life of Christian Pedersen, an immigrant who married a certain Rachel in Chicago and was very unhappy with her. He found peace in a shack on the edge of the Dakota farmlands. When in 1931 the book was printed in English as *I Sit Alone,* critics deplored its tedious moralizing but conceded that Ager had depicted his boyhood and his early years in Chicago with extraordinary skill.

The most controversial of Ager's works was *Kristus for Pilatus* (Christ Before Pilate), which appeared in 1910. The plot concerns a pastor who, in view of a disturbed conscience, seemingly washed his hands before Christ. It brought out uncomfortably the religious bigotry and prejudice among the immigrants. Ager's mastery of the social and psychological approaches in literature, together with his keen insight and ironical humor, marks him as deserving of a high place in Norwegian-American creative writing.[14]

Simon Johnson, a North Dakotan who arrived from Norway at the age of eight, produced *Et Geni* (A Genius) as his first effort. The tale is a depressing but intensely absorbing account of a young man who fails in an effort to sell his invention. He takes to drink. Later novels by Johnson present pioneer life with keen perceptiveness. One of several, *Fallitten paa Braastad* (The Braastad Bankruptcy), appeared in 1922 as a voluminous portrayal of aspiration, tragedy, and misunderstanding in an immigrant family. The generation gap was foreshadowed. In *Frihetens Hjem* (The Home of Freedom), published in 1925, the author focused upon the life of the second generation. He attributed American postwar isolationism to the rantings of "bombastic patriots."

One who composed mainly lyrics and biblical dramas was Jon Norstog, poet and peasant of remote Watford City, in northwestern North Dakota. Born in Telemark province of Norway in 1877, he emigrated in 1902. Newspaper editing first engaged his attention. Through his mother he was related to Aasmund Vinje, the bard who wrote in *Landsmål* (now called *Nynorsk*). Norstog inherited this propensity for New Norwegian, which unfortunately lacked popularity in Norwegian communities in the United States. His use of the as yet unaccepted medium also cost him his degree at the University of Christiania, where he refused to write in *Riksmål*, the prescribed Dano-Norwegian language.

Until his death in 1942 Norstog used his own hand printing press. He was his own salesman, carting his books over the farm and ranchland country. Waldemar Ager had an eye on him and saw great possibilities in his literary qualities. At the same time, he found it difficult to understand Norstog, suggesting that much learning had made him mad. Norstog is perhaps best remembered for his pedestrian but powerful dramas based upon biblical characters: *Cain, Moses, Joshua, Israel, Joseph,* and *King David*, all between 1912 and 1923. In his *Exodus* (1928) he finally turned to the novel, emphasizing cultural conflict in America, and between America and the world. His narration proved to have less impact upon readers than his impressive use of the rugged *Nynorsk*. It appears that his total work was appreciated more in the Old World. Among the immigrants he was praised but seldom read.[15]

Better known for his long and influential editorial career with *Decorah-Posten*, Johannes B. Wist is nevertheless worthy of a niche in the relatively obscure pantheon of Norwegian-American letters. In 1905 he and Kristian Prestgard began the annual publication of *Symra*, a literary magazine containing original contributions of the highest order, including some by Ager, Rölvaag, Simon Johnson, Knut Gjerset, and George T. Flom. This superb cultural periodical ceased publication in 1914.

Wist's trilogy of immigrant life, completed by 1922, included *Nykommerbilleder* (Newcomer Scenes), *Hjemmet paa Prærien* (The Home on the Prairie), and *Jonasville*. Unpretentiously written, the novels reflect often overlooked details of life in the settlements, personified in one Jonas Olsen. Wist's *Reise til*

Rochester (1922) relates comically the story of a journey in a 1913 model Ford.

The immigrant saga is not recorded by men only. Thanks to the Norwegian-American Historical Association, diaries and novels by women have also come to light. Elise Wærenskjold of Texas kept an accurate and informative diary almost from the time of her coming in 1847 to her death in 1895. Published under the title *The Lady With the Pen* (1961), it reveals her as the mother of a large family, the wife of a Confederate soldier, and herself a leader in the community. It is a personal document of considerable historical value.

A second Civil War mother, Gro Svendsen, has left letters of deep human interest which have been published in *Frontier Mother* (1950). Like Elise Wærenskjold, she wrote in Norwegian, but not as a Confederate sympathizer. She begins with the transition from Hallingdal in Norway to Estherville, Iowa, where she arrived in the troublesome year of 1861. In one of the last letters, in 1880, her bereaved husband explains that he has planted a tree on her grave in South Dakota, to which they had recently moved. Again, the family was large, the soil often stingy, and the locusts at times voracious.

American-born Aagot Raaen embellished her reminiscences to read like a historical novel. She gives a fascinating first-hand account of the pioneers in *Grass of the Earth* (1950). The setting is Mayville, in eastern North Dakota. As Theodore C. Blegen states in the foreword, rooms in the house of history are often cold and poorly furnished. These reminiscences supply warmth and life. The scene belongs not to the sod-breaking period but to the middle period, when the railroad, the saloon, and the farm mortgage were part of the social milieu. The author wrote in English, which in her childhood days was not her natural tongue.

One who emigrated from the vicinity of Bergen in 1902 at the age of two would call Winnipeg, in the Canadian province of Manitoba, her home. Martha Ostenso (the family name was Östensjö) enjoyed a wide circle of readers at home and abroad in the 1930s and thereafter. Writing in English, she entered a contest sponsored by a New York newspaper in 1925. In competition with 1,100 others, she won first prize, a sum of

$13,500, and assurance of publication. The novel, her first and best, appeared as *Wild Geese* and soon was translated into many languages (*Grågås* in Norwegian). The theme was familiar —the hardships of prairie life in Manitoba for an Icelandic farming family. Here one reads of internal family strife and the eternal search for sustenance and security in the great wheat country. Human creatures were, like the migrating geese, dependent upon the inexorable forces of nature. And besides, they were afflicted with the profit-seeking motivations of their own species.

Reviewers were less than generous in their appraisal of *Wild Geese*. Some thought that it was about the soil, but not of the soil, and that the novel did not stand on its own merits. There was too much dependence upon Edna Ferber, Selma Lagerlöf, and Knut Hamsun. Martha Ostenso's subsequent contributions continued to portray Scandinavians in minor roles. Only in *O River, Remember!* (1943) do three generations of Norwegians emerge as central figures. People of Norwegian stock were not, as a rule, her leading characters. Several of her novels were translated, however, into Norwegian by C. J. Hambro, Norway's distinguished newspaper editor and world statesman.

In the field of Norwegian-American fiction the names of Hjalmar Hjorth Boyesen (1848–1895) and Ole Edvart Rölvaag (1876–1931) carry a special luster. Both were schoolmen, Boyesen at Cornell and Columbia universities and Rölvaag at St. Olaf College. Boyesen, a professor of Germanic literature, became a realistic novelist, a literary critic, and a social Darwinist. Although he emigrated at the age of twenty-one he quickly attained a mastery of the English language and chose to write in that medium. His combined works would total about thirty-five volumes, including full-length novels, short stories, essays in literary criticism, poetry, and history. American journals were glad to accept whatever came from his pen. He was a significant liaison between European and American litterateurs. Though he was an immigrant, his interest in his fellow Norwegian countrymen in America appears to have been purely incidental.

Two years after his coming to America Boyesen had a rare opportunity to meet William Dean Howells, soon to become editor of the *Atlantic Monthly*. Fortunately, his manuscript of *Gunnar* was accepted for publication serially in that journal. The bound volume followed in 1874. Doors were opened to a professional career. In the course of a European tour in 1873 he had met the distinguished Russian novelist Ivan Turgenev in Paris. Correspondence and a lifelong friendship developed. The influence of Björnson is also discernible, as evidenced in *Gunnar*, which had its setting in Norway. *Gunnar* was well received by Americans in the East. An eighth edition was printed in 1895, the year of Boyesen's death.

Among Boyesen's countrymen in the Middle West *Gunnar* was hardly popular. He had imitated Björnson, it was said disparagingly, in his romantic approach and even in the topographical background, in which the mountainous and pastoral environment of Norway predominated. Unspoiled goatherds and peasants and scary trolls were nothing new to the initiated Norse of the Middle West. In any event, the European trip and a continuous association with Howells would change Boyesen. He turned from romanticism toward realism, away from the idyllic, the fanciful, and the legendary, and toward subjects of study in contemporary life, however sterile and unpicturesque they might be. In this period of transition Boyesen completed his second novel. *A Norseman's Pilgrimage*, based upon his own life.

In 1879 Boyesen ventured into immigrant life in Minnesota in *Falconberg*. Apparently out of touch with the situation in the West, he revived the issue, largely resolved, of the common school and the stubbornness of Norwegian pastors. He spoke of canyons and ravines, both foreign to Minnesota. Yet his picture was not entirely distorted. His opinions of the clergy were shared by Marcus Thrane and Kristofer Janson, who were thoroughly familiar with conditions in the North Star state. Granted that Boyesen's Swedenborgian upbringing was showing —his father had been forced to resign his army commission in Norway when he joined that denomination—there was strength and vigor in *Falconberg*. In producing the novel, Boyesen was the first to portray Norwegian immigrant life effectively to an American audience. Some critics believe that the book was mainly inspired by the desire to support the liberal views of his exemplar, Björnson, who was then about to visit the United States in order to lecture before Norwegian-American audiences.[16]

Boyesen's *Mammon of Unrighteousness* (1891) is generally recognized as being among the first of the sociological novels in American literature. He had recently complimented Björnson, Janson, and Rasmus B. Anderson for their exposure of ecclesiastical hypocrisy, alleged to prevail in the Norwegian Synod. He himself joined the Episcopal Church. The heroine in his *Mammon*, beautiful but cold of manner, was possibly a fictional replica of his wife, who descended from aristocratic native American stock. He now wrote not of immigrants but of the American social scene. In *The Golden Calf* (1892) and in *Social Struggles* (1893) he emphasized the worship of money. Boyesen was caught up in the acquisitive Gilded Age. He also suspected that unrestricted immigration, particularly from the economically distraught countries of southern and eastern Europe, threatened American moral and economic standards. Native Americans, he feared, were forsaking manual labor and even skilled craftsmanship. In so doing they were losing their pride in good workmanship.[17]

The American-oriented Boyesen died a year before the Norwegian-minded Rölvaag reached the shores of America and the farmland of South Dakota in 1896. The two men were not of the same generation, nor had they ever met. In the cosmos of literature dealing with Americans of Norwegian descent Rölvaag would emerge as the more scintillating of the two.

Prior to the publication of *Giants in the Earth* (1927) Rölvaag had produced several novels, many essays, and a few textbooks for instruction in the Norwegian language. *Paa Glemte Veie* (On Forgotten Paths) appeared in 1914. It described a daughter's efforts to convert her father to the true Christian faith. In 1921 *Længselens Baat* (The Ship of Longing) he presented sketches of life in Norway and in America. *To Tullinger* (Two Fools), later published as *Pure Gold* (1930), exposed the tragedy of money madness in wartime America.

Rölvaag's creativity took on new life in the 1920s. The war was over. In the words of Einar Haugen, Rölvaag resented the antiforeignism generated in America during that struggle and "found the Norwegian people succumbing to the effects of mass suggestion, and like Peter of old fervently denying their origin." Cultural activities were being revived. Rölvaag's textbook program was about completed, and he was free to swing back to the novel. These years of his maturity as an artist also coincided with much literary output in Norway, where Sigrid Undset, Johan Bojer, and Knut Hamsun were at their peaks.

Giants in the Earth, its title taken from the Old Testament story of the flight of the Israelites to the Promised Land, first appeared in two volumes in Norway, as *I De Dage* (In Those Days) and *Riket Grundlægges* (The Kingdom Is Founded). It relates the experience of a simple farming couple and their family in South Dakota. Per Hansa and his wife Beret, as homesteaders, are threatened with famine, cold, and loneliness. Readers come to identify Per Hansa with Rölvaag himself, and Beret with Rölvaag's mother. Only Beret's body was transported to the bleak midwestern prairie, not her soul and mind. Sequels to the story are found in *Peder Victorious,* in part a psychological study of the son's rise from youth to maturity, and in *Their Father's God,* in which Rölvaag scrutinized American political practices.[18]

Those who knew Rölvaag, and others who have studied him, point to certain factors which may have shaped his philosophy. They cite the influence of the province of Nordland upon him as a boy and as a young man. Here was a land of marvels and a playground of natural forces. A dramatic boyhood escape from a storm which took many lives in the Lofoten Sea probably strengthened his conviction in a divine providence governing his life. There were impressions from his first American home, where Elk Point, South Dakota, spread before him, in miniature, the panorama of the Northwest. Finally, European and American authors caught his imagination at an early age. James Fenimore Cooper, to mention only one, fascinated him with his *Last of the Mohicans.*[19]

Reviewers of Rölvaag's *magnum opus* were often lavish in their praise. One suggested that it made "almost all other novels of the Western frontier seem cheap." Another called it "a firmly woven tapestry of coarse texture wrought by a master." An

American scholar who specializes in the role of immigrants in American fiction puts it this way:[20]

> Years ago Percy Boynton observed that Rölvaag in *Giants in the Earth* had presented the classic contrast of the two main types of immigrants: the lusty, boastful extrovert in Per Hansa, the sensitive, fearful, suspicious introvert in Beret Holm. . . . It is the great dramatic irony of the novel that the husband, ideally equipped for the new life, perished in a blizzard on a futile quest for a minister, and that his wife, inadequately prepared for the role of matriarch which was suddenly imposed upon her, was destined to survive until a third generation was on the threshold.

Henry Steele Commager points to the symbolic import of Per Hansa's body being found leaning against a haystack in the spring, facing west. "Surely *Giants in the Earth*," he concludes, "records earth's humbling of man, but just as surely it exalts his incomprehensible courage."[21]

There are parallels and divergences in the personal lives and philosophies of Boyesen and Rölvaag. Educated in Norway, Boyesen wrote in English, while Rölvaag, educated in America, wrote in Norwegian. Both were concerned with assimilation, but with different aspects of it. Boyesen focused upon the dangers of non-Nordic immigration, Rölvaag upon the gloomy prospect of loss of Norwegian identity in the New World. Boyesen came to be associated with leading American novelists and identified with American literature, Rölvaag with the Norwegian scene. Boyesen conversed with Easterners and was somewhat removed in his thinking from the center of Norwegian population in the Middle West. Rölvaag not only benefited from personal proximity with the bulk of Norwegiandom in America but also achieved recognition among immigrant churchmen and pressmen that was denied the more rapidly assimilated Boyesen, absorbed as he was in American society. Both writers were critical, though constructively so, of American institutions. Neither was convinced that political and social democracy would be furthered by the leveling influence of the frontier. Rather, they conceived the cradle of Western democracy to lie in the Teutonic and Anglo-Saxon traditions of Northern Europe.

Ethnic groups tend to exaggerate the importance of certain

men and events that bolster their pride in their national origins. Norwegians are no exception to this tendency. They too have had their hero worshipers and their champions of the authenticity of the Kensington Stone, the Newport Tower, the Viking artifacts, and the Vinland Map. But of greater importance have been their literary contributions in imparting a sense of greatness of the Scandinavian culture, yes, but also the drama inherent in the movement of a people from Europe to America.[22]

Norwegian-American literary production is difficult to measure quantitatively with accuracy, and even more difficult to assess fairly in a qualitative sense. If second and third generations are included, and if publications with English titles are added, the aggregate, as estimated some ten years ago, would be around 250 works of fiction and about 120 volumes of poetry.[23]

One might inquire why and how Norwegian-American writers succeeded so remarkably in composing fine literature, in view of the relatively small immigrant population and readership to which their writings were directed. It must be seen as an advantage that Norwegians in America were concentrated in their own settlements and retained their language and customs in some measure even into later generations. Moreover, Norway's struggle for nationhood gave impetus to a cultural renaissance at home and abroad. Talented immigrants sought to keep pace with the Norwegian vanguard in Europe. They found encouragement and opportunity in the immigrant press, ever ready to accept their contributions, and in turn the newspapers inspired kindred minds in Norwegian communities. The effect was cumulative.

Granted that favorable circumstances prevailed for creative writing, the personal factor ought to be remembered. Seldom in so miniscule a universe as the Norwegian-American world could so many gifted folk be found, ready to play their part in the field of letters. Motivations ranged from cultural nationalism to unexplainable inner drives, perhaps the desire to become a Clio, a Homer, or a supreme biographer like James Boswell. It is to the credit of these literary artists that they persisted against odds in a pioneering society where survival was the first priority.

CHAPTER 12

Leadership in Business, the Professions, and the Arts

THE PREFACE STRESSES THE UNHERALDED ROLE OF MULTITUDES OF simple men and women in the American cities, villages, and countryside. It was often through the inspiration of inconspicuous folk, and frequently through the self-sacrificing efforts of the pioneers, that sons and daughters achieved prominence in one or another realm. One hears that successful men stand upon the shoulders of their fellows. Without the impetus given by relatives and friends, and by the community, many who achieved a measure of greatness might never have been moved to take the all-important initial step that led to significant accomplishment, and thus to personal fulfillment.

The record of Norwegian-Americans is difficult to trace without engaging in arbitrary selection of personalities. The story is partially covered in our earlier references to the leaders in the settlements, soldiers, public officials, churchmen, educational administrators, and literary figures. Yet men, and sometimes women, performed notably in business and professional enterprises and in many other ways. In this connection a dilemma of sorts presents itself. Is the definition of immigrant to be viewed narrowly or broadly? The author wishes to construe the word broadly, including not only the foreign born, but also the American offspring who, in point of time and social background, were not far removed from those who had arrived in the steerage and who had known the tensions of Ellis Island, the fears of economic insecurity, the half-serious and half-amusing bout with the English language and, for most, the solace of faith and fellowship in the Lutheran communion. Attention will therefore be directed toward actual migrants and, in some instances, toward their children in the New World.

In the expanding world of American business after the Civil War immigrants of all national origins, save perhaps the British, played the part of laborers rather than managers or owners. There were of course some exceptions. Abundance of labor generally meant lower wages. It also guaranteed greater returns for entrepreneurs operating within a laissez-faire system. Strikes were frequent, and usually unsuccessful. High tariffs benefited industry but ate into the meager profits of agriculture, the very segment of the economy in which the majority of Scandinavians found themselves. Free competition tended toward monopoly, a detriment to consumers. It was scarcely checked by governmental antitrust legislation. Strong labor unions and collective bargaining were still in the future. Big Business was king, buttressed by a pseudo-scientific belief that Darwin's biological theory of the survival of the fittest was equally applicable to social and economic phenomena.

It is noteworthy that among America's immigrant population some of those who rose to prominence in business ventures, or who wrestled with economic or mechanical problems, expressed concern for the welfare of the working masses. Before turning the searchlight on those who combined business acumen with progressive reform ideas, we might attempt to estimate the importance of Wisconsin-born Thorstein Veblen, one who neither toiled nor spun nor invested but who surveyed the economic scene from the vantage point of a social critic.

Fortified with intellectual weapons sharpened by his education at Carleton College and The Johns Hopkins University, Veblen attacked the "predatory" institutions which, in his opinion, stifled all productive forces. He burst upon the American scene with a disturbing exposure of "the establishment" in *The Theory of the Leisure Class* (1899). Sardonically he lambasted the "pecuniary culture," whether in business or in university administration. Some call him the American Karl Marx, but he rejected the doctrines of historical determinism and the ultimate triumph of the proletariat. This man, seemingly detached from an earlier immigrant milieu, raised questions but gave no answers. Yet his hard-nosed condemnation of economic practices and social institutions proved to be of considerable significance for twenti-eth-century progressivism. It is possible that the New Deal of the 1930s owes much to Veblen's penetrating insights.[1]

While Veblen exposed injustices in factory and field, his contemporary Andrew Furuseth fought abuses on the high seas. Unlike Veblen, he knew hard physical labor at first hand. Furuseth had entered upon the life of a seaman in Norway. During his rough stints on ships of various nations he learned that, outside territorial waters, no law was above the captain's. Shabby living quarters and poor food were all too common for the toilers of the sea. Many ships were unseaworthy. Discipline was severe. And if a crewman attempted to disengage himself from a merchantman in port he forfeited his pay for services rendered. The complaining sailor might be bludgeoned back into duty.

Furuseth eventually took "'French leave" of a British ship in San Francisco harbor. In 1885 he organized the Pacific Coast Seamen's Union and became its secretary. For much of his long life he lobbied in Washington, D. C., on behalf of seamen. His interest was universal, favoring neither Scandinavians nor native Americans, although he knew that thousands of Norwegians were employed in the American merchant service.[2]

Largely because of Furuseth's perseverance and persuasive-ness, Congress was made to wrestle with the problem of justice for the men at the bottom of the nautical ladder. Following several minor successes, the La Follette Seamen's Act of 1915 recognized the need for reform. Specifically, imprisonment for desertion was abolished. Penalties for disobedience or neglect were reduced. Food requirements were specified, both as to quantity and quality, and hours of work were limited. The law made mandatory that henceforth in the American merchant marine at least 65 percent of the crew must be able-bodied seamen, and at least 75 percent must be able to understand the language in which commands are given.

Furuseth's acquaintance with Senator Robert M. La Follette began in 1909, when he first requested of the Solon from Wisconsin the privilege of telling the story of men who were shackled by repressive laws and practices. He called them unfree. La Follette, incredulous, listened and learned. When at last the seamen's bill was being read in the Senate, La Follette paused at one point to explain that as a Midwesterner he was only a landlubber and that he owed his knowledge of maritime affairs to Furuseth, who was sitting in the gallery. As head of the International Seamen's Union, centered in Washington, D. C., the Norwegian argonaut made himself available as a resource man to the nation's legislators. Over the years this aggressive humanitarian continued to speak and write on behalf of the marine underdogs.[3]

In the struggle between exploited labor and conscienceless capital there were the philosophical Veblens and the pragmatic Furuseths. Management-worker relationships often bore resemblance to the feudal lord-vassal connections. But among owners and managers in America some, including Norwegians, were able to envision a more amicable personal tie between the head office and the work bench.

As examples of enlightenment among managers the names of Nelson Olsen Nelson, John A. Johnson, Carl G. Barth, Victor F. Lawson, Arthur E. Andersen, Joakim Lehmkuhl, and Haakon I. Romnes may be cited.

Backed by military experience in the Union Army, Nelson O. Nelson founded in 1877 in St. Louis a company for the manufacture of building and plumbing supplies. Influenced in part by French experiments and by the Rochdale plan of workers' cooperation in England, he embarked upon a profit-sharing program. Nelson's total impact upon the St. Louis community was highly beneficial. For the urban children of want he provided free boat excursions on the Mississippi River and free swimming pools. He is credited with starting mobile library service in the county school districts of Missouri.[4]

In comparison with America's captains of industry and finance, Norwegian-Americans achieved only minor success. Yet not all of them had been limited in Norway to single digits in evaluating their assets. John A. Johnson, for one, organized in Madison, Wisconsin, a farm equipment firm and later a precision-tool manufacturing company, replete with an auditorium and a library for his employees. Ole Evinrude, inventor of the outboard motor, was one of his trainees. Johnson served in the state legislature in the 1850s and assumed the almost unheard-of position that the freed Negro in Wisconsin should have the right to vote. He also contended that the American public school deserved priority over the parochial institution. In an age of labor unrest, when government invariably sided with Big Business, he courageously held out for the workingman's right to organize and to strike, and for employers' liability for the welfare of their employees.[5]

At the turn of the century America was in need of leadership in the expanding fields of social and economic betterment. Carl G. Barth sympathized with the workingman at a time when little attention was paid to the human factor in production. He spent most of his working life in the employ of the Bethlehem Steel Company. As a protege of Frederick Winslow Taylor, who is generally acclaimed as the father of scientific management, Barth demonstrated the practicability of scientific methods in the treatment of industrial workers. He pioneered in the field of wage incentives. He searched for an answer to what constituted a full day's work for an efficient laborer.[6]

Victor F. Lawson, whose father was among the first Norwegian immigrants in Illinois, inherited an interest in the Chicago *Skandinaven*, published in the same building as the *Chicago Daily News*. He bought out the *Daily News* from Melville E. Stone, and when Stone retired as editor in 1888, Lawson assumed that responsibility. He strongly supported postal savings banks (adopted in 1910), of benefit mainly to the rural folk. He urged civic reforms such as free public lectures, a fresh-air sanitarium, and the maintenance of a symphony orchestra.[7]

Arthur E. Andersen, who headed a nationally known auditing and accounting firm bearing his name, found time also to engage in civic affairs in Chicago and, in no small measure, to encourage Norwegian-American historical studies. For many years he was associated with Northwestern University, eventually as professor of accounting and chairman of the board of trustees. During the depression of the 1930s he declared that there could be no greater economic reward than to accept the task of making the world a better place for all mankind. He harbored a bit of skepticism for the New Deal. Let not the individual person be forgotten, he urged, in the national movement toward social reform.[8]

There is abundant evidence that Arthur Andersen, an expert in finance, was a man of heart as well as mind in his business activities. The same may be said of Joakim Lehmkuhl, who made his mark in watchmaking. Lehmkuhl came to the United States as a refugee from Norway, then being invaded by Hitler's forces. Originally he was assigned by the Norwegian government in exile, in London, to help organize the Norwegian shipping office in New York for the purpose of making maximum shipping facilities available to the Allies. In 1942 he and a few associates bought out the Waterbury Clock Company of Connecticut.

Speaking as president of the United States Time Corporation, Lehmkuhl believes that the American consciousness of time has been largely instrumental in transforming the nation from a wilderness into a great power. He has made Timex a watchword. Although he earned degrees in American universities before settling permanently in the United States, he places little value upon education as such. Some of his ablest employees are dropouts. Eighteen percent of his workers in his widely disseminated factories and research laboratories are Negroes. Partisans of pure democracy may quarrel with his management methods. In a close-knit organization, he spurns the committee approach for reaching decisions and getting action. Honesty, says Lehmkuhl, is the most important quality in an executive.[9]

Many share owners of today are familiar with the name of Haakon I. Romnes, who rose from lineman to top executive in the Bell Telephone System. His progress was facilitated by his work on the coaxial cable, necessary to radio and later to television transmission. After serving as chief engineer for the American Telephone and Telegraph Company, he was elected president of the Western Electric Company and, in 1965, of A. T. & T. In his time he witnessed a revolution in the number of conversations that could be carried over a pair of wires, from only three in 1928 to 100,000 in 1972.

In addition to Romnes's technical and professional achievements, he saw clearly the need for equal opportunity among the races. He once stated that management needs to demonstrate not merely good faith but practical initiative in support of the basic tenet of human equality. He realized that prejudice is

economically and humanly wasteful. However, the more com-
pelling reason for granting equal opportunity to all lay in the
fact that it was right.[10]

For many Norwegian-Americans, engineering became a field
in which they could excel. Kenneth Bjork's *Saga in Steel and
Concrete* documents many of their successes. This important
segment of immigrant history defies condensation and excerpting.
Nevertheless, a few representative persons should be mentioned,
bearing in mind that the men of Norwegian birth who left
monuments in steel and concrete were but a fraction of the
total American engineering force, whether immigrant or
American-born.

Bjork rightly points out that the industrial revolution in
Norway, exemplified in large part in railroad construction under
the most adverse conditions in that mountainous land, called
forth the best in technological skills. Before the year 1900, therefore, technical schools at Horten, Trondhjem (now Trondheim),
Bergen, and Christiania (now Oslo) were graduating well prepared personnel. While the demand for engineers remained
constant in Norway, the phenomenal economic growth of the
United States attracted numerous Norwegian graduates into
the fields of transportation, mining, and construction. A migration of skills was under way.

In the New York area Ole Singstad, Olaf Hoff, Sverre Dahm,
and Hans Rude Jacobsen specialized in bridge, tunnel, and
skyscraper construction. As chief engineer of the New York
Tunnel Authority, Singstad pioneered in applying new techniques
in building the Holland Tunnel, the first for automobiles, under
the Hudson River. His unique ventilating system carried away
gasoline fumes. Hoff, later consulting engineer for the Harlem
River Tunnel, built the railroad tunnel under the Detroit River.
He introduced the sunken-tube method, which American engineers adopted. Dahm, after a turn at raising skyscrapers in
Chicago, applied himself to subway engineering in Greater New
York from 1900 to 1932. He was later supported in that effort
by Jacobsen, known as the dean of Norwegian engineers in
New York, who headed the engineering staff of the New York
subway system from 1922 to 1934.[11]

Some demonstrated their genius functionally in the con-

struction of tall buildings. Necessary to the new operation was
the use of caisson and pile undergirdings instead of spread-
footing foundations, and the use of structural steel instead of
wrought-iron framework. Joachim Giaver of Chicago proved
to be a master in this field. Among his monuments are the
Equitable Building of New York, the Field Museum of Natural
History in Chicago, the Washington Post Office, and the Frick
Building in Pittsburgh. Magnus Andersen continued Giaver's
excellent work in Chicago, with the Wacker Drive Building
among others. Meanwhile, in New York Gunvald Aus and Kort
Berle erected the imposing Woolworth Building, employing the
new structural steel technique, besides numerous apartment
buildings, hotels, and office buildings. In Sacramento, the
capital of California, Christian Buestad erected several large
state buildings. Not the least of his other achievements was
the Chinese Village at the Golden Gate International Exposition in 1939.[12]

Prior to the "brain drain" from European lands after World
War II, relatively few immigrants came ready-made for professional pursuits. Not only was the English language a formidable deterrent both in studying and in practicing, but only the
most fortunate reached their trans-Atlantic destinations with
sufficient funds to establish themselves in a specialty. Yet a
few immigrants, and many more descendants, gained distinction
in medicine, dentistry, and in the natural sciences.

Ludvig Hektoen, Adolf Gundersen, and Alfred Owre come to
mind not only because of their outstanding contributions in
medicine and dentistry but for their identity with and service
to the Norwegian community of the Middle West as well as
to the general public. Hektoen's intensive studies in Uppsala,
Prague, and Berlin stimulated a lifelong interest in pathology.
It was the beginning of a career which was to lead him into
cancer research. From 1898 to 1933 he served as professor of
pathology at Rush Medical College in Chicago. For nearly
forty years he directed the John McCormick Institute for
Infectious Diseases. Some 300 scientific articles are said to have
come from his pen. For better than three decades he edited
The Journal of Infectious Diseases and, for a shorter period of
time, *The Archives of Pathology.* His discovery of the principle

of cross-matching of blood before transfusions was epochal. This man was honored on his eightieth birthday in 1943 with the dedication of the Hektoen Institute of Medical Research at Cook County Hospital in Chicago.[13]

Adolf Gundersen and his six sons, as well as some grandsons, have ministered to the health needs of patients in La Crosse, Wisconsin, and throughout America. One of the sons, Trygve, an ophthalmologist on the staff of Boston University, has treated patients from over the world, principally because of his skilled treatment of detached retinas and his new insights into a dreaded eye disease, glaucoma.

The elder Gundersen, following his medical preparation in Norway, came to America in 1891. In time he established, with several associates, the Gundersen Clinic, which today has a staff of sixty doctors and a hospital of 350 beds. As a regent of the University of Wisconsin he helped to lay the plans for its medical school and also left a sizable legacy for young Norwegian surgeons to study in English-speaking countries. The Medical Society of Norway elected him to honorary membership. The Gundersen family have maintained an active interest in Norwegian literature, art, and history.[14]

Alfred Owre spent his first fourteen years in Norway. Upon graduating from the University of Minnesota's school of dentistry he went on to earn a degree in medicine. In 1905 he was appointed dean of the dental school. In the course of his career he was engaged in battle on two fronts. The one was the struggle against commercialism and nonscientific practices. The other was as a forerunner in promoting the science of dietetics. Vested interests opposed him for advocating state control, which to them was identical with socialism. Owre preferred social planning to insistence upon private professional rights.

Owre's second theater of action was in publicizing the direct relationship of foods to personal health and national well-being. In a small book entitled *Prunes and Pancakes* (1926), he discussed the problem of diet and listed the caloric values of various common foods. He recommended eating only breakfast and dinner each day, and plenty of walking. Ahead of his time, he declared that "any physical salvation for civilized man must be in dietetic reform." After his death in 1935 the University of Minnesota named their school of dentistry for him.[15]

Several Norwegian immigrants, or men of immigrant stock, devoted a major part of their lives to work in the Library of Congress and other archival collections. All were active in research, over and above their library responsibilities. Torvald Solberg, the first chief of the copyright bureau of the Library of Congress, gave 46 years of service. James C. M. Hanson inaugurated the cataloging system in the same library and played a personal role in extending improved library methods to the University of Chicago and the Vatican. Juul Dieserud, after gaining valuable insights in Chicago's Newberry Library, was employed for over thirty years as a cataloger and a foreign-language expert in the Library of Congress. Thorstein Jahr was also connected with that institution. Collectively, he and his Norse friends left their mark upon the rapidly growing science of book classification on both sides of the Atlantic.[16]

Some American-born scholars of immigrant heritage, and endowed with bilingual facility, made special contributions in linguistics as well as in literature. A trio of highly competent professors, Rasmus Björn Anderson, Julius E. Olson, and Einar I. Haugen, all of the University of Wisconsin, furnish a prime illustration of superior native ability, industrious application, and a fortunate combination of circumstances. Theirs was a state with a considerable Norwegian representation (over 40,000 by 1870, or about 35 percent of all Norwegian immigrants at that time) in which the public generally exhibited good will toward the Scandinavian minority. These talented men sensed the feelings and aspirations of their people.

Rasmus B. Anderson was to spend his life of ninety years in Madison, the hub of Norwegian cultural activity in America in the 1880s and 1890s. He filled the newly founded chair of Scandinavian languages and literature at the University. In the course of time he forsook the classroom to take to journalism, lecturing, and politics. Anderson could claim two major achievements. First, he popularized the saga accounts of Norse discoveries in the New World and advanced the knowledge of Norwegian literature. Second, he aided in reconciling the immigrant's sentimental and cultural ties with his homeland with his loyalty to America. Not all Norwegian literature, however, came within the scope of his admiration. The realism and naturalism of contemporary Norwegian works annoyed him, particularly the creations of Ibsen and Bjørnson.[17]

Julius Olson and Einar Haugen have maintained the Rasmus B. Anderson tradition. Olson began as an instructor in German and Scandinavian under the senior professor. His lectures on Scandinavian literature proved very popular. Unlike Anderson, he was willing to cite Norway's contemporary writers, while still concentrating on their literary forebears. His 47 years of continuous teaching left little time for publication, but his stimulating personality struck fire in a legion of students, among them Laurence M. Larson and George T. Flom, who were to keep the fires lit on the altar of Norsedom in their teaching careers at the Universities of Illinois and Iowa.[18]

A fitting tribute is paid to Einar Haugen in a *festschrift* carrying numerous examples of the latest scholarship within his broad field of interest. Cited by the editors as a recognized international authority in linguistics, they describe him as being "fascinated by language as a medium of cultural growth and cross fertilization." They credit this scholar with aggressively promoting the study of Nordic civilization in America, and American civilization in Scandinavia.[19]

Haugen has brilliantly filled the roles of teacher and scholar. Among his contributions are two landmarks: *The Norwegian Language in America: A Study in Bilingual Behavior* (two volumes, 1953 and 1969) and a *Norwegian-English Dictionary* (1965) containing 60,000 words and with a masterly introduction presenting the development of the Norwegian language. In 1964 Haugen accepted an invitation to the chair of Germanic Languages and Literatures at Harvard University.

Few women in the nineteenth century were able to break the professional barrier. Agnes Mathilde Wergeland, an emigrant of 1890, succeeded in a man's world as chairman of the department of history in the University of Wyoming. For her the road was at times barricaded with extreme hardship. Although she was a cousin of the great national romanticist Henrik Wergeland and of his sister Camilla Collett, a champion of women's rights in Norway, Miss Wergeland descended from people of humbler circumstances. The young woman who once studied piano with Edvard Grieg earned a Ph.D. from the University of Zurich before leaving for America. Two books of Norwegian poetry came from her pen. After her death, three substantial monographs on medieval European topics were published, with the assistance of friends. The American West, with its stimuli of majestic mountains and a freer social atmosphere, afforded Agnes Wergeland opportunities in higher education which might well have been denied her in the land of her birth and in America's older settlements.[20]

Some achieved fame in the universal language of music. Ole Windingstad and F. Melius Christiansen have been mentioned, as leaders in symphonic and choral music. One who stands quite alone as an operatic performer is Olive Fremstad. Of Swedish and Norwegian parentage, she was born in Stockholm, where her father was serving with the Norwegian palace guard of the king of Sweden-Norway. At the age of six, after four years in Norway, she accompanned her parents to St. Peter, Minnesota, and subsequently to Minneapolis and to Grantsburg, Wisconsin. Her father appears to have been a self-ordained preacher and gospel singer. The family were active in the little Norwegian Methodist congregation in Grantsburg. Olive (baptized Anna Olivia) joined her father as a singer in revival meetings.

Encouraged by a friendly vocal teacher, Miss Fremstad came to New York in 1890. Three years later she became a pupil of Lilli Lehmann in Berlin. The way led to concert appearances in Munich and Vienna. Her debut at Covent Garden in London was the prelude to eleven seasons with the Metropolitan Opera Company of New York, beginning in 1903. There the dramatic soprano sang the Wagnerian roles of Isolde and Brünnhilde, though her repertoire easily embraced the roles of Sieglinde and others. Critics ascribed to Olive Fremstad rare histrionic talent, extraordinary versatility, and a remarkable voice range. A discerning listener declared, "Her interpretations were a standard by which later Wagnerian sopranos were measured."[21]

Jacob and Paul Fjelde, father and son, rank with the best in American sculpturing. In Jacob's forty years of life, of which the final nine were spent in Minneapolis, the list of his three-dimensional creations is impressive: a group of figures above the main entrance to the University of Minnesota Library, a monument at Gettysburg dedicated to the First Minnesota Regiment, a bust of Henrik Ibsen in St. Paul, and a figure of Hiawatha and Minnehaha in Minneapolis. His last work was a statue of Ole Bull, erected in Loring Park, Minneapolis, the site of many a 17th of May celebration.[22]

Minneapolis-born Paul Fjelde studied under the distinguished sculptor, Loredo Taft. Among his more notable works is a statue of Colonel Hans C. Heg, which stands in Lier, Heg's birthplace in Norway. Replicas are to be seen in Madison and Muskego, Wisconsin. Paul's esthetic contributions in stone extend to a monument to the poet Julius Baumann in Cloquet, Minnesota, and one to Ivar Aasen at Concordia College, Moorhead, Minnesota. A bronze tablet of Paul Hjelm-Hansen, promoter and land agent for the Great Northern Railway, hangs in the Minnesota Historical Society Building in St. Paul. His bust of Abraham Lincoln, donated by the people of North Dakota, was erected in Oslo's famed Frogner Park.[23]

For sheer adventure the varied experiences of Oskar J. W. Hansen, a sculptor, are unparalleled. As a lad in Norway he discovered a Viking grave in the nearby Lofoten Islands and delighted in exploring the mysterious site time and again. At thirteen he went to sea. As he sailed the Mediterranean, life took on new excitement with an opportunity to examine ancient Greek ruins. While still in his teens, Hansen joined the French Foreign Legion, and met an English sculptor. Through the Englishman he came to know Auguste Rodin and to work in the Paris studio of the famous realist.

In 1909, at the age of seventeen, Oskar Hansen came to America as a seaman. Caught in the Mexican revolution, he escaped by way of Yucatan. He graduated from the United States Military Academy at West Point, New York, and served his adopted country in World War I. He attained the rank of lieutenant colonel.

Hansen's boyhood efforts at wood carving, and above all his association with Rodin, opened the way to a rich career. Three of his works are displayed in Urbana, Illinois, in the International Hall of Fame. A war monument carved from Italian marble may be seen in Hinsdale, Illinois. The Rand Tower in Minneapolis houses his "Spirit of Aviation." The Museum of Fine Arts in Dayton, Ohio, exhibits his bust of Orville Wright. When in 1938 President Franklin D. Roosevelt dedicated Boulder Dam (now Hoover Dam), he was also bowing, in a sense, to Hansen's prize-winning decorative sculpture featured thereon.[24]

In the field of Norwegian-American painting there has been no Ole Rölvaag. Yet we focus attention upon Herbjörn Gausta, who appears to have been the first of his national origin to become a professional artist in America. Gausta emigrated at the age of thirteen. From Luther College his path led to European art studios. Funds contributed by friends enabled the promising young man to visit Norway, where the folk music tradition of his native Telemark had a second chance to cast its spell over him. At the Royal Academy in Munich he met a benefactor. Isabelle E. Singer, widow of the sewing machine manufacturer, found him copying one of Murillo's paintings and asked to purchase it. When she ordered copies of other paintings, Gausta's future was rendered secure for the time being. In 1888 he returned to Minneapolis and, except for another interval in Europe, remained there until his death.

Gausta's creative work proved to be of enduring value, although many of his earlier paintings perished in a Minneapolis fire. His paintings were exhibited at the Art Institute of Chicago. In the 1890s he managed to produce "The Lay Preacher," sketched in Norway probably with the intention of updating Adolf Tidemand's "Haugianerne." Over a score of years the clergy proved to be his most dependable patrons, helping him to keep financially solvent by commissioning him to paint altar pieces by the hundreds. Gausta also demonstrated real talent in caricatures and satirical sketches. In short, he established a place for art in the growing culture of Norwegian America.[25]

A second painter, Jonas Lie, arrived later on the American scene and lost no time identifying himself with native Americans. As a nephew of the great Norwegian novelist of the same name, Jonas enjoyed a spiritual kinship with his uncle. His mother brought him to the United States in 1893. He eventually became president of the National Academy of Design in New York, where several of his paintings are on display. He was fascinated with the building of the Panama Canal, the result being twelve paintings, ten of which now hang on the walls of the United States Military Academy at West Point.[26]

The purpose of this chapter is to recognize some of the more successful Norwegian immigrants and their descendants and to indicate their role in the total business and professional life of America. Some arrived as children from Norway. Their lives are more a part of the American story than of the Norwegian saga. Such a one is Knute Rockne, a perennially successful football coach at the University of Notre Dame and, perhaps more important, a moral inspiration to the youth of America.[27]

Some were born to or descended from immigrants but made their marks outside and beyond the Norwegian frame of reference. Their names are legion, as in the case of most national groups in America. They labored in many fields of endeavor, including science, journalism, politics, and many others. We cite an example or two. Ernest O. Lawrence invented the cyclotron, or atom smasher, and directed the radiation laboratory at the University of California, Berkeley, from 1935 until his death in 1958. It was his rare distinction to receive both the Nobel Prize in physics and the Enrico Fermi Award. Eric Sevareid has long been known for his special news analyses in television broadcasting. One hesitates to make even a symbolic selection in the field of politics. An earlier chapter considers the participation of Norwegian pioneers in political affairs. During the past generation or two, a large number of American-born men and women of Norwegian descent have sought, and often won, political office. They have proved their loyalty to principles and their concern over public issues.[28]

In his definitive work on Norwegian engineers in America, Kenneth Bjork cites their idealism and their excellent technical preparation in Norway's schools. Despite their superior skills, none appear to have felt superior toward their fellow men. On the contrary, in the age of the "robber barons," Norwegian engineers and businessmen alike displayed unusual sympathy and understanding toward the workingman, in large part because as immigrants they had personally known poverty and insecurity. Moreover, employers' associations were already active in the Scandinavian lands by 1900, and their existence implied no prejudice against employees. Norwegian-American entrepreneurs were conscious of the workingman's struggle on both sides of the great salt-water gulf and had no difficulty in identifying with the common man.

Norwegian scientists and artists, like the men familiar with building and bridge and tunnel construction, were caught up in the spirit of American democracy. Those of American birth usually adjusted more quickly to the American social and economic patterns. Yet those born in Norway were not slow to assume the responsibilities of United States citizenship and to demonstrate in their careers charitable impulses derived, to a considerable extent, from childhood religious instruction in the old country.

It would be misleading to suggest that the personal impact of a comparatively small handful of immigrants from the European North affected American business and professional circles profoundly. Whatever the actual numbers of Norsemen in America, they were at first inundated by the millions of Yankees, Germans, and Irish, and later by the Italians and Poles. Among Americans of all ethnic strains, thousands could claim distinction in their chosen occupations. Nevertheless, the Norwegians who excelled in business, or those who sat at the drawing boards or manipulated the slide rules, or others who dexterously handled the scalpel or the drill, or yet again others who decorated with lilywork the starkly practical columns of a materialistic civilization, all of them approached more nearly than their compatriots the heights of human striving. The New World presented the opportunity. Gifted, devoted, educated, and inspired persons responded to the challenge.

CHAPTER 13

America at War and in Isolation

ON THE EVE OF WORLD WAR I, IMMIGRANTS FROM EUROPE WERE, as a rule, better informed than their Yankee neighbors about affairs in the Old World, thanks to the foreign-language press and to a stream of personal correspondence over the years. Commenting upon their mental attitude, Marcus Lee Hansen, the historian of immigration, once declared that the so-called hyphenates were almost as prepared for war psychologically as were the Europeans themselves. This is not to say, however, that the events of July, 1914, did not catch them unawares. Not knowing what lay ahead, they went about their daily business as usual. In the case of the Norwegians, no distant rumblings disturbed their plans for celebrating the centennial of the Eidsvold Constitution and Norway's independence. Three thousand visiting Norwegian-Americans paraded up Christiania's Karl Johansgate to the royal palace on May 17, the national holiday. In America others were observing the occasion in like fashion in New York, Chicago, Minneapolis, and Seattle. On July 4 the governor of North Dakota unveiled the Lincoln bust, the work of Paul Fjelde, in Frogner Park in Christiania. As yet, war played a negligible part in Norwegian thinking.[1]

Confronted with a European war, President Woodrow Wilson found that not all Americans were capable of assuming the neutrality of thought that he requested when hostilities erupted. For those who still had relatives in Europe, a calm and reasonable point of view proved to be even more difficult. In the previous century the poet Oliver Wendell Holmes had stated the matter aptly when he wrote, "We are all tattooed in our cradles with the beliefs of our tribe. The record may seem superficial, but it is indelible." Wilson himself had long been suspected of prejudice toward the foreign-born. He had alienated sizable ethnic groups, among them Poles and Italians, in his *History of the American People*, published in 1902. "Some Americans need hyphens in their names," he had declared, "because only part of them has come over." Theodore Roosevelt was in Wilson's company, for a change, when he too suggested that "when two flags are hoisted on the same pole, one is always hoisted undermost."

These statements were not altogether erroneous. Irish-Americans found it impossible to cheer the war efforts of England, a country which for centuries had been oppressing and dominating their ancestors. German-Americans faced the dilemma, temporarily, of choosing between the fatherland and their adopted country. But when the United States intervened in the war, almost all 50 percent Americans, as some labeled them, became 100 percent loyal to Uncle Sam.[2]

Men and women of Norwegian descent did not consider Norway to be dominated by a powerful foreign state, nor were they gripped with the nationalistic fervor that borders on imperialism. Granted that Norway's separation from Sweden in 1905 played a part in stimulating national consciousness, for Norwegians at home and abroad the great war of 1914–1918 brought less change in orientation than for the Irish and for ethnic groups whose origins lay in the German, Austro-Hungarian, or Turkish empires.

As indicated, few Americans sensed imminent danger in the European conflict. In North Dakota, somewhat removed from the main channels of interoceanic communication, Norwegian political leadership was primarily concerned with domestic affairs. The plight of the farmers merited first consideration. The Non-Partisan League was the answer. But as war clouds were reflected in the news items of Norse journals, the Norwegian element in North Dakota and the Middle West expressed their determination not to endorse American intervention. Financial moguls, they warned, must be thwarted in their international schemings. Suspicion fell upon the munitions industries. These uneasy Norsemen also condemned the federal government's practice of extending long-term loans to Britain and France. They dubbed Wilson's administration pro-British and denounced John Bull's interference with American shipping. Seven of eight Norwegians in the House of Representatives supported resolutions calling for denial of passports to United States citizens seeking passage on armed vessels flying the flags of belligerent powers. Four of the eight congressmen, and one of two Norwegian-American senators, voted against the war resolution of April 2, 1917.[3]

Newspapers in North Dakota as an example, confirmed the nationwide noninterventionist point of view. Editorially the Non-Partisan *Fargo Fram* and the Republican *Normanden* of Grand Forks voiced appreciation of the hardships and indignities endured by their German-American neighbors. Norwegians agreed with German immigrants and their children on war issues. Distrusting the British at first, they regarded news releases from Germany as more reliable. Were it not for British violations of international law, they implied, Germany would not have reacted so drastically in the form of the U-boat campaign. Could it be that England had planned the sinking of the British passenger liner *Lusitania* in May of 1915 in order to arouse American feelings against Germany? Let Theodore Roosevelt cry out against the Kaiser and his government. William Jennings Bryan was behaving more reasonably, they felt, than the belli-cose ex-president by tendering his resignation as secretary of state rather than serving as a yes-man for the Anglophile Wilson. But the election of 1916 found many Norwegians still preferring Wilson over his Republican opponent, Charles Evans Hughes. Aware that the President had "kept us out of war" thus far, they opted for continued neutrality. Beware of fighting for national honor. This was the common theme of the Norwegian-American press, and probably of its reading clientele.[4]

Once war had been declared against Germany on April 6, 1917, most naturalized citizens and their progeny responded as patriotic Americans. Editors of foreign-language journals appealed for loyalty and, in contrast with their earlier tolerance, stressed Germany's barbaric violations of human rights at sea with the death-dealing submarine. A new instrument of warfare was on the loose, unrestrained by current international rules. In the hitherto noninterventionist Middle West Congressman Nils P. Haugen of Wisconsin broke with his pacifist friend, United States Senator Robert M. La Follette.[5]

Ties with neutral Norway grew stronger as Norwegian merchantmen descended with alarming frequency into Davey Jones's locker. Already in September of 1914 the directors of the Sons of Norway had decided to participate in a joint Norwegian-American committee to assist Norway. In 1916 Norwegian-Americans raised $2,600,000 for relief measures in the distressed homeland.[6]

The attitude of the United States government toward maritime Norway was somewhat strained. Washington complained that Norwegian merchant vessels were carrying contraband goods. Norway was accused of feeding the Germans. To these charges Norway replied that such carrying trade was inevitable, since the British had widened the definition of contraband to include practically all kinds of commodities. It was rumored also in the American press that Norway permitted submarines to be built for Germany in Norwegian ports.[7]

The future looked darker for Norway when the *New York Times* recommended an embargo on wheat to the almost starving country. Headed by the explorer-statesman Fridtjof Nansen, a Norwegian commission arrived in Washington in the summer of 1917. Nansen explained to American officials that England had agreed that Norway might export specified quantities of fish to Germany. Norway was willing to put a million tons of shipping at the disposal of the Allies. Furthermore, Norwegian shipping had been available in all seas for Allied use since the war began. Norway's vessels were not owned by England, as the German ambassador to the United States had claimed. It was not for that reason, Nansen explained, that so many ships were the victims of German U-boats. The Germans, he went on, had destroyed one-third of Norwegian shipping (about one million tons), most of which was in Allied service. After seven months in America, Nansen was able to reach a satisfactory agreement on American exports to Norway.[8]

The case of Christoffer Hannevig also exemplifies friction with Norway. Hannevig was a shipbuilder of Norwegian citizenship who envisioned great profits in America when the demand for cargo vessels reached its maximum. In August, 1917, the Emergency Fleet Corporation requisitioned all merchant ships over 2,500 tons then under construction. In Hannevig's opinion his shipyards had been seized and his contracts cancelled. He was forced to declare himself bankrupt. He denied that he had been compensated. Eventually, in 1958, the government of Norway dropped its claims on his behalf, involving $63,000,000 and compound interest since 1917. A United States court of claims had ruled that Norway had no valid grounds for prosecuting the United States. Norwegians at home and abroad had mixed feelings over the Hannevig litigation. Many in the United States were inclined to classify the protesting shipbuilder as one of many wartime profiteers, while in Europe his countrymen tended to side with their government in a formal charge of confiscation.[9]

Venom directed against allegedly unneutral Norway reflected upon Americans of Norwegian descent. In the East, the area press accused Scandinavian "shipyard slackers" of making big money while evading military service. Some Norwegian supervisors were pro-German, it was said. In the Middle West, as late as 1919 the *Des Moines Capital* was vilifying the foreign-born. Editor Johannes B. Wist of *Decorah-Posten* found it necessary to defend his compatriots.[10]

The war years proved difficult for foreign-language news media generally. Not only was exchange of papers forbidden, and government censorship applied, but agitation against hyphenated Americans continued unabated. Incensed by the implied lack of patriotism, over 700 publishers of foreign-language newspapers, serving some 18,000 readers, endorsed a statement of loyalty addressed to President Wilson.[11] For the most part, a change had already taken place in their periodicals, from emphasis upon ethnic and cultural topics to news and commentary in support of American national interests.

Next to suffer attacks by avowed patriots was the teaching of foreign languages. German was dropped from high school and college curricula. Had Norse been more generally taught, it might have met with the same fate. It was under attack in the Minneapolis high schools. Moreover, the wartime spirit created a determination among Norwegian editors to introduce more English into their dailies and weeklies. More and more the English language crept into church services and fraternal rituals also.

The Sons of Norway accepted the substitution of English in their lodge meetings, although this was not necessarily the result of the war. Many younger members were by then unfamiliar with the Norwegian tongue. In keeping with the patriotic trend, in 1918 the organization added to its aims the promotion of knowledge of and loyalty to their new fatherland. However, this modification expressed no fundamental change of attitude. Members had never sensed any conflict between American ideals and the Norwegian democratic tradition. American wartime pressures, however, undoubtedly facilitated the partial shift in language and the revision of declaration of purpose.[12]

When events of early 1917 precipitated America's decision for war against Germany, nearly all Americans joined in what Wilson described as a crusade for saving democracy. The subtleties of British propaganda, plus the resumption of overt acts of aggression by Germany, had done their work. In view of the Hunnish image of Emperor William II, it was easy to believe the most fantastic rumors. German soldiers, it was echoed about, were nailing Belgian babies to barn doors. Polish priests were being hanged upside down in their steeple bells, their heads serving as clappers. And the few Norwegians in the South and West became disturbed when the Zimmerman Note, sent from Berlin to Mexico City, disclosed designs of persuading Mexico and Japan to declare war against the United States.

The Norwegian-American response to the nation's call for all-out effort varied only in details from that of the general public. Service flags adorned the walls of church sanctuaries and school auditoriums. For each death, whether from combat, disease, or accident, a gold star appeared in the rectangle of silver stars. There was no Fifteenth Wisconsin Infantry Regiment, as in the Civil War, but Minnesota had its 151st Field Artillery, largely Scandinavian, and Greater New York was proud of the 308th Infantry, trained on Long Island. The National Lutheran Council estimated that 90,000 Norwegian-Americans were in uniform, approximately 2½ percent of the total United States forces of 4,000,000.[13]

Through its Committee on Public Information, for which there was a Scandinavian Bureau, the government scheduled Loyalty Days for the respective ethnic stocks. Skeptics sneered that the program could only further Europeanize the immigrants. Norwegians and others, in turn, joined in patriotic demonstrations. Sons of Norway lodges conducted Liberty Loan rallies with considerable success. At first hesitant because their Americanism might be questioned, Norse leaders in the New York City area announced the annual 17th of May parade in 1917. Already the Irish had observed St. Patrick's Day without serious incident. Some 10,000 Norwegians participated in the march, recognizing the 103rd anniversary of Norway's independence.[14]

That Norwegians were aware of the cost in human lives for Norway became clear to everyone in the East when more than 3,500 folk of Norwegian descent joined in the big New York Fourth of July parade of 1918. They provided three bands and two floats, one of which portrayed German treatment of Allied and neutral ships and sailors. The case for Norway, virtually an Allied power though technically neutral, was stated in striking figures: "53 Norwegian ships with 704 seamen have been sunk without a trace." "Norway holds the seas open for civilization." "Norway, a country with only 2½ million inhabitants, has lost 830 ships of a total tonnage of 1,500,000 and 2,000 seamen because of the U-boats." The Norwegians of New York were assigned a special day (October 13) in 1918 for the Fourth Liberty Loan drive. Results spoke eloquently for their loyalty. Pledges totaled $6,000,000.[15]

On the personal side, engineers and other civilians of Norwegian birth served their adopted country with high distinction. Andrew Christenson, a product of Horten's Technical School, was engaged in the development of rolling stock after his arrival in America in 1893. He is credited with designing the first all-steel passenger car in 1906. During World War I he supervised the designing of all railroad cars for the United States Army in France. In 1917 he was placed in charge of engineering and construction of about a thousand 9½-inch gun carriages. Magnus Swenson, with an engineering degree from the University of Wisconsin, served as defense administrator for the State of Wisconsin and as chairman of the American Relief Administration for Northern Europe under Herbert Hoover in 1919.[16]

Loyalty to Wilson's Democratic administration flagged as the war drew to a close and wartime idealism became dissipated. Wilson's defeat at the polls in the Congressional elections of 1918 signaled not only new Republican strength but also the beginnings of an isolationist point of view. Contentious haggling at the Paris Peace Conference strengthened the suspicion that the Allied victors were out to win advantages for themselves. Wilson's insistence upon representing his country personally at the conference detracted from the magnetism that he had once possessed. For many of Scandinavian blood the decision in the election of 1920 was "to return to normalcy," to borrow the phrase of Warren G. Harding, Republican presidential candidate. They and their fellow Americans voted Republican for the most part.[17]

In the early 1920s Congress exceeded the bounds of mere precaution against foreign ideologies, notably Russian Communism and Italian Fascism, by enacting restrictive legislation against immigrants of "undesirable" national origin. First, an act of 1921 stipulated that the number of nationals allowed to enter the country in any one year should not be more than 3 percent of that particular nationality resident in the United States in 1910. In 1924 the law was revised in favor of Northern and Western Europeans by reducing the annual number to 2 percent and, more importantly, basing the number on the census figures for 1890 for the respective nationalities. In 1890 there were relatively few immigrants from Southern and Eastern Europe resident in America. In addition, the measures of the 1920s virtually closed the doors to further entrance of Asiatics, which meant mainly the Japanese and the Chinese.

In the opinion of one scholar of immigration, the country was eager to integrate a shaken social order, in which for several years ethnic nationalism, bordering on disloyalty, had been not only allowed to flourish but in some degree was encouraged by American authorities. Not all would agree, however, with this ratiocination. Evidence is overwhelmingly on the side of loyalty of the foreign-born, regardless of country of origin. All endured the hardships of wartime. All participated willingly in observing heatless, meatless, and wheatless days. Many were given official notification that sons, fathers, or husbands had perished. Love for the motherland and loyalty to the promised land were not in conflict.[18]

Norwegian immigration in the 1920s was little affected by the new restrictive legislation. The normal flow of immigrants from the North fell considerably short of the quota. Even when the quota was reduced from ca. 12,000 in 1924 to ca. 2,400 in 1927 there was no reason for concern. The postwar arrivals, more urban-minded than their predecessors, settled chiefly in Brooklyn's Bay Ridge and Sunset Park districts. Hamilton Avenue, their former community, had been taken over by the Italians. Times were hard. Sons of Norway lodges set up an employment service. Some churches did likewise. It was of some comfort to know that, while shipbuilding and maritime enterprise were down, building construction was on the rise. And among Norwegian church members there were a fair number of building contractors looking for dependable and eager hands.

The adversity of the decade of the 1920s further stimulated group consciousness. Brooklyn's 16-page *Nordisk Tidende*, the voice of Norsemen in the East and one of the few surviving papers in the 1970s, had enjoyed "seven fat years" (1922–1929) and had opened up its own bookstore. This journalistic spurt was occurring just prior to the beginnings of a "Hoover City," whose wretched inhabitants, numbering 200 or so, were mostly Norwegians who frequented missions and prayer meetings for a cup of coffee. Norwegian churches and lodges found it impossible to meet the total needs of their countrymen.[19]

As if to lend further color to the inauguration of an age of expansion in radio, movies, and automobiles, Norwegian-Americans nationwide celebrated in 1925 the centennial of the arrival of the Sloopers. In New York Leif Erikson Square was dedicated, and 10,000 marched in the 17th of May parade. Seattle and Minneapolis also made much of the centennial. In Minneapolis Nicollet Avenue was decked with American and Norwegian flags. Americans who traced their lineage from Norway's west coast city of Stavanger met there 3,000 strong. *Bygdelags*, whose members came from a particular valley or province in Norway, had their special day on June 6. President Calvin Coolidge delivered the main address at the Minnesota State Fair Grounds on June 8. The audience of over 60,000, hardly impartial on such an occasion, was pleased to hear the otherwise taciturn chief executive say, "Norsemen have exercised a great influence upon our modern history and Western civilization." And again, the ship *Restauration* (Restoration) of 1825 brought "representatives of a stalwart race, men and women of fixed determination, enduring courage, and high character, who were to draw in their retinue a long line of their fellow countrymen, destined to . . . contribute to the salvation of a great nation." The United States government issued commemorative 2- and 5-cent postage stamps in honor of the centennial.[20]

The Republican triumvirate of Harding, Coolidge, and Hoover stood well with the Scandinavian element. The protective tariff walls (1922 and 1930) and the cautious gestures in international cooperation, such as the naval disarmament conference of 1922 and the signing of the innocuous Pact of Paris of 1928, met with general approval. But with the stock market crash of 1929 and the ensuing economic doldrums Hoover lost popularity.

Shaken out of their conservatism, Norwegian editors and other spokesmen urged support for Franklin D. Roosevelt. Even his opposition to legalized prohibition of the manufacture, distribution, and sale of intoxicating beverages failed to turn most Scandinavians away from a confident leader with his "happy days are here again" theme. At this late stage, the vast majority of Norwegian-Americans had never seen Norway or spoken its language. There were few fresh arrivals from abroad. More were returning to rather than departing from Norway annually. Immigration was cancelled out not primarily by the quota system but by old man Depression.

Between the two world wars interest in the European homeland among Americans of Norwegian heritage may have reached its nadir. Once proud newspapers lost circulation drastically. Linguistic and psychological ties with Norway were weakening. Editors found their influence waning, and their subscribers shrinking in number. *Minneapolis Tidende* turned over its mailing list to *Decorah-Posten* in 1935, as did *Skandinaven* of Chicago in 1941. Some Norwegians found satisfaction in Norway's active role in the League of Nations, where Carl J. Hambro served for many years, some of the time as president of the Assembly. Isolationism seemed to prevail, however, in the Middle West, where isolationist Henrik Shipstead was elected four times to the United States Senate from Minnesota, the last in 1940.

The year 1940 brought a sudden revival of American interest in the European North, mainly in Denmark and Norway. Well before the Nazi invasion of the two Scandinavian states on April 9 and 10, Germany was seen to be a totalitarian juggernaut with aggressive designs. Pure isolationism, where it existed, went out the window. Norwegian-Americans agreed with the Roosevelt policy of aid to the Allies short of war. Hence Lend-Lease, the destroyer-for-bases deal with Britain, and the sending of American troops to once Danish-owned Iceland for its protection drew no significant opposition.[21]

Norwegians in America followed closely reports of Norway being caught in the power struggle. Its favorable location for air and submarine bases was clear. Moreover, Germany's industrial and military needs seemed to demand continued flow of Swedish iron ore, via the North Norwegian port of Narvik. Control of Norway was therefore vital to the belligerents, especially to Britain and Germany. Narvik was retaken by a combined Allied and Norwegian force, then lost for a second time to the Nazis. By June 8, 1940, Allied forces had evacuated Norway. They would be required, it was thought, for preventing a German conquest of France. A day earlier, on June 7, King Haakon VII and his cabinet boarded a British vessel, headed for London and a five-year exile.

The Norwegian government in exile maintained communications with and gave instructions to Milorg, the Norwegian resistance organization. A British secret organization operated independently. There were suspicions and misunderstandings between them. Both efforts were greatly assisted in their communication with London by the unofficial cooperation of Sweden. Messengers and agents were shuttled across the rugged Norwegian terrain. In 1942 the Germans gave up the pretense of popular Norwegian support and of the legality of their occupation. Collaboration was wanting. Reichscommissar Josef Terboven then turned to Major Vidkun Quisling, the Norwegian Nazi leader, who acquired the title Minister President. The German occupation became firmly established, but so did the resistance.[22]

Norway's reputation suffered unjustly among Americans during the first year or two of the German occupation. Leland Stowe, foreign correspondent for the *Chicago Daily News,* had reported one-sidedly in *Life* magazine that Norwegians had been indifferent toward or cooperative with Nazi armies during the invasion.

Gradually a truer picture emerged with the help of British officials with whom the exiled Norwegian government in London cooperated. The Norwegian Information Agency in Washington, D. C., Norwegian churches and fraternal organizations, and congressmen and senators of Norse blood also supplied rather authentic information. Among those who succeeded in altering the picture for the better in the national capital were Senators Henry M. Jackson of Washington, Henrik Shipstead of Minnesota, and Alexander Wiley of Wisconsin. Wiley was known to be a close friend of Crown Prince Olav. Others who presented the Norwegian cause positively were Governors Earl Warren of California and Harold Stassen of Minnesota. Americans learned, among other things, that Norway's merchant fleet, fourth largest in the world, was almost entirely in Allied service.

President Roosevelt's "Look to Norway" address of September 16, 1942, gave public recognition to the Norwegian resistance movement. "If there is anyone who still wonders why this war is being fought, let him look to Norway. . . . And if anyone has doubts of the democratic will to win, again I say, let him look to Norway." Later in the year the Department of State raised the Norwegian legation in the nation's capital to the rank of embassy. Favorable opinion in America was most welcome to Norwegians in both Europe and North America.[23]

Norwegians in America came to the aid of their friends in Norway with huge donations of food and clothing. Johan Arnd Aasgaard, head of the American Lutheran Church, served actively as chairman of a drive which netted $27,000,000. Numerous helpers assisted him. William T. Evjue, founder, editor, and publisher of *The Capital Times* of Madison, Wisconsin, was representative of the many able fund raisers. On a smaller scale, but commensurate with their numbers, church congregations and organizations did their part. The Norwegian Club of San Francisco, as one of these, first raised money to aid the Norwegian Red Cross in its Finnish Relief Program, then for Norwegian Relief. The American-Scandinavian Foundation in New York provided emergency loans for Scandinavian fellows stranded in the United States and sent out many lecturers to bespeak the cause of relief. Norwegian sailors, now homeless because of enemy occupation of Norway, were befriended in

American ports, frequently by their Norwegian-American brothers and sisters.[24]

As in the hostilities of 1917–18, so in World War II the Norwegian-American military role can hardly be considered in detachment from the national effort as a whole. Officers and enlisted men, far removed in time from the pioneers, were scattered throughout the military, naval, and air forces. The 99th Infantry Battalion was an exception. Activated in July, 1942, at Camp Ripley, Minnesota, it originally comprised a thousand men of Norwegian descent, some of them born in Norway. Courses in the Norwegian language and training in skiing were compulsory, with readiness for the Allied invasion of Norway in mind. Captain Harold D. Hansen's battalion suffered many casualties in the Normandy invasion and at Aachen. Eventually the survivors landed in Drammen and Oslo and paraded, with selected American units, in the victory celebration in the Norwegian capital.[25]

In recognizing individual performances of the men in khaki or blue, tribute should be paid to legions of unnamed soldiers and sailors and airmen of varied national backgrounds. Our task is to cite a few men of Norwegian heritage. There were Army men like Torger Tokle and Leif Sverdrup. Tokle, an immigrant of 1939 who made his home in Brooklyn and was unrivaled as a skijumper in the United States, was killed in March of 1945 in an attack against the Germans in the mountains of northern Italy. The sports editor of the *New York Times* once called him the Babe Ruth of the skiing world. Before his death Tokle is reported to have said, "I will do everything for my adopted country to help it remain the champion of the small and downtrodden nations of Europe." His words reflect good sportsmanship, and real patriotism.[26]

Major General Leif Sverdrup was closely associated with General Douglas MacArthur in the Pacific theater of war. He emigrated in 1914 at the age of sixteen. His military contribution was with the Army Corps of Engineers. Sverdrup came by his rank deservedly. B-17 bombers followed the route to Far Eastern destinations laid down by him. He became commanding general of the Engineer Construction Command.[27]

Lauris Norstad, promoted to full general in 1952, was born in

Minneapolis. He was active in executing the North African campaign and in directing Allied air force operations in the Mediterranean while still only 36 years of age. For better or for worse, he is connected with the strategy that lay behind the atomic bombing of Hiroshima and Nagasaki, at which time he was chief of staff of the Twentieth Air Force. Norstad was largely instrumental in bringing about a unification of the armed services after the war. From 1956 to 1962 he headed the Supreme Headquarters of the Allied Powers in Europe (SHAPE). General Norstad is reputed to have engaged in a running argument with the Pentagon over the deployment of tactical nuclear weapons on West German soil, in preference to conventional weapons favored by Washington. His retirement in 1962 is seen as a consequence of this difference of opinion.[28]

Colonel Bernt Balchen, born in Norway in 1899, embarked upon a career in aviation that in time won him the title of "King of the Arctic." Roald Amundsen, Admiral Richard Byrd, and Lincoln Ellsworth, all polar explorers, valued his skill. In 1929 he piloted Byrd's plane to the South Pole. He taught the Royal Canadian Mounted Police to fly hyroplanes in the bush country. He became a United States citizen in 1931 by special act of Congress, an honor granted only to the Marquis de Lafayette before him. During World War II he commanded a secret underground operation within the British Royal Air Force, ferrying some 2,000 Norwegians to England under the most hazardous conditions. As an officer in the Army Air Forces of the United States, after service with the British, he developed the air base at Thule in Greenland, the strategically located Danish possession. At the conclusion of the war Balchen directed the evacuation of 70,000 slave laborers from liberated countries. President Eisenhower later commended him for his contribution to the commercial utilization of the Arctic air routes and to national defense. With his expertise and counsel the Scandinavian Airlines System pioneered in scheduling flights on the polar routes.[29]

The internationally cataclysmic years from 1914 to 1945 witnessed relatively little movement of foreigners to the United States. The wars, the quota system, and the depression all combined to decelerate the human flow westward from Europe, and eastward from Asia. Norwegian immigration reached its lowest point not only because of the legal and economic deterrents imposed by American conditions but because there was little reason for the natural overflow of the nineteenth century to continue. As America's drawing power waned, Norway gained in stature. The explanation lay in the fact that free land was no longer available to the descendants of the fjord-to-prairie peasants of an earlier generation, and that living conditions in Norway, on the other hand, were improving. The "immigrants" spoken of in this chapter are therefore usually sons and daughters, or grandsons and granddaughters, of the pioneers. They were well assimilated into the society of the New World.

The general attitude of wartime America toward citizens of Norwegian descent was one of trust and friendliness. It was known that Norway sought no advantage from the war, other than the preservation or recovery of her freedom. No doubt the nearness of New York to the old country and the uninterrupted communication with Norway through persons and news media served to strengthen ethnic ties. Frequent calls of Norwegian vessels and young seamen in Atlantic ports and in the seamen's missions of New Orleans, San Diego, San Francisco, and Seattle also furnished living reminders not of the past alone but of a thriving and struggling Norwegian nation, bent upon maintaining a democratic way of life.

World War I had hastened the decline of the Norwegian language in America. Lutheran congregations turned rapidly toward fuller use of the English tongue in hymns, rituals, and sermons. The struggling minority communions like the Baptists and the Methodists moved closed toward merger with the parent American denominations. Norwegian journals shared the withering experience of the immigrant press as a whole. The year 1917 had been the peak year, with 1,350 separate foreign-language publications. By 1940 the total had fallen to 1,047, in 38 different languages. The government stood aloof in this metamorphosis of the news media. With practically no immigration, newspapers died a natural death. But the few people who could not read English usually managed to find a foreign-language paper to their liking.[30]

By what some might call a strange perversity of human nature, immigrant groups in their turn assumed a superior attitude toward those who came after them. Certainly during the great wars nearly all "hyphenates" strove to identify with America and Americanism. In the interwar period isolationism, an aspect of nationalism, made possible the enforcement of quota legislation, based upon national origins. People of Norwegian descent were no exception in their posture on the immigration issue. They favored the keep-out policy. It was as though the lady in New York harbor had turned her face the other way.

Yet the patriotic smugness reflected in isolationism and in immigration restriction did not preclude periodic revivals of Norwegianness. The centennial celebration of 1925 and the German invasion of Norway in 1940 stirred memories and hopes that had lain dormant. Carl Söyland frankly declared that World War II gave the Norwegian community in Brooklyn a ten-year lease on life. This may have been an understatement. Today there are forces not only binding Americans and Norwegians closer together but also making Norwegian-Americans more aware and more appreciative of their European heritage.

CHAPTER 14

America and Norway: Ideas in Transit

NORWEGIAN IMMIGRANTS KEPT ONE FOOT IN THE HOMELAND, AT least temporarily. While their propensity for looking backward may not have been altogether beneficial to themselves, it was not permanently detrimental to an appreciation of things American. When Carl J. Hambro published a book on North Atlantic travel and Norwegian emigration to America he emphasized the importance of the Atlantic passenger vessels in maintaining communication and helpful relations between America and Norway. He suggested that the hyphen connecting the two nations was older than American history itself. Reminders are to be found in the Icelandic sagas and in the story of North Atlantic exploration. Hambro, once president of the Assembly of the League of Nations and himself in a measure an incarnation of world citizenship, credited the ocean liners with creating and preserving a mutual trust between the emigrants and those who remained at home. He believed that the majestic passenger carriers represented a gain for Norway, insofar as they united the Norwegian people of two continents.[1]

If Americans of Norwegian birth cast over-the-shoulder glances into their Nordic past, what can be said of those who remained at home? Did they give constant and serious attention to the affairs of their departed relatives and neighbors in the distant land to the west? Apparently not. In the 1890s Nicolai Grevstad of Chicago's *Skandinaven* spoke for many readers when he complained to the distinguished Norwegian statesman, Johan Sverdrup, that they were not appreciated in the land of their birth. It is known that officials and well-to-do-folk in Norway were not reconciled to the emigration of their fellow Norwegians. Often they stigmatized the departed ones as ungrateful and uncultured. Some Norwegians sought to correct this one-sided judgment, as when one editor questioned whether Norsemen at home had made sufficient effort to communicate with alleged plebeians and upstarts in America.[2]

Prior to 1890 several influential Norwegians displayed friendship for America. There come to mind once more Sören Jaabæk, Johan Sverdrup. Björnstjerne Björnson, and Kristofer Janson. Jaabæk, an effective parliamentarian and newspaper publisher, admired the American governmental system and American institutions generally. Sverdrup is reported to have described political democracy, as early as the 1840s, as government of, by, and for the people, a generation before Lincoln's epochal Gettysburg Address. Björnson and Janson, as literary men and intellectuals, found spiritual kinship with their counterparts in the New World.

What was it that had brought Norwegian-Americans more vividly into the consciousness of those who had remained in Europe? Was it common blood, speech, or culture? If so, why then did not the rapprochement occur sooner? Was it the consequence of political developments in Norway prior to the break with Sweden in 1905? Or was the pull-factor accentuated only with the coming of World War I, when Norwegians in America and their neutral but suffering friends in Norway agonized together? Surely these were factors in strengthening Norwegian-American relations.

Apart from ethnic affinity and common political and social goals, however, the weightier factors in promoting cohesion between Norwegians everywhere were the cumulative effect of millions of America letters, the more frequent America journeys by observant and articulate Norwegians, the informal ecclesiastical relations between Lutheran and other church bodies, the flow of ideas through newspapers and periodicals, and the active programs of Norwegian and other Scandinavian cultural organizations.

The overwhelming effect of immigrant correspondence upon the people of Norway has been cited. The first wave of emigrants responded to an inner compulsion to describe and to analyze American society. Their descendants and later arrivals usually contented themselves with recitals of personal experiences, often trivial. They were less certain that what was different in America was better. Nevertheless, *Amerikabreve* constitute a unique reservoir of source material which may provide a more adequate answer to the question of America's influence during Norway's period of transition.[3]

Hans Tambs Lyche, an admirer of America, epitomizes the personal influence in relations between America and Norway. Unlike Knut Hamsun, he wrote glowingly of his life in America between 1881 and 1892. As a Unitarian minister and a contributor to Christiania's *Dagbladet* and the literary magazine *Samtiden* (Our Times), he helped to present the world of American literature to compatriots at home. His founding of *Kringsjaa* (Survey) brought American culture to the reading public of Norway. To him Boston was the Paris of the New World, full of beauty and light. He idolized Ralph Waldo Emerson. He identified Americanism with courage, optimism, and democracy. Lyche built bridges between his two loves, the land of his childhood and the land of his choice.[4]

With reference to personal ties, seldom has a representative of the United States government performed as effectively in Norway as Lauritz S. Swenson. The Minnesota-born banker, educated in history and political science at the graduate school of The Johns Hopkins University, carried a lifelong impression from his student days of Björnstjerne Björnson's visit to Luther College in 1880. In 1911 President William H. Taft named Swenson as United State minister to Norway. There he remained until 1930, with the important exception of eight years, during Woodrow Wilson's Democratic administration. He acquired a remarkable facility in the Norwegian language and became familiar with Norwegian history and literature. King Haakon VII often sought him out, as one in whom he could confide. Swenson served altogether thirty-seven years in diplomatic posts While he appears to have disseminated only the official view of the American government while in Norway, he contributed most significantly as a radiant and intelligent medium of goodwill and understanding.[5]

In Norwegian-American relations books and periodicals, as always, transcended national boundaries. Hans Tambs Lyche, back in Norway, frequently editorialized on the subject of American libraries. He joined with others in calling for a reorganization of Christiania's Deichmanske Bibliotek, Norway's leading public library. Haakon Nyhuus, with fresh experience as a cataloger at Chicago's Newberry Library, returned to Norway in 1897 to carry out the proposed innovations at Deichman.[6]

Arne Kildal, a graduate of an American library school, gained valuable experience in the Library of Congress. In 1910 he accepted the directorship of Bergen's public library. While in America, he had read widely in Norwegian-American newspapers. He confessed to having a whole new world of immigrants opened up to him. In 1925 he became head of the library division of the Norwegian government's department of church and education. Through Kildal and his colleagues the Dewey decimal system, the open-shelf idea, and a library extension program were introduced. He found time also to serve as secretary-general of Nordmanns-Forbundet, an office which he ably filled for a quarter of a century. His American interests are further reflected in such works as *De gjorde Norge större* (They made Norway greater).

Kildal's thesis in the above-mentioned work is that successful emigrants produced a wholesome effect upon Norwegians who remained at home. Emigration made all Norwegians prouder of their national heritage. This most profound event in recent Norwegian history also brought significant social and economic consequences. Kildal's perceptive observations carry special weight because he loved America. His active promotion of the study of American history and literature in Norway forms a legacy of incalculable worth.[7]

Another Norseman who consistently associated himself with the United States was Halvdan Koht, an eminent historian and biographer. Following his initial visit to America in 1908 he wrote rather disparagingly, yet not without hope, concerning the power of the monied interests in American life. But he enjoyed his stay, as he said, because he believed in the American people. Koht turned his attention to Norway. There, he related critically, American history was little known and poorly understood. He was determined to correct this deficiency. Dutifully, he traced the rise of America in world perspective. America, he believed, supplied the opportunity for advancement of Europe's lower classes.[8]

Perhaps Koht's adulation of the new Norway overseas appears at its best in his ground-breaking volume entitled *The American Spirit in Europe*. Here again he points up America's leadership. He reminds readers that Alexis de Tocqueville had observed more than a century earlier, in his *Democracy in America* (1835), that America and Russia would one day determine the fate of the world. The strength of America lies not in its population or in its natural resources but in the expansive energy that animates its activities. Only in America will one find collectivism and individualism side by side, and solidarity coexisting with freedom. He predicts that supposedly irreconcilable views and systems will coalesce, for the benefit of all mankind. He cites an example in his own country, where the Ibsen spirit of individualism did not prevent the introduction of a collectivist national solidarity.[9]

Koht attributed Norway's material progress to many American inventions. He recognized in Captain Matthew Maury's book, *Lanes of Steamers Crossing the Atlantic* (1853), a boon to the safety and efficiency of ships of all nations. The Swedish-American John Ericsson and several American and English engineers introduced various types of the screw propeller, which replaced the cumbersome paddle wheel. Samuel F. B. Morse gave the telegraph to the world, as Thomas A. Edison did the incandescent lamp, the phonograph, and the motion picture, the last of which Koht believed had a democratizing effect in all countries where it penetrated. American argricultural machinery revolutionized European farming, he said, and Isaac M. Singer's sewing machine was hardly less sensational in its way. The Remington typewriter and the Bell telephone captured Europe, to the advantage of business on both sides of the ocean. American business reached its apex with the infiltration of capital. In short, the eyes of Europeans opened wider and wider after the World's Fair in London in 1851. Previous to the marvelous American displays there, Europeans had associated America with P. T. Barnum and humbug. After the fair it became evident that America had arrived industrially as a mature economic power.[10]

Not everything struck Koht favorably, but he confessed to America being his second fatherland. It had freshened and freed his mind. On the occasion of his first visit he felt that he stood on the threshold of a thrilling experience. To one who inquired what the difference might be between England and America he replied unhesitatingly that England lived on her past, America on her hopes for the future. No finer tribute to Halvdan Koht can be found than that of his son-in-law, Sigmund Skard, on the occasion of Koht's death at 92 in 1965. Koht made United States history, says Skard, an obligatory part of the curriculum in the University of Oslo at a time when European institutions rarely required it. He pioneered in the promotion of American studies, the field in which Skard himself is engaged. Halvdan Koht not only knew America, says Skard, he loved it. Through it all he was fully aware that European conservatives and traditionalists fought the forces of change emanating from America. His sympathy lay with the lower classes, who looked hopefully to the United States.[11]

Reformers and newspapermen also demonstrate the transit of ideas. Marcus Thrane has been cited as a socialist who left his imprint on both Norway and America. His successor, Martin Tranmæl, affected the course of American socialist development only slightly perhaps, but he became the strong man of the labor movement in Norway. He learned from Eugene Debs, the American socialist, the wisdom of employing parliamentary methods rather than the direct-action approach of the Industrial Workers of the World. For a brief interval he chaired a committee in the Socialist party of Debs and edited *Socialisten* for Scandinavian readers in Chicago. His efforts to win seats for Labor party candidates in the Norwegian parliament, after his return from the United States in 1905, may have turned the Norwegian labor movement in a different direction from that of Sweden and Denmark. In Norway universal manhood suffrage and full parliamentary government came earlier, in all likelihood because Labor worked independently, not with *Venstre* (the Liberals), as in the sister Scandinavian states. Tranmæl learned much from Debs.[12]

The temperance movement is an example of less tangible reforming forces with international ties. In the 1830s one Robert Baird, a Presbyterian minister, traveled widely in Europe in the interests of temperance and religious freedom. So successful was he in Norway that, in the estimation of the historian Wilhelm Keilhau, brandy disappeared as the national beverage. It was replaced by coffee. Baird is described not only as a temperance missionary but as "a prophet of American Manifest Destiny, believer in the voluntary principle of American Protestantism, supporter of Anglo-Saxon supremacy, and *de facto* immigrant agent with neither title nor commission." His influence upon Scandinavians and prospective emigrants was formidable.[13]

The American temperance movement, although not of immigrant origin, affected Norway. Beginning with the founding of the Independent Order of Good Templars (1851) in Utica, New York, the movement spread to England, and from there to Norway. In 1967, when Norway celebrated the 90th anniversary of its first chapter, some one thousand chapters were active in the country.[14]

Reference has been made to Aasta Hansteen and the feminist crusade. As an admirer of Lucy Stone, Miss Hansteen returned to her native Norway to become a worthy successor to Camilla Collett. Undoubtedly Ibsen had helped to prepare the way. In *A Doll's House* he shocked his contemporaries by having Nora forsake her husband and children for a career. Others saw in his drama a portent of the future relations of the sexes.

That Lutheranism was exported to America with the emigrants is a highly important factor within the context of relations between Norway and America. The shuttling back and forth of clergymen helped to maintain a strong spiritual tie. Moreover, the same ritual was followed in both countries. Hymns were sung in common, although from different hymnals. From Tromsö in North Norway to Seattle on America's Pacific Coast could be heard, on any given Sunday morning, the strains of Bernhard S. Ingemann's "Deilig er jorden" (Fair is the earth), Nicolai F. S. Grundtvig's "Kirken den er et gammelt hus" (freely translated as "Built on a rock the church doth stand"), or Hans A Brorson's "Den store hvide flok vi se" (The great white host we see), sung to Edvard Grieg's majestic melody.

In the case of non-Lutherans, who received their original inspiration from American Protestant denominations, they became to a minor extent a part of Norway's ecclesiastical structure. To attribute their organization and growth in Norway solely to American impetus, however, is not defensible. As in America, so in the homeland there were favoring circumstances. The democratic spirit was rising. People were turning more and more for spiritual comfort and guidance to less formalized forms of Christianity, which promised greater prospects for personal expression and fulfillment. In fact, ever since the resurgence of pietism with Hans Nielsen Hauge and others, a trend toward personal holiness characterized certain groups within the state church itself.

The east-west flow of ideas is represented as well in the press, on two continents. Norway's newspapers naturally emphasized national and local affairs, but seldom did they totally ignore the United States. Liberal editors and correspondents, particularly, portrayed America as the land of freedom and opportunity. After Jaabæk's pro-American *Folketidende* reached the end of its days in 1880, *Dagbladet* and *Verdens Gang* crusaded on behalf of the less privileged for parliamentary reform. They pointed admiringly to American democracy. There was, of course, no unanimous response to emigration and to American customs and institutions. Certain journals, like the conservative *Morgenbladet* of Christiania, all but flaunted their indifference to their departed countrymen and to the American scene.

Whereas Norwegians of the European North have been made increasingly aware of the experiences of emigrated sons and daughters in the twentieth century, the immigrants have likewise been kept informed of their heritage through newspapers, periodicals, and other media. In this respect the Norwegian-American *Skandinaven, Decorah-Posten,* and *Nordisk Tidende,* to mention the more influential journals, have played a very effective role. The newspapers must be regarded as important ties between the Norwegian people on both sides of the ocean. Significantly, the weekly visitors to the mail boxes in town and country also disseminated information from American news sources. Often immigrant publishers and editors were virtually institutions in themselves. Who would deny the influence of a Nicolai Grevstad of *Skandinaven,* a Kristian Prestgard of *Decorah-Posten,* or a Carl Söyland of *Nordisk Tidende?*

Grevstad during his editorship (1892–1911) and for many years thereafter promoted the idea of fulfilling the duties of American citizenship. But within the context of citizenship he urged a deeper appreciation of Norwegian contributions to civilization. Foreshadowing the current interest in ethnic studies, he argued in the 1930s for a fairer picture of the Norwegian immigrant, too often stereotyped as a hewer of wood and a drawer of water. Let it be known, he declared, that not only had the new citizens excelled in many ways but they had proved their loyalty to their adopted land. The immigrants, he said, were psychologically Americans even before they set foot upon American soil.[15]

Kristian Prestgard, associate editor and editor in chief of *Decorah-Posten* from 1898 to 1946, held the Norwegian community of the Middle West together as few would have been able to do. Norway's Halvdan Koht put it well when, a year before Prestgard's death, he remarked upon the rich collection of local news from Norway in the Iowa paper. By that time it had outlived almost all Norwegian-language journals. Not even in Norway, said Koht, did any newspaper carry items from communities throughout the entire land. It was Prestgard's love for Norway, he believed, that motivated this work. *Decorah-Posten* also nourished a love for Norway among its readers.

Prestgard commanded a profound knowledge of Norwegian literature, a knowledge which he imparted to hundreds of thousands of subscribers over the years. Yet he held America in high esteem. Having arrived in this country to report on the Columbian Exposition of 1893 in Chicago, he remained for the rest of his life. A visit to Norway in 1927 bolstered his pride in both countries, as he wrote upon his return in *En sommer i Norge*. Both flags were his, and he felt the better for it.[16]

Carl Söyland, who assumed the chief responsibility for editing Brooklyn's *Nordisk Tidende* from 1940 to 1963, also personifies an intimate relationship between America and Norway. An early interest in music turned his steps away from his native Bergen to the studios of the capital city, Christiania. From there he traveled to America (for two years, he thought) and to many other points on the globe, sometimes as seaman and then again as vagabond. Entering the field of journalism as a free-lance writer, he expanded his influence to the Greater New York Norwegian community and to Norwegian readers everywhere. Broad in his mental horizon, he saw "The World of Tomorrow," the slogan of New York's world exposition of 1939, as a challenge to break with ethnic provincialism. "We can no longer live on Norwegianness as a kind of treasure-chest satisfaction," he warned, "in which one delves into the past to revive old memories." The revolutions in communication and transportation, he noted, had annihilated time and distance. Personal and literary exchanges between Norway and America had brought a new relationship.[17]

As has been noted in a previous chapter, cultural and social organizations aided not only in the adjustment to life in America but also in maintaining ties with Norway. The Sons of Norway and the Norwegian-American Historical Association have performed outstandingly well in both respects. While covering the larger region of the European North, *Scandinavian Studies*, published by the Society for the Advancement of Scandinavian Study, has enlightened many Americans on aspects of the Norwegian language, literature, and history. We cite once more the accomplishments of The American-Scandinavian Foundation and of its influential quarterly, *The American-Scandinavian Review*. Norway's parallel to the *Review* is *The Norseman*, published in English by Nordmanns-Forbundet in Oslo, in addition to its Norwegian-language journal *Nordmanns-Forbundet*.

The leadership of The American-Scandinavian Foundation largely explains its success. Besides its two Norwegian-American editors referred to in Chapter 10, Hanna Astrup Larsen and Erik J. Friis, the Foundation has enjoyed the leadership of three non-Scandinavians, Henry Goddard Leach, Lithgow Osborne, and C. Peter Strong. Leach, a specialist in Scandinavian literature and history, directed many of the foundation's activities until his retirement in 1947. Osborne, formerly United States ambassador to Norway, succeeded Leach as president in that year.[18] C. Peter Strong became president when Osborne became chairman of the board.

Between Norway and the United States forces of attraction have proved stronger than forces of repulsion. At the close of the nineteenth century both nations were approaching self-realization. Norway's new liberal party helped to introduce ministerial responsibility to the people's representatives and, before the century ran its course, universal manhood suffrage became a reality. The struggle for separation from Sweden, the stronger

Scandinavian neighbor to the east, inspired a deeper feeling of national oneness.

For the United States, national unity was severely tested in the Civil War. "Reconstruction" failed to heal the nation's wounds. But in the final quarter of the century the "bloody shirt" was less seldom waved. Constitutionally the nation stood united, but spiritually not fully so. The people of Norway understood. For them separation from Sweden was the last step in national fulfillment, or so it seemed. For America the word was preservation. Ideologically, Norway and America operated on the same wavelength.

Twentieth-century ties are no less binding. Two world wars found America and Norway in agreement, both nonaligned in 1914 and 1939 and both asserting a desire to be neutral. The Norwegian merchant marine proved its value for the European Allies, and for America, in both wars. When selected American soldiers paraded in Oslo to mark the liberation from German occupation, they impressed the greatly relieved Norwegian onlookers. Norwegians shouted cheers of joy, and shed tears of appreciation.

Other factors are contributing to a common understanding. Common membership in NATO, mutual visits by leaders in state and church, cultural exchanges, international trade, and cooperative business and scientific ventures are strengthening North Atlantic bonds. America is on the lips of more Norwegians than ever before, while more and more Americans, of whom a large percentage are of Norwegian heritage, are helping to bring prosperity to Norway's tourist trade.

Anniversary celebrations have preserved and fostered Norwegian fellowship at home and abroad. They will continue to do so. In the summer of 1972 the people of the Telemark region, famous for its skiing, honored Snowshoe Thompson, who carried a fifty-pound sack of mail on skis for twenty years through scenic but grim Sierra Nevada terrain, between Placerville in California and Carson Valley in Nevada. The fiftieth anniversary of the Norwegian-American Historical Association will be properly recognized in 1975. And now that in 1975 the sesquicentennial of Norwegian group migration is about to be observed on both sides of the ocean, Americans of Norwegian descent are prompted to reinforce the bonds with overseas cousins, to re-evaluate their common Scandinavian traditions, and to reemphasize the similar social and political objectives of the United States and Norway.[19]

While the Norwegian-American Historical Association, the Swedish Pioneer Historical Society, and other learned societies are preparing to participate in the bicentennial observances of 1976 in America, there is one disturbing feature on the domestic scene. Perhaps justifiably, various ethnic groups are claiming social and economic discrimination and are making urgent demands for alleviation of their complaints. There may be a brighter side to the situation. In the long run the prospect of cultural diversity, when accompanied by mutual appreciation of the many and varied ethnic customs and aspirations, need hold no fears for America. In the spirit and intention of the founding fathers, the *e pluribus unum* (from many one) may be realized, insofar as immigrants and their progeny demonstrate respect for Old World cultures, sympathetic recognition of each other's customs, and a constant loyalty to American ideals. Unity is possible, with the mingling of peoples of diverse national origins, and democracy may prove most productive when individual and group differences are accepted and even encouraged.[20]

Turning our attention to Norway, questions may be raised concerning the effects of emigration. Is there a correlation between mobility and social change? Are movement and communication essential to progress? Are the people who remain at home stimulated by emigration? Do they acquire a broader outlook and a feeling of contact with a bigger world? The answers appear to be in the affirmative. Frequently emigrants return to inject new life and to introduce the latest techniques in farming, engineering, and other areas. Not that emigration alone is the explanation for the occurrence of desirable change in the country of origin but, given the magnitude of the Norwegian exodus to America in the nineteenth and twentieth centuries, it was a prime factor.[21]

Einar Haugen, a specialist in the field of Norwegian linguistics and literature, once remarked that America needed friends and that Norway was ready to respond to that need. Aside from the practical considerations of national security and trade, spiritual ties have been strengthened, while ties of ancestry have been weakened. Haugen aptly concluded, as do we, with these lines from the Elder Edda:

> If a friend you have
> Whom well you trust,
> And from whom you wish returns,
> Trade your ideas, Give each other gifts,
> And go to see him often.

Notes and References

Chapter One

1. Ingrid Semmingsen, *Veien mot vest: Utvandringen fra Norge til Amerika, 1825–1865* (Oslo, 1942), 234 and 245. The main title in translation: *The Road Westward*. As Professor of American History in the University of Oslo, Dr. Semmingsen is also the author of a second volume (1950), covering 1865 to 1915.

2. Franklin D. Scott, "The Dual Heritage of the Scandinavian Immigrant," *Americana Norvegica: Studies in Scandinavian-American Interrelations*, III, 35 (Oslo, 1971). Nicolai Grevstad in *Nyt Tidsskrift* (New Journal) 4:122–40 (Christiania, 1885). In the opinion of a later prominent member of *Dagbladet's* staff, Hagbard Berner, editor in the 1870s, Grevstad had caught the America fever and was inclined toward reforming the Norwegian jury system. See Ragnar Vold, *Dagbladet i Tigerstaden* (Dagbladet in the Tiger City), 7 (Oslo, 1949).

3. *Verdens Gang*, June 15, July 15, and August 28, 1880.

4. T. K. Derry, *A Short History of Norway* (London, 1957), 167–70 and 188.

5. T. K. Derry, *A Short History of Norway*, 190. Ingrid Semmingsen, *Veien mot vest*, I, 249.

6. Ingrid Semmingsen, I, 199, 202, 205, and 210.

7. Theodore C. Blegen, *Norwegian Migration to America, 1825–1860* (Northfield, Minnesota, 1931), 133–38. The sequel to this volume is *Norwegian Migration to America: The American Transition* (Northfield, Minnesota, 1940). Hereafter they will be designated as Volumes I and II.

8. Theodore C. Blegen, *Norwegian Migration to America*, I, 307. Halvdan Koht, *Henrik Ibsen, Eit Diktarliv* (A Poet's Life), II, 35 (Oslo, 1929).

9. Ingrid Semmingsen, II, 88, 96, 98, 104, and 120. Theodore C. Blegen, I, 287–307.

10. Ingrid Semmingsen II, 130 and 134.

11. Ingrid Semmingsen, II, 258 and 261.

12. Sigvald Støylen in *Nordisk Tidende* (Brooklyn, New York), March 4 and 5, 1965. Carl Søyland, long-time editor of *Nordisk*

Tidende, recommended in 1947 that Thrane's remains be removed to Norway from a simply marked grave in Eau Claire, Wisconsin. The Labor government carried out this proposal in 1949, the centennial year of the labor movement.

13. Aksel Zachariassen, *Fra Marcus Thrane til Martin Tranmæl* (Oslo, 1962), 35–42.

14. Ingrid Semmingsen, II, 58, 63, 183, 223, 234, and 373.

15. Einar Molland *Church Life in Norway 1800–1950* (Minneapolis, Minnesota, 1957). Translated from the Norwegian by Harris Kaasa.

16. For the most recent work on Hauge see Sverre Norborg, *Hans Nielsen Hauge* (2 volumes, Oslo, 1966 and 1970), based largely upon a vast collection, hitherto unutilized, of Hauge letters. An excellent interpretation of Grundtvigianism from a theological and spiritual perspective is that of Ernest D. Nielsen, entitled *N. F. S. Grundtvig: An American Study* (Rock Island, Illinois, 1955).

17. Andrew Jenson, *History of the Scandinavian Mission* (Salt Lake City, Utah, 1927), 62–75. Jenson's volume is an important source for an excellent chapter in Kenneth Bjork's *West of the Great Divide: Norwegian Migration to the Pacific Coast, 1847–1893* (Northfield, Minnesota, 1958), 74–134.

18. Andrew Jenson, *History of the Scandinavian Mission*, 90. Arnold Mulder, "Mormons from Scandinavia: A Shepherded Migration, 1850–1900," *Pacific Historical Review*, XXIII, 227–46 (August, 1954). Mulder derives his information from *Skandinaviens Stjerne* (The Star of Scandinavia), a Mormon newspaper published in Copenhagen, beginning in 1851.

19. Carl Frederick Eltzholtz, *Livsbilleder af O. P. Petersen* (Pictures drawn from the life of O. P. Petersen), 8–18 (Chicago, 1903). Andrew Haagensen, *Den Norsk-Danske Methodismes Historie paa begge sider havet* (The history of Norwegian-Danish Methodism on both sides of the ocean), 213 (Chicago, 1894). Arlow W. Andersen, *The Salt of the Earth: A History of Norwegian-Danish Methodism in America* (Nashville, Tennessee, 1962), 25–29 and 63 ff.

20. *77th Annual Report of the Missionary Society of the Methodist Episcopal Church* (New York, 1895).

21. Johan Thorkildsen, *Den Norske Metodistkirkes Historie* (Oslo, 1926), 189 and 224.

22. Ingrid Semmingsen, II, 446.

23. Ingrid Semmingsen, II, 506 and 509.

24. Birger Osland, *A Long Pull from Stavanger: The Reminiscences of a Norwegian Immigrant* (Northfield, Minnesota, 1945), 58–61. Osland, a prominent Chicago businessman who had emigrated in

1888, framed the resolution. Grevstad's words appeared in Trondhjem's *Dagsposten*, June 18, 1905.

25. *The North American Review*, CLXXXI, 281–95 (August, 1905). *The Independent*, LIX, 92–94 (July 13, 1905). *The Outlook*, LXXX, 413 (June 17, 1905) and LXXX, 558 (July 1, 1905).

26. *The Independent*, LX, 1538–42 (June 28, 1906).

27. *Dagsposten*, October 22 and December 5, 1905.

28. Arne Hassing, "Norway's Organized Response to Emigration," *Norwegian-American Studies*, XXV (1972), 54–79.

Chapter Two

1. From Theodore C. Blegen, *Grass Roots History* (Minneapolis, Minnesota, 1947), 44–45.

2. For a brief yet comprehensive treatment of the transition from the Old World to America see Theodore C. Blegen, *Norwegian Migration to America*, II, 3–36 (Northfield, Minnesota, 1940). Blegen believes the best Norwegian presentation of the emigrant traffic to be that of Jacob S. Worm-Müller and Fredrik Scheel, *Den norske sjøfarts historie* (The history of the Norwegian merchant marine), II, part 1, 547–635 (Oslo, 1935). Excellent on technical phases of the ocean voyage, mainly from the British point of view, is Edwin C. Guillet, *The Great Migration: The Atlantic Crossing by Sailing-ship since 1770* (Toronto, Canada, 1963; originally published, 1937).

3. *Morgenbladet*, January 14, 1854; letter dated November 30, 1853, from New York. Cited in Blegen, *Norwegian Migration*, II, 21.

4. Marcus Lee Hansen, *The Atlantic Migration, 1607–1860* (Cambridge, Massachusetts, 1961), 172–78; originally published in 1940. The percentage of deaths is given by Maldwyn Jones in his *American Immigration* (Chicago, Illinois, 1961), 107.

5. C. A. Clausen, "An Immigrant Shipload of 1840," *Norwegian-American Studies and Records*, XIV, 54–77 (Northfield, Minnesota, 1944). The name of this series was changed to *Norwegian-American Studies* in 1962.

6. Knud Langeland, *Nordmændene i Amerika* (The Norwegians in America), 51–56 (Chicago, Illinois, 1888).

7. *The Diary of Elisabeth Koren, 1853–1855*, translated and edited by David T. Nelson (Northfield, Minnesota, 1955), 1, 6, 14, 18, 62, and 64.

8. Laurence M. Larson *The Log Book of a Young Immigrant* (Northfield, Minnesota, 1939), 17–19.

9. George Svejda, *Castle Garden as an Immigrant Depot, 1855–1890*, 31–39; an administrative report of 1968 by the Division of

History, Office of Archeology and Historic Preservation, United States Department of the Interior. Edward Corsi, *In the Shadow of Liberty: The Chronicle of Ellis Island* (New York, New York, 1970), 59. Originally published in 1935.

10. George Svejda, *Castle Garden*, 43–53, 83, and 105.

11. Paul Knaplund, *Moorings Old and New: Entries in an Immigrant Log* (Madison, Wisconsin, 1963), 131–49.

12. Fiorello La Guardia, *The Making of an Insurgent: An Autobiography, 1882–1919* (New York, 1948 and 1961), 62–75.

13. Edward Corsi, *In The Shadow of Liberty: The Chronicle of Ellis Island* (New York, 1970), 9, 15, 31, and 296.

14. Ingrid Semmingsen, *Veien mot Vest*, II, 280–83. Theodore C. Blegen, *Norwegian Migration to America*, II, 333. Reports of the Swedish-Norwegian Consul General's Office in New York and Records of the United States Shipping Office provide a basis for estimates of the number of deserters and repatriates.

15. *Thirtieth Annual Report of the Missionary Society of the Methodist Episcopal Church* (New York, 1847), 93.

16. Gunnar Christie Wasberg, "Centennial of the Norwegian Seamen's Mission," *The Norseman* (Oslo, 1964), no. 4, 109–12. T. K. Derry cites the costliness of the change from sail to steam as an explanation for Norway's drop by 1890 from third to fifth place in tonnage among the maritime nations. At that time 75 percent of Norwegian tonnage still consisted of sailing vessels. *A Short History of Norway*, 181.

17. Drachmann's poem is translated by John Volk in Aage Heinberg, *Over Atlanten fra og til Danmark gennem Tiderne* (Over the Atlantic from and to Denmark through the Ages), 181 (Copenhagen, 1936).

Chapter Three

1. Theodore C. Blegen, *Grass Roots History* (Minneapolis, Minnesota, 1947), 49.

2. From the introduction to *Frontier Mother: The Letters of Gro Svendsen*, v. Translated and edited by Pauline Farseth and Theodore C. Blegen (Northfield, Minnesota, 1950).

3. *Utvandringsstatistikk* (Emigration statistics), 100–103. From a chart in possession of *Den Norske Amerikalinie* (The Norwegian America Line), Oslo. The chart is reproduced in Theodore C. Blegen, *Norwegian Migration to America*, I, 18.

4. Knud Saavesen Arker to his son Saave Knudsen Groven, January 20, 1847. Published in *Drammens Adresse* (Drammen's Advertiser), May 18, 1847.

5. Knud Langeland, *Nordmændene i Amerika* (Norwegians in America), 97 (Chicago, Illinois, 1888).

6. Bayrd Still, "Norwegian-Americans and Wisconsin Politics in the Forties," *Norwegian-American Studies and Records*, VIII, 59 (Northfield, Minnesota, 1934). Laurence M. Larson, "The Norwegian Element in the Northwest," *American Historical Review*, XL, 77 (October, 1934).

Chapter Four

1. On Anneken Henriksen, Hans Hansen, and Claes Carstensen see John O. Evjen, *Scandinavian Immigrants in New York, 1630–1674* (Minneapolis, Minnesota, 1916), 51–68. Carl Joachim Hambro, *Amerikaferd: Av Emigrasjonens Historie* (America Travel: From the History of Emigration), 1–10 (Oslo, 1935).

2. A rather convincing essay on the influence of the stranded Germans is Ingrid Semmingsen's "A Shipload of German Emigrants and their Significance for the Norwegian Emigration of 1825," *The Swedish Pioneer Historical Quarterly*, XXV (July–October, 1974), 183–92. On the Sloopers see Theodore C. Blegen, *Norwegian Migration to America*, I, 24–56, and Carleton C. Qualey, *Norwegian Settlement in the United States* (Northfield, Minnesota, 1938), 17–39.

3. Alfred Hauge, a cultural writer for *Stavanger Aftenblad*, some years ago completed a three-volume fictionalized biography of Cleng Peerson. Their separate titles are *Hundevakt* (Dog Watch), *Landkjenning* (Landsighting), and *Ankerfeste* (Anchorfast); published in Oslo, 1964–1966. In 1970 a Cleng Peerson Memorial Institute, headed by George Joa, was established in Stavanger. Its purpose is to collect and classify books and other information pertaining to Norwegian emigration to America.

4. Richard Canuteson, "A Little More Light on the Kendall Colony," *Norwegian-American Studies and Records*, XVIII (Northfield, Minnesota, 1954), 82–101. Mario S. DePillis, "Still More Light on the Kendall Colony." *Ibid.*, XX (1959), 24–31.

5. Richard Canuteson traces the subsequent career of Larsen in "Lars and Martha Larson: 'We Do what We Can for Them.' " *Ibid.*, XXV (1972), 142–66. The spelling of "Larsen" varies.

6. Theodore C. Blegen, *Norwegian Migration to America*, I, 63–67. Knud Langeland, *Nordmændene i Amerika*, 16 and note.

7. Carlton Qualey, *Norwegian Settlement in the United States*, 21–28 and 38.

8. The description of early Chicago is from Leola Nelson Bergmann, *Americans From Norway* (Philadelphia and New York, 1950), 63.

9. Hjalmar Rued Holand, *De Norske Settlementers Historie* (Ephraim, Wisconsin, 1908), 100–102. Carlton Qualey, *op. cit.*, 37–39.

10. Carlton Qualey, *op. cit.*, 40–51. For an informal centennial review by a later pastor see N. N. Rønning, *The Saga of Old Muskego* (Waterford, Wisconsin, 1943).

11. Theodore C. Blegen, *Grass Roots History* (Minneapolis, Minnesota, 1947), 42.

12. Fred Swansen, *The Founder of St. Ansgar* (Blair, Nebraska, 1949), preface and pages 65–71, 105, and 115.

13. David T. Nelson, editor and translator, *The Diary of Elisabeth Koren, 1853–1855* (Northfield, Minnesota, 1955), 232. The reference is to Adolph C. Preus, who served the Koshkonong parish from 1850 to 1860. Frederick Swansen, *op. cit.*, 118–20.

14. Gunnar J. Malmin, translator and editor, *America in the Forties: The Letters of Ole Munch Raeder* (Minneapolis, Minnesota, 1929), a publication of the Norwegian-American Historical Association.

15. Reiersen's 166-page guide was entitled *Veiviser for norske Emigranter til de Forenede Nordamerikanske Stater og Texas* (Christiania, 1844). Rasmus B. Anderson, *First Chapter of Norwegian Immigration* (Madison, Wisconsin, 1915), 369–82. "Behind the Scenes of Emigration: A Series of Letters from the 1840s," by Johan Reiersen; translated by Carl O. Paulson and Verdandi Study Club of Minneapolis, and edited by Theodore C. Blegen, in *Norwegian-American Studies and Records*, XIV, 78–116 (1944).

16. *America in the Forties: The Letters of Ole Munch Raeder*, 38–40.

17. Carlton Qualey, *Norwegian Settlement in the United States*, 62–67 and 70–72.

18. Carlton Qualey, *op. cit.*, 82–87. Dane County, Wisconsin, takes its name not from the Danes but from Nathan Dane, a member of the Confederation Congress who assisted in drafting the Northwest Ordinance of 1787.

19. Carlton Qualey, *op. cit.*, 97–99, 101–102, and 114.

20. Carlton Qualey, *op. cit.*, 129, 131, and 139. *Emigranten*, February 16, 1861. South Dakota and North Dakota became states in 1889.

21. Kenneth Bjork, *West of the Great Divide: Norwegian Migration to the Pacific Coast, 1847–1893* (Northfield, Minnesota, 1958), 29–38. Thomas I. Benson, "Gold, Salt Air, and Callouses," *Norwegian-American Studies*, XXIV, 193–220 (1970).

22. Kenneth Bjork, *West of the Great Divide*, 136–41 and 274–99.

23. Carlton Qualey, *Norwegian Settlement in the United States,* 198–202.

24. Theodore C. Blegen, *Norwegian Migration,* I, 288–307.

25. Theodore C. Blegen, *Norwegian Migration,* I, 351 and II, 360, 371–72, and 381.

Chapter Five

1. Gunnar J. Malmin, editor, *America in the Forties: The Letters of Ole Munch Raeder,* 88–90.

2. Gjert Gregoriussen Hovland to Niels Sivertsen, April 23, 1835; published in *Christianssandsposten,* February 23, 1843. Hovland also to a friend, April 28, 1835; published in *Den Norske Rigstidende* (The Norwegian National News), May 25, 1837. These letters are filed in the Theodore C. Blegen collection in the library of the University of Minnesota.

3. From Four Mile Prairie, Kaufman County, Texas, to T. A. Gjestvang, July 27, 1852; published in *Arbeider-Foreningernes Blad* (Newspaper of the Workers' Association), January 15, 1853; from the Blegen collection. Reiersen's "Norwegians in the West in 1844" appeared in English translation in 1926 in the *Norwegian-American Studies and Records,* I, 110–25. The article was first published in Christiania.

4. An anonymous writer in Waukesha County, Wisconsin, to Christiania's *Morgenbladet,* May 5, 1856; letter dated February 18, 1856.

5. *Drammens Adresse,* May 18, 1847.

6. *Nordlyset,* August 5, 12, and 19; September 2, 1847; February 10, 1848. Reymert and Even Heg were co-owners of this pioneer newspaper at the outset. By 1849 the paper was sold to Knud Langeland and O. J. Hatlestad. They changed the name to *Democraten,* but politically it remained Free-Soil.

Strictly speaking, the first Scandinavian newspaper in America was *Skandinavia,* with mainly Norwegian subscribers. It began publication in New York City on January 1, 1847, as a semi-monthly. Its eight issues came to an end on May 15. Editor Hans Peter Christian Hansen, a Danish immigrant of 1846, returned to Denmark in 1852. It is difficult to attach much political significance to this short-lived journal.

7. *Emigranten,* January 23, 1852. The role of *Emigranten* in the campaign of 1852 is discussed by Harold M. Tolo in *Norwegian-American Studies and Records,* VIII, 92–111 (1934).

8. *Emigranten,* August 15, 1856. H. Fred Swansen, *The Founder of St. Ansgar,* 123–26.

9. George M. Stephenson, "The Mind of the Scandinavian Immigrant," *Norwegian-American Studies and Records*, IV, 71 (1929).

10. Milo Quaife, *The Convention of 1846* (Madison, Wisconsin, 1919), 704.

11. Donnal V. Smith, "The Influence of the Foreign-Born of the Northwest in the Election of 1860," *Mississippi Valley Historical Review*, XIX, 197 (September, 1932). The thesis that Scandinavian and German votes swung the election in Lincoln's favor has been examined and found wanting by Joseph Schafer in his "Who Elected Lincoln?," *American Historical Review*, XLVII, 51–63 (October, 1941).

12. *Emigranten*, September 16, 1857; February 21, 1859.

13. *Emigranten*, October 17 and 24, 1859.

14. Ole Rynning, *True Account of America for the Information and Help of Peasant and Commoner*, 87; translated and edited by Theodore C. Blegen (Minneapolis, Minnesota, 1926); originally published in Christiania, 1838.

15. Laurence M. Larson, "A Century of Achievement, 1825–1925: The New Norway in the New World," *American-Scandinavian Review*, XIII, 346 (June, 1925). Kendrick C. Babcock, *The Scandinavian Element in the United States*, in "Illinois University Studies in the Social Sciences," III, 158 (Urbana, Illinois, 1914); reprinted by the Arno Press, New York, 1970.

16. *Nordlyset*, April 6, 1848; May 10, 1849; March 9, 1850.

17. *Democraten*, March 8, 1851.

18. *Emigranten*, July 9, 1852. See H. M. Tolo, "The Political Position of *Emigranten* and the Election of 1852," *Norwegian-American Studies and Records*, VIII, 102 (1934). *Emigranten*, July 11, 1856.

19. *Emigranten*, May 13, June 24, July 15, and August 12, 1857.

20. *Den Norske Amerikaner*, June 14, 1856; May 13, 1857. *Nordstjernen*, June 10, 1857.

21. *Emigranten*, January 23 and September 17, 1860.

22. *Folkebladet*, September 22, 1860.

23. Theodore C. Blegen offers an excellent general treatment of the slavery controversy among Norwegian-Americans in his *Norwegian Migration to America*, II, chapter 14.

24. H. Fred Swansen, *The Founder of St. Ansgar*, 155. J. Magnus Rohne, *Norwegian-American Lutheranism up to 1872* (New York, 1926), 206.

25. A recent study is that of Wallace Turner in his *The Mormon Establishment* (Boston, Massachusetts, 1966); see especially pages 218–25.

Chapter Six

1. Norwegian-American writers claim that in the North one Norwegian male in every six enlisted, and that one in eight volunteered among native-born Americans. Olof N. Nelson, editor, *History of the Scandinavians and Successful Scandinavians in the United States* (Minneapolis, Minnesota, 1897), I, 304. Carl G. O. Hansen, in *Norsk-Amerikanernes Festskrift 1914* (Decorah, Iowa, 1914), 39. See also C. A. Clausen and Derwood Johnson, "Norwegian Soldiers in the Confederate Forces," in *Norwegian-American Studies*, XXV (1972), 105–41. Their study is limited to Norwegians in Texas and reveals that 53 Norwegian Texans served in the Confederate Army.

2. Carl Fredrik Solberg, "Reminiscences of a Pioneer Editor," *Norwegian-American Studies and Records*, I, 141 (1926); edited by Albert O. Barton. John A. Johnson, later a successful Madison, Wisconsin, industrialist, also joined Heg and Solberg in appealing for the formation of a Norwegian regiment. See Agnes M. Larson, *John A. Johnson: An Uncommon American* (Northfield, Minnesota, 1969), 41.

3. *Emigranten*, November 18, 1861. Theodore C. Blegen, *Norwegian Migration*, II, 392. Among the histories of the Fifteenth Wisconsin Regiment are John A. Johnson, *Det Skandinaviske Regiments Historie* (La Crosse, Wisconsin, 1869); O. A. Buslett, *Det Femtende Regiment Wisconsin Frivillige* (Decorah, Iowa, no date); and Waldemar Ager, *Oberst Heg og Hans Gutter* (Colonel Heg and his Boys) (Eau Claire, Wisconsin, 1916).

4. Waldemar Ager, *Oberst Heg og Hans Gutter*, 7.

5. Waldemar Ager, *op. cit.*, 15–60.

6. Waldemar Ager, *op. cit.*, 9–10.

7. Waldemar Ager, *op. cit.*, 10–14.

8. Waldemar Ager, *op. cit.*, 166–78.

9. Waldemar Ager, *Oberst Heg og Hans Gutter*, 227. According to William De Loss Love, 49 of the Fifteenth Wisconsin were killed in action, 33 died of wounds, and 217 died from disease, a total of 299; *Wisconsin in the War of the Rebellion* (Chicago, 1866), 1083. Edwin B. Quiner, *Military History of Wisconsin* (Chicago, 1866), 324. Personal glimpses of the war are found in many America letters. For a wife's reactions to her soldier-husband's letters see *Frontier Mother: The Letters of Gro Svendsen* (Northfield, Minnesota, 1950), especially part 3 on "The Union Soldier, 1865"; translated and edited by Pauline Farseth and Theodore C. Blegen.

10. Andrew Nilsen Rygg, *Norwegians in New York, 1825–1925* (Brooklyn, New York, 1941), 43–45. One who joined the Union

Navy was Peter C. Asserson, an immigrant of 1859. His main contribution came after the war, as a naval engineer. He retired in 1903 with the rank of rear admiral. See Kenneth O. Bjork, *Saga in Steel and Concrete: Norwegian Engineers in America* (Northfield, Minnesota, 1947), 335–38.

11. Waldemar Ager, *op. cit.*, 244. Arlow W. Andersen, *The Salt of the Earth: A History of Norwegian-Danish Methodism in America* (Nashville, Tennessee, 1962), 74–77, 160, and 181. During his longtime editorship of *Reform*, Ager attended Norwegian Methodist meetings in Eau Claire, Wisconsin. He first encountered Methodism in his native city of Fredrikstad, Norway.

12. *Emigranten*, March 2 and July 20, 1863; February 27, 1865.

13. *Life Story of Rasmus B. Anderson* (Madison, Wisconsin, 1915), 69.

14. Ole and Ingeborg Aslesen to Helge Gundersen, December 27, 1861. Luther College collection of America letters.

15. Anders Helgesen Schare to relatives, August 8, 1862. Luther College collection.

16. From the letters of Sergeant Nils J. Gilbert, in Waldemar Ager, *op. cit.*, 91.

17. Theodore C. Blegen, editor, *The Civil War Letters of Hans Christian Heg* (Northfield, Minnesota, 1936), 135.

18. *Emigranten*, January 14, 1866. *Fædrelandet*, March 29, 1866. *Skandinaven*, July 26, 1866.

19. *Fædrelandet*, September 6, 1866. *Skandinaven*, September 6 and 20, 1866.

20. *Skandinaven*, October 31, 1867. *Fædrelandet og Emigranten*, March 16, 1871. Four short-lived Democratic journals appeared in 1868: *Den Skandinaviske Democrat* of La Crosse, Wisconsin, *Fremad* (Forward) of Milwaukee, *Amerika* of La Crosse, and *Folkevennen* (The Friend of the People) of Winona, Minnesota.

21. *Skandinaven*, August 11, 1869; June 28 and December 20, 1871.

22. *Amerika*, August 13 and November 4, 1872. This paper should not be confused with *Amerika* of La Crosse, Wisconsin.

23. *Minnesota*, September 27, 1872. Although this newspaper, published in Minneapolis, survived only two years, it possessed two seasoned editors in Carl F. Solberg, formerly of *Emigranten*, and Hjalmar Eger, formerly of *Nordisk Folkeblad*.

24. *Skandinaven og Amerika*, September 13 and November 13, 1873. *Skandinaven*, June 11, 1874. *Skandinaven* changed its name to *Skandinaven og Amerika* in 1873, then returned to the earlier name in 1874.

25. *Skandinaven*, September 28, 1874; June 27, July 11, and 25, and August 1, 1876.

26. *Skandinaven*, October 17 and November 8 and 14, 1876; February 27, 1877.

Chapter Seven

1. Laurence M. Larson, *The Changing West and Other Essays* (Northfield, Minnesota, 1937), 39–48.

2. For an elaboration of this theme see John Higham, "Origins of Immigration Restriction, 1882–1897," *The Mississippi Valley Historical Review*, XXXIX, 77–88 (June, 1952).

3. Ingrid Semmingsen, *Veien mot vest*, II, 242–49, 273–77, and 376–84.

4. Jon Michael Wefald, *From Peasant Ideals to the Reform State: The Political Ideas and Attitudes of the Norwegians in the American Middle West, 1890–1917*, ii–vi. This doctoral dissertation (University of Michigan, 1965) was published in 1971 by the Norwegian-American Historical Association as *A Voice of Protest: Norwegians in American Politics, 1890–1917*. The author presently serves as Commissioner of Agriculture for the State of Minnesota.

5. Jon Wefald, *op. cit.*, 27, 45, and 55.

6. Ingrid Semmingsen, *Veien mot vest*, II, 288–90. Elwyn B. Robinson, in speaking of Norwegian domination of the eastern and northern sections of North Dakota around 1910, affirms that they tended toward radicalism in politics, a result of their experience in Norway as peasants striving for various reforms. *History of North Dakota* (Lincoln, Nebraska, 1966), 288.

7. Merle Curti, *The Making of an American Community: A Case Study of Democracy in a Frontier County* (Stanford, California, 1959), 334. Nils P. Haugen, *Pioneer and Political Reminiscences*, edited by Joseph Schafer (Madison, Wisconsin, n.d.), 61, 80, 108, and 111; reprinted from the *Wisconsin Magazine of History*, XI–XIII (1927–1929). Robert Maxwell, *LaFollette and the Rise of the Progressives in Wisconsin* (Madison, Wisconsin, 1956), 87–92.

8. Martin Ulvestad, *Normændene i Amerika: Deres Historie og Rekord* (Minneapolis, Minnesota, 1907) I, 359 and 368.

9. Odd Sverre Lovoll, "The Norwegian Press in North Dakota," *Norwegian-American Studies*, XXIV, 78–101 (1970).

10. *Skandinaven* finally ceased publication in 1940. For further information on Thrane's career in America see Aksel Zachariassen, *Fra Marcus Thrane til Martin Tranmæl* (Oslo, 1962), 43–44; a rather personalized history of the Norwegian Labor party. Also Leola Nelson

Bergmann, *Americans from Norway* (Philadelphia, Pennsylvania, 1950), 190–94, and Carl G. O. Hansen, "The Story of Marcus Thrane," *Sons of Norway*, XLVI (1949), 17–19.

11. *Dagslyset*, September, 1870. Johannes B. Wist, "Pressen efter Borgerkrigen" (The Press after the Civil War), *Norsk-Amerikanernes Festskrift* (Decorah, Iowa, 1914), 93.

12. Halvdan Koht, *Marcus Thrane. Til Hundreaarsdagen. Oktober 14* (Christiania, 1917), 31–50. Aksel Zachariassen, *op. cit.*, 44. Waldemar Westergaard, translator and editor, "Marcus Thrane in America: Some Unpublished Letters, 1880–1884," *Norwegian-American Studies and Records*, IX, 68 (1936).

13. Sigvald Støylen, "Streiflys over Marcus Thranes liv og omskiftende virke i Amerika" (Glimpses of the Life and Varied Activities of Marcus Thrane in America), *Nordisk Tidende* (Brooklyn, New York, March 4, 1965). Henriette C. K. Naeseth, formerly of Augustana College, Rock Island, Illinois, is in possession of microfilm copies of Thrane's plays, journals, and letters, obtained from the Norwegian-American Historical Association, Northfield, Minnesota. It is her intention to publish some of this in book form.

14. For brief sketches of Knute Nelson's career see Solon J. Buck, "Knute Nelson," *Dictionary of American Biography*, VII, 418–19 (New York, 1934); Juul Dieserud, "Nordmænd i det Offentlige og Politiske Liv" (Norwegians in Public and Political Life), *Norsk-Amerikanernes Festskrift*, 311–21; and "The Unelected President," *The Norseman*, no. 1, 1971 (Oslo, Norway). The standard biography is Martin W. Odland's *The Life of Knute Nelson* (Minneapolis, Minnesota, 1926).

15. *St. Paul Pioneer Press*, June 8, 1887. H. G. Stordock to Knute Nelson, March 19, 1892, in the Nelson Papers, Minnesota Historical Society, St. Paul; cited in Jon Wefald, *From Peasant Ideals to the Reform State*, 72, 77, and 86.

16. *Skandinaven*, February 24, 1892. *Nye Normanden*, October 12, 1897. In Wefald, *op. cit.*, 101, 108, and 122.

17. *Skandinaven*, April 1, 1896. Evelyn Nilsen, "Buslett's Editorship of *Normannen* from 1894 to 1896," *Norwegian-American Studies and Records*, XII, 128–43 (1941). *Decorah Posten og Ved Arnen* (Decorah, Iowa), November 6 and 10, 1896, and November 12, 1912. *Ved Arnen* was a regular literary supplement to this paper, which was founded in 1874 and ceased publication in December, 1972.

18. Louis L. Gerson, *The Hyphenate in Recent American Politics and Diplomacy* (Lawrence, Kansas, 1964), 4 and 6.

19. Hjalmar Hjorth Boyesen, "The Scandinavians in the United States," *North American Review*, CLV, 526–35 (November, 1892),

and "The Dangers of Unrestricted Immigration," *The Forum*, III, 533–42 (July, 1887).

20. A scholarly biography of Boyesen, with emphasis upon his literary qualities and contributions, is that of Clarence A. Glasrud, entitled simply *Hjalmar Hjorth Boyesen* (Northfield, Minnesota, 1963). Francis Amasa Walker, "Immigration and Degradation," *The Forum*, XI, 634–44 (August, 1891).

21. Edward Alsworth Ross, "Scandinavians in America," *Century*, LXXXVIII, 291–98 (June, 1914). That it is possible to be nativist toward "undesirable" ethnic groups and charitable toward others is well illustrated in Julius Weinberg's "E. A. Ross: The Progressive as Nativist," *Wisconsin Magazine of History*, L, 242–53 (Spring, 1967).

22. *Skandinaven og Amerika*, October 2 and November 6, 1873. *Skandinaven*, September 4, 1877.

23. Odd Sverre Lovoll, "The Norwegian Press in North Dakota," *Norwegian-American Studies*, XXIV, 78–101 (1970).

24. Jon Wefald, *op. cit.*, citing Andrew E. Lee's letter of July 6, 1899, to Joseph D. Sayers.

25. Jon Wefald, *op. cit.*, 157 and 159. Gilbert Fite, *Peter Norbeck: Prairie Statesman* (Columbia, Missouri, 1948), 93.

26. Odd Sverre Lovoll, "The Norwegian Press in North Dakota," *Norwegian-American Studies*, XXIV, 84–89 (1970).

27. *Skandinaven*, October 24, 1902; January 14, 1903; August 1, 1906. Cited in Jon Wefald, *op. cit.*, 127 and 135.

28. Sten Carlsson, "Scandinavian Politicians in Minnesota Around the Turn of the Century," *Americana Norvegica: Studies in Scandinavian-American Interrelations*, III, 237–71 (Oslo, 1971).

Chapter Eight

1. Einar Molland, *Church Life in Norway, 1800–1950* (Minneapolis, Minnesota, 1957), 38; translated and edited by Harris Kaasa. A recent biography of Hans Nielsen Hauge, based upon some 300 hitherto unused letters, is that of Sverre Norborg, *Hans Nielsen Hauge: Biografi, 1771–1804* (Oslo, 1966) and *1804–1824* (Oslo, 1970).

2. Einar Molland, *op. cit.*, 61 and 64.

3. Ernest D. Nielsen, *N. F. S. Grundtvig: An American Study* (Rock Island, Illinois, 1955). The above paragraph is excerpted from Nielsen's recapitulation, pages 148–64.

4. Gunnar J. Malmin, translator and editor, "Bishop Jacob Neumann's Word of Admonition to the Peasants," *Norwegian-American Studies and Records*, I, 108 (Minneapolis, Minnesota, 1926).

5. Laurence M. Larson, "The Lay Preacher in Pioneer Times," in *The Changing West and Other Essays* (Northfield, Minnesota, 1937), 147–73.

6. Rasmus B. Anderson, *First Chapter of Norwegian Immigration* (Madison, Wisconsin, 1915), 431.

7. Th. Eggen, "Oversigt over den Norsk-Lutherske Kirkes Historie i Amerika" (Survey of the History of the Norwegian Lutheran Church in America), in *Norsk-Amerikanernes Festskrift* (Decorah, Iowa, 1914), 227. N. N. Rönning, *Fifty Years in America* (Minneapolis, 1938), 112–14. The standard biography of Eielsen is Christopher O. Brohaug and J. Eisteinsen, *Kortfattet beretning om Elling Eielsens liv og virksomhed* (A Brief Presentation of Elling Eielsen's Life and Work), Chicago, 1883.

8. H. Fred Swansen, *The Founder of St. Ansgar* (Blair, Nebraska, 1949), 13–40; a biography of Claus L. Clausen.

9. Einar Haugen, "Pastor Dietrichson of Old Koshkonong," *Wisconsin Magazine of History*, XXIX, 301–18 (March, 1946). Dietrichson related his experiences in *Reise blandt de norske Emigranter i "De forenede nordamerikanske Fristater"* (Christiania, 1846). Dietrichson's travel narrative and his Koshkonong prairie journal are now available in translation as *A Pioneer Churchman: J. W. C. Dietrichson in Wisconsin, 1844–1850* (Norwegian-American Historical Association and Twayne Publishers, New York, 1973).

10. Helene and Peter A. Munch, translators, *The Strange American Way: Letters from Wiota, Wisconsin, 1855–1859, by Caja Munch and An American Adventure, by Johan Storm Munch* (Carbondale, Illinois, 1970), 115, 157, 185, and 259. Theodore C. Blegen, *Norwegian Migration to America*, II, 167.

11. Helene and Peter A. Munch *The Strange American Way*, 211, 227, 238, and 240. Nelson and Fevold, *The Lutheran Church Among Norwegian Americans: A History of the Evangelical Lutheran Church* (Minneapolis, Minnesota, 1960), I, 119.

12. H. Fred Swansen, *The Founder of St. Ansgar*, 107, 152, 158, 164, and 168.

13. H. Fred Swansen, *op. cit.*, 180–85, 220, and 223–24.

14. Theodore C. Blegen, *Norwegian Migration to America*, II, 532. "Free Church" is given a different meaning in a recent essay by J. C. K. Preus. He refers to the Norwegian Lutheran organization in America of the 1850s as operating without state support, as do all religious bodies in America. See "From Norwegian State Church to American Free Church," *Norwegian-American Studies*, XXV (1972), 186–224.

15. Olaus Fredrik Duus, *Frontier Parsonage: The Letters of Olaus*

Fredrik Duus, Norwegian Pastor in Wisconsin, 1855–1858 (North-field, Minnesota, 1947), vii. Translated by the Verdandi Study Club of Minneapolis and edited by Theodore C. Blegen.

16. Nelson and Fevold, *The Lutheran Church Among Norwegian Americans, 1890–1959*, 229, 238, and 251. A *Lutheran Hymnary* was published in 1912, and a new *Lutheran Service Book and Hymnal* in 1958.

17. Kenneth O. Bjork, *West of the Great Divide: Norwegian Migration to the Pacific Coast, 1847–1893* (Northfield, Minnesota, 1958), 480.

18. Kenneth O. Bjork, "Hvistendahl's Mission to San Francisco, 1870–75," *Norwegian-American Studies and Records*, XVI (1950), 1–63. Bjork, *West of the Great Divide*, 482–94 and 505.

19. Leola Nelson Bergmann, *Americans From Norway*, 212.

20. Carl Söyland, *Skrift i Sand* (Writing in the Sand), 25 (Oslo, 1954).

21. Andrew Nilsen Rygg, *Norwegians in New York, 1825–1925* (Brooklyn, New York, 1941), 268.

22. *Ibid.*, 88, 92–95, and 105.

23. Peder Stiansen, *History of the Norwegian Baptists in America* (Wheaton, Illinois, 1939), 21–23 and 27–28.

24. *Ibid.*, 34, 57, 76, 80, 86, and 107.

25. For the early history of Norwegian Methodists see Andrew Haagensen, *Den Norsk-Danske Methodismes Historie paa begge Sider Havet* (The History of Norwegian-Danish Methodism on Both Sides of the Ocean), Chicago, 1894, and Arlow W. Andersen, *The Salt of the Earth: A History of Norwegian-Danish Methodism in America* (Nashville, Tennessee, 1962), 11–81. The Washington Prairie congregation built a church structure in 1868. In 1973, largely through the efforts of Vesterheim, the Norwegian-American Museum in Decorah, the original structure was restored and dedicated, with Methodist Bishop Ole E. Borgen of the Northern European Area and veteran pastor Carl W. Schevenius of Minneapolis participating.

26. On Tank and Iverson see Joseph Schafer, "Scandinavian Moravians in Wisconsin," *Wisconsin Magazine of History*, XXIV, 25–38 (September, 1940), and Hjalmar Rued Holand, *My First Eighty Years* (New York, 1957), 131–44.

27. William Mulder, "Mormons from Scandinavia, 1850–1900: A Shepherded Migration," *Pacific Historical Review*, XXIII, 227–46 (August, 1954), and "Norwegian Forerunners among the Early Mormons," *Norwegian-American Studies and Records*, XIX, 46–61 (1956). The two articles are incorporated in Mulder's *Homeward*

to Zion: The Mormon Migration from Scandinavia (Minneapolis, 1957).

28. William Mulder, Homeward to Zion: The Mormon Migration from Scandinavia, 102 and 106.

29. C. A. Thorp, "Danske blandt Adventisterne i Amerika," in Peter S. Vig, Danske i Amerika, II, 251–61 (Minneapolis and Chicago, 1908).

30. Jacob Hodnefield, "Erik L. Petersen," Norwegian-American Studies and Records, XV, 176–84 (1949).

31. Nina Draxten, "Kristofer Janson's Beginning Ministry," Norwegian-American Studies, XXIII, 126–74 (1967).

32. Per Sveino, "Kristofer Janson and His American Experience," Americana Norvegica, III (Oslo, 1971), 88–104; subtitle: Studies in Scandinavian-American Interrelations. George T. Flom, "Kristofer Nagel Janson," Dictionary of American Biography, V, 612 (New York, 1932). Nils Bloch-Hoell discusses Janson, Björnson, and Hamsun on a related theme in "Norwegian Ideas of American Christianity," Americana Norvegica, IV (Oslo, 1973), 69–88.

Chapter Nine

1. Ole Rynning, True Account of America, 89. C. N. Stangeland to relatives, August 9, 1844, in Stavanger Amtstidende og Adresseavis (County News and Advertiser) of October 10, 1844.

2. Johannes W. C. Dietrichson, Reise blandt de norske Emigranter i "De forenede nordamerikanske Fristater" (Travel among the Norwegian emigrants in the United Free States of North America), 40. Raeder, America in the Forties, 136. Nordlyset (The Northern Light), November 8, 1849.

3. Democraten, July 27, 1850. Skandinaven, May 26, 1869. Fædrelandet og Emigranten, October 15, 1868. See also Laurence M. Larson, "Skandinaven, Professor Anderson, and the Yankee School," The Changing West and Other Essays, 118–25.

4. Skandinaven, January 9, 1874; January 9 and 16, and March 2, 1875.

5. Skandinaven, October 27, 1869; October 17, 1876; March 5, 1878. Rasmus B. Anderson, Life Story, 598. Laurence M. Larson, "Skandinaven, Professor Anderson, and the Yankee School," The Changing West and Other Essays, 139–42.

6. Hjalmar Hjorth Boyesen, "The Dangers of Unrestricted Immigration," The Forum, III, 533–42 (July, 1887) and "The Scandinavians in the United States," The North American Review, CLV, 526–35 (November, 1892).

7. Nils P. Haugen, *Pioneer and Political Reminiscences*, 95. Louise Phelps Kellogg, "The Bennett Law in Wisconsin," *Wisconsin Magazine of History*, II, 3–25 (September, 1918). Roger E. Wyman, "Wisconsin Ethnic Groups and the Election of 1890," *Wisconsin Magazine of History*, LI, 269–93 (Summer, 1968).

8. Lynwood Oyos, Professor of History at Augustana College, to Arlow W. Andersen, December 31, 1971, based upon Emil Erpestad's history of Augustana College.

9. Paul Knaplund, *Moorings Old and New: Entries in an Immigrant's Log* (Madison, Wisconsin, 1963), 183–99. For an appreciative appraisal see *Paul Knaplund* (Madison, Wisconsin, 1967), edited by Merle Curti, a long-time friend and colleague. This book contains essays on Knaplund as teacher, historian of the British Empire, his relations with the University of Wisconsin, and his publications.

10. Thorbjörn Eggen, "Oversigt over den Norsk-Lutherske Kirkes Historie i Amerika," *Norsk-Amerikanernes Festskrift*, 22–25. N. N. Rönning, *Fifty Years in America* (Minneapolis, 1938), 137–46. For an up-to-date history, see Carl H. Chislock, *From Fjord to Freeway: 100 Years of Augsburg College* (Minneapolis, 1969).

11. Leola Nelson Bergmann, *Americans From Norway*, 163–67. M. K. Bleken, "De Norsk-Amerikanske Skoler," *Norsk-Amerikanernes Festskrift*, 255. Theodore C. Blegen, *Norwegian Migration to America*, II, 519–26. David T. Nelson's *Luther College, 1861–1961* (Decorah, Iowa, 1961), a centennial publication of over 400 pages, fills the need of a comprehensive history.

12. Theodore C. Blegen, *Norwegian Migration to America*, II, 537. N. N. Rönning, *Fifty Years in America*, 121–30. Erik Hetle's *Lars Wilhelm Boe* (Minneapolis, 1949) covers the years of Rölvaag and Christiansen, who will be considered later in Chapters 10 and 11.

13. Lars W. Boe's introduction to P. M. Glasoe's *The Landstad-Lindeman Hymnbook* (Minneapolis, 1938), 3. Leola Nelson Bergmann, *Americans From Norway*, 167. See also Mrs. Bergmann's *Music Master of the Middle West: The Story of F. Melius Christiansen and the St. Olaf College Choir* (Minneapolis, 1944). The official history of the college is William C. Benson's *High on Manitou: A History of St. Olaf College, 1874–1949* (Northfield, 1949) and Joseph M. Shaw's *History of St. Olaf College* (Northfield, 1974).

14. For a helpful study, see Bert H. Narveson, "The Norwegian Lutheran Academies," *Norwegian-American Studies and Records*, XIV, 184–226 (1944).

15. Excellent biographies of Boyesen and Anderson have been published within the past few years. See Clarence A. Glasrud,

Hjalmar Hjorth Boyesen (Northfield, Minnesota, 1963) and Lloyd Hustvedt, *Rasmus Björn Anderson: Pioneer Scholar* (Northfield, 1966).

Chapter Ten

1. Birger Osland, *A Long Pull From Stavanger* (Northfield, Minnesota, 1945), 33–35. Arne Garborg (1851–1924), Norwegian poet and novelist, championed the use of *Landsmål*, language of the peasants rather than of the cities and the elite, in a movement toward language reform. The struggle continues today between *Nynorsk* (new Norwegian, formerly *Landsmål*) and Bokmål (book language, formerly *Riksmaal*).

2. Upon Hansen's death at the age of 89 in 1960, he was eulogized in the *Sons of Norway Viking*, LXVIII (March, 1971), 67, and in *Nordmanns-Forbundet*, LIII (Oslo, July, 1960), 176. As editor of the *Sons of Norway* he made English the official language and defended the change of name from *Sönner af Norge*. For Carl G. O. Hansen's article on organizational affairs see "Det norske foreningsliv i Amerika," *Norsk-Amerikanernes Festskrift* (Decorah, Iowa, 1914), 266–91.

3. See *Ygdrasil, 1896–1971* (Madison, Wisconsin, 1971), an anniversary booklet of 48 pages written by Olaf A. Hougen, assisted by Gerhard B. Naeseth. Over 600 Ygdrasil lectures, bound in a single volume, are deposited in the archives of the State Historical Society of Wisconsin. For a 75th anniversary evaluation see Harald S. Naess, "Ygdrasil Literary Society, 1896–1971," *Americana Norvegica* IV, 31–46. In 1967 Mrs. Gerhard (Milma) Naeseth wrote a history (mimeographed) of the Gudrid Reading Circle. *Western Viking* of Seattle (May 18, 1973) reports on a smaller Ygdrasil society, organized about twenty years ago in LaCrosse, Wisconsin.

4. Erik J. Friis, ed., *The Norwegian Club, Inc., 1904–1964* (Brooklyn, 1964). For the historical sketch by Friis see pages 13–27.

5. Karsten Roedder, *Av en Utvandreravis' Saga: Nordisk Tidende i New York gjennom 75 År* (From the Saga of an Emigrant Newspaper: *Nordisk Tidende* in New York through 75 Years), 18 and 42 Brooklyn, 1966).

6. Carl G. O. Hansen, *op. cit.*, 275. Jorgen Dahlie, *A Social History of Scandinavian Immigration, Washington State, 1895–1910*, 151; an unpublished doctoral dissertation, Washington State University, 1967.

7. Carl G. O. Hansen, *op. cit.*, 290.

8. Theodore C. Blegen, *Norwegian Migration to America*, II, 563. Arthur C. Paulsen and Kenneth Bjork, *"A Doll's House* on the

Prairie: The First Ibsen Controversy in America," *Norwegian-American Studies and Records*, XI (1940), 16. Arlow W. Andersen, "American Politics in 1880: Norwegian Observations," *Scandinavian Studies*, XL (August, 1968), 233–47. Thrane's plays are being prepared for publication by Henriette C. K. Naeseth.

9. Theodore C. Blegen, *Norwegian Migration to America*, II, 567. Carl G. O. Hansen, *op. cit.*, 277. *Minnesota Posten* (Minneapolis), January 11, 1974.

10. Carl Söyland, *Skrift i Sand* (Writing in the Sand), 254 (Oslo, 1954). Carl G. O. Hansen, *op. cit.*, 277.

11. Carl Söyland, *op. cit.*, 255–57.

12. Theodore C. Blegen, *Norwegian Migration to America*, II, 573–75. Jorgen Dahlie, *op. cit.*, 167. Frank Elkins, "Norwegian Influence on American Skiing," *The American-Scandinavian Review*, XXXV, 335–40 (December, 1947).

13. Carl G. O. Hansen, *op. cit.*, 286.

14. *Ibid.*, 287. Andreas Nilssen Rygg, *op. cit.*, 173.

15. Two official histories of the Sons of Norway have been published: Carl G. O. Hansen, *History of the Sons of Norway, 1895–1945* (Minneapolis, 1945) and Sverre Norborg, *An American Saga* (Minneapolis, 1970). For the later statistics see a report in *Decorah-Posten*, June 1, 1972.

16. Sverre Norborg, *An American Saga*, 97, 107, and 191.

17. Sverre Norborg, *op. cit.*, 184 and 187.

18. Johan Hambro, "The League of Norsemen," *The Norseman*, no. 4, 1964, 113–17. This magazine began publication in 1963 for the benefit of English readers.

19. Jacob Hodnefield, "The Norwegian-American Bygdelags and Their Publications," *Norwegian-American Studies and Records*, XVIII (1954), 163–232. See also Carl T. and Amy Narvestad, "The Bygdelags of Norse America," *American-Scandinavian Review*, LVIII (December, 1970), 376–79. Both articles have now been superseded by Odd Sverre Lovoll's "The Bygdelag Movement," in *Norwegian-American Studies*, XXV (1972), 3–26.

20. Earl Christmas, "Heirs to the Vikings in America," *Current History Magazine*, XXIII (October, 1925), 61–66.

21. Carl T. and Amy Narvestad, "The Bygdelags of Norse America," *American-Scandinavian Review*, LVIII (December, 1970), 376–79.

22. For specific information on the Foundation see Erik J. Friis, *The American-Scandinavian Foundation, 1910–1960: A Brief History* (New York, 1961).

23. Walter Johnson, "Fifty Years, 1911–1960," *Scandinavian Studies*, XXXII (February, 1960), 1–6.

24. Lloyd Hustvedt, "The Norwegian-American Historical Association and Its Antecedents," *Americana Norvegica*, III (Oslo, 1971), 294–306; the subtitle reads *Studies in Scandinavian Interrelations, Dedicated to Einar Haugen*, edited by Harald S. Naess and Sigmund Skard.

25. Knut Gjerset, "The Norwegian-American Historical Museum," *Norwegian-American Studies and Records*, VI (1931), 153–61. David T. Nelson, "The Norwegian-American Museum," *Sons of Norway Viking*, LXII (December, 1965), 300–301. In 1972 the Vesterheim Museum was notified of its accreditation by the American Association of Museums. At that time only 177 of about 7,000 museums in Canada and the United States had been so recognized.

Chapter Eleven

1. Waldemar Ager's essay, entitled "Norsk-amerikansk Skjönliteratur," appeared in *Norsk-Amerikanernes Festskrift* (Decorah, Iowa, 1914), 292–306.

2. Theodore C. Blegen, *Norwegian Migration to America: The American Transition* (Northfield, Minnesota, 1940), 585–86. Useful as surveys are three articles, all appearing in the *Norwegian-American Studies and Records* (*Studies* beginning in 1962): Aagot D. Hoidahl, "Norwegian-American Fiction, 1880–1928," V (1930), 61–83; Gerald H. Thorson, "First Sagas in a New World: A Study of the Beginnings of Norwegian-American Literature," XVII (1952), 108–29; and Dorothy Burton Skårdal, "The Scandinavian Immigrant Writer in America," XXI (1962), 14–53.

3. Laurence M. Larson, "Tellef Grundysen and the Beginnings of Norwegian-American Fiction," in *The Changing West* (Northfield, Minnesota, 1937), 49–66.

4. Aagot Hoidahl, "Norwegian-American Fiction," 65 and 67.

5. Waldemar Ager, "Norsk-amerikansk Skjönliteratur," in *Norsk-Amerikanernes Festskrift 1914*, 304.

6. *The Cultural Life of Modern America* was published in the Norwegian language in Copenhagen in 1889, upon Hamsun's return from abroad. A recent translation and edition is that of Barbara Morgridge (Harvard University Press, 1969). For an up-to-date comprehensive commentary see Harald Naess, *Knut Hamsun og Amerika* (Oslo, 1969). Hamsun's American connections are also presented in Sverre Arestad's "Hamsun and America," in *Norwegian-American Studies*, XXIV (1970), 148–92, and in Harald Naess's "American

Attitudes to Knut Hamsun," in *Americana Norvegica: Studies in Scandinavian-American Interrelations,* III (Oslo, 1971), 338–60. Paul Knaplund estimates the literary role of Hamsun in "Knut Hamsun, Triumph and Tragedy," in *Modern Age,* IX (Spring, 1965), 165–74. For press reactions in Norway see my "Knut Hamsun's America," in *Norwegian-American Studies,* XXIII (1967), 175–203.

7. Sverre Arestad, in the article cited above, analyzes five short stories by Hamsun: *Vagabonds Dager* (Vagabond Days), *Kvindeseir* (Feminine Victory), *Rædsel* (Fear), *Paa Prærien* (On the Prairie), and *Zachæus,* all America-based but written near the turn of the century in Norway. Tore Hamsun, *Knut Hamsun* (Oslo, 1959).

8. Waldemar Ager, *op. cit.,* 300. Aagot Hoidahl, *op. cit.,* 68. Einar Haugen, *Norge i Amerika* (Oslo, 1939), 104.

9. Gerald Thorson, "The Novels of Peer Strömme," *Norwegian-American Studies and Records,* XVIII (1954), 141–62. An English translation of *Halvor* by Inga B. Norstog and David T. Nelson was published in Decorah in 1960. It carries the title *Halvor: A Story of Pioneer Youth.* Strömme's reminiscences, never translated, were published posthumously as *Erindringer* (Minneapolis, Minnesota, 1923).

10. Theodore Jorgenson and Nora Solum, *Ole Edvart Rölvaag: A Biography* (New York, 1939), 301.

11. John Heitmann, "Julius B. Baumann: A Biographical Sketch," *Norwegian-American Studies and Records,* XV (1949), 140–75.

12. Aagot Hoidahl, *op. cit.,* 69.

13. Theodore C. Blegen, *Norwegian Migration to America,* II, 592. Aagot Hoidahl, *op. cit.,* 70.

14. Aagot Hoidahl, *op. cit.,* 75. Einar Haugen, *Norge i Amerika* (Oslo, 1939), 109.

15. Waldemar Ager, "Norsk-amerikansk Skjönliteratur," 298. Carl Söyland, *Skrift i Sand,* 151–53. Einar Haugen, *Norge i Amerika,* 110. Norstog's hand printing press is now on exhibit in the Vesterheim Museum in Decorah, Iowa.

16. On Boyesen see Clarence A. Glasrud, *Hjalmar Hjorth Boyesen* (Northfield, Minnesota, 1963); Laurence M. Larson, "Hjalmar Hjorth Boyesen," in *The Changing West* (Northfield, Minnesota, 1937), 82–115; and, Neil T. Eckstein, "The Marginal Man as Novelist: The Norwegian-American Writers, H. H. Boyesen, and O. E. Rölvaag as Critics of American Institutions" (An unpublished Ph.D. dissertation, University of Pennsylvania, 1965).

17. Per E. Seyersted appraises Boyesen in "Hjalmar Hjorth Boyesen: Outer Success, Inner Failure," *Americana Norvegica: Norwegian Contributions to American Studies,* I, 206–38 (Philadelphia, 1966).

Boyesen's skeptical attitude toward women is the subjèct of Per Seyersted's "The Drooping Lily: H. H. Boyesen as an Early American Misogynist," in *Americana Norvegica: Studies in Scandinavian-American Interrelations*, III (Oslo, 1971), 74–87. Cecyle S. Neidle presents a useful overview in *Great Immigrants* (New York, 1971), 181–202.

18. Aagot Hoidahl, *op. cit.*, 79–80. Lincoln Colcord, an intimate friend of Rölvaag, assisted in the translation into English. His eleven-page introduction is a masterful analysis of Rölvaag's mind and purpose.

19. See Theodore Jorgenson, "The Main Factors in Rölvaag's Authorship," *Norwegian-American Studies and Records*, X (1938), 135–51. Two memorial articles are helpful: Einar Haugen, "O. E. Rölvaag: Norwegian-American," *Ibid.*, VII (1933), 53–73, and Julius E. Olson, "Ole Edvart Rölvaag, 1876–1931: In Memoriam," *Ibid.*, VII (1933), 121–31. Jorgenson collaborated with Nora O. Solum to produce *Ole Edvart Rölvaag* (New York, 1939). More recent works are those of Gudrun Hovde Gvaale, *O. E. Rölvaag: Nordmann og amerikanar* (Bergen, 1962) and Paul Reigstad, *Rölvaag: His Life and Art* (Lincoln, Nebraska, 1972).

20. John T. Flanagan, "The Immigrant in Western Fiction," in *Immigration in American History* (Minneapolis, Minnesota, 1961), 79–95.

21. Henry Steele Commager, "Human Cost of the West," *Senior Scholastic*, LVIII (February 28, 1951), 10–11.

22. Kenneth O. Bjork, "Literature in Its Relation to Norwegian-American History," *Scandinavian Studies*, XXXVIII (February, 1966), 13–19.

23. Dorothy Burton Skårdahl, "The Scandinavian Immigrant Writer in America," 27. For a systematic listing of books and articles pertaining to Norwegians in America, readers are referred to the section on "Some Recent Publications" in the volumes of *Norwegian-American Studies*. Here one finds publications of many kinds: historical, biographical, poetic, and fictional. It is interesting to note that women of the second and third generations seem to have usurped the field of the immigrant novel, with contributions by Borghild Dahl, Kathryn Forbes, Lillian Gamble, Agnes Roisdal, Erna Oleson Xan, and Margarethe Erdahl Shank.

Chapter Twelve

1. Max Lerner, "Thorstein Veblen," *Dictionary of American Biography*, X, 241–44 (New York, 1936). Lerner recommends most

favorably Joseph Dorfman's *Thorstein Veblen and His America* (original edition, New York, 1934). Not available at the time of Dorfman's writing was Douglas F. Dowd, *Thorstein Veblen* (New York, 1966). See also Carlton Qualey's introduction to *Thorstein Veblen: The Carleton College Veblen Seminar Essays* (New York, 1968), 1–15. Veblen attacked the "captains of erudition" in *The Higher Learning in America: A Memorandum on the Conduct of Universities by Business Men* (1918).

2. Most authoritative and exhaustive on Norwegian immigrant seafaring are Knut Gjerset's two monographs: *Norwegian Sailors on the Great Lakes: A Chapter in the History of American Inland Transportation* (Northfield, Minnesota, 1928) and *Norwegian Sailors in American Waters: A Study in the History of Maritime Activity on the Eastern Seaboard* (Northfield, Minnesota, 1933).

3. Herman Weintraub, *Andrew Furuseth, Emancipator of the Seamen* (Berkeley, California, 1959) appears to be the only biography. See also Leola Bergmann, *Americans From Norway*, 225-33; Carl Söyland, *Skrift i Sand*, 47–50; Sören Röinestad and Conrad Wahle, "Andrew Furuseth," *Sons of Norway Viking*, LXV (1968), 242–43; George P. West, "Andrew Furuseth and the Radicals," *Survey*, XLVII (November 5, 1921), 207–209, and "Andrew Furuseth Stands Pat," *Survey*, LI (October 15, 1923), 86–90.

4. George W. Stephens, "Nelson Olsen Nelson," *Dictionary of American Biography*, VII, 419–20 (New York, 1934). Between 1902 and 1912 Nelson contributed many short articles to *The Independent*, a popular weekly national publication. They dealt with profit-sharing and related topics.

5. For the complete biography see Agnes M. Larson, *John A. Johnson: An Uncommon American* (Northfield, Minnesota, 1969). On Evinrude see Kenneth O. Bjork, "Ole Evinrude and the Outboard Motor," *Norwegian-American Studies and Records*, XII (1941), 167–77.

6. Florence M. Manning, "Carl G. Barth, 1860–1939: A Sketch," *Norwegian-American Studies and Records*, XIII (1943), 114–32. Kenneth O Bjork, *Saga in Steel and Concrete: Norwegian Engineers in America* (Northfield, Minnesota, 1947), 281–308.

7. Edward A. Duddy, "Victor Freemont Lawson," *Dictionary of American Biography*, VI (1936), 60–61. The best known biography is Charles H. Dennis, *Victor Lawson: His Time and Work* (Chicago, 1935).

8. Arthur E. Andersen, *Behind the Figures: Addresses and Articles by Arthur Andersen, 1913–1941* (Chicago, 1970); see pages

201–11 and 231–37. Birger Osland, *A Long Pull From Stavanger* (Northfield, Minnesota, 1945), 216.

9. "Making the Most of Time," *Nation's Business*, LVI (September, 1968), 80–86. "What Makes the Norwegian-American Watch King Tick?", *Sons of Norway Viking*, LXVI (1969), 39.

10. One of the more recent appraisals of Haakon Romnes's career is Richard L. Tobin's "Ma Bell's Long-Distance Runner," in *The Saturday Review* (January 22, 1972), 59–60. *The Saturday Review*, after canvassing over 250 businessmen, educators, and editors, named Romnes "businessman of the year 1971." Romnes retired in 1972. The American press reported his death in 1973.

11. Kenneth O. Bjork, *op. cit.*, 173–85, 185–206, and 209–12. Part of Hans Rude Jacobsen's personal story appears in *Growing Up in Norway* (New York, 1971; privately published).

12. *Ibid.*, 207–208 and 227–43. Sören C. Röinestad, *A Hundred Years with the Norwegians in the East Bay* (Oakland, California, 1963), 73.

13. "Ludvig Hektoen," *Encyclopedia Americana*, XIV (1969), 76. *Sons of Norway Viking*, LXVI (1969), 278. An excellent reference article on "Norwegian Emigrants with University Training, 1830–1880," is the work of Oystein Ore in the *Norwegian-American Studies and Records*, XIX (1956), 160–88. Ore himself was an internationally known mathematician, who served on the faculty of Yale University from 1927 to 1945.

14. Henning Sinding-Larsen on Trygve Gundersen in *Decorah-Posten*, November 2, 1972. "Adolf Gundersen" in *Who's Who in America*, XX (1938–1939), 1084.

15. The only biography appears to be Netta Wilson's *Alfred Owre: Dentistry's Militant Educator* (Minneapolis, 1937). Leola Bergmann, *op. cit.*, 252–54. Brenda Ueland on Alfred Owre in *Minnesota Posten* (Minneapolis), April 15 and 22, 1971. Miss Ueland, a granddaughter of Ole Gabriel Ueland, Norway's great peasant leader, writes from first-hand acquaintance with Dr. Owre.

16. A convincing work is J. Perriam Danton, *American Influences upon Norwegian Librarianship, 1890–1914* (Berkeley and Los Angeles, California, 1957). Arne Kildal, a citizen of Norway and one who also worked for a time in the Congressional library, played a stellar role in disseminating library techniques in Norway. He has featured Jahr in "Thorstein Jahr: A Norwegian-American Scholar," in *Americana Norvegica: Studies in Scandinavian-American Interrelations*, III (Oslo, 1971), 223–34. Jahr's many articles are listed by Thor Andersen in the same source, 235–36.

17. Lloyd Hustvedt, *Rasmus Björn Anderson, Pioneer Scholar*

(Northfield, Minnesota, 1966), 352. For a brief survey see Paul Knaplund, "Rasmus B. Anderson, Pioneer Crusader," *Norwegian-American Studies and Records*, XVIII (1954), 23–43.

18. See Einar Haugen's eulogy of his onetime mentors in "Wisconsin Pioneers in Scandinavian Studies: Anderson and Olson, 1875–1931," *Wisconsin Magazine of History*, XXXIV (1950), 28–39. Also George T. Flom, "Norwegian Language and Literature in American Universities," *Norwegian-American Studies and Records*, II (1929), 78–103.

19. Harald S. Naess and Sigmund Skard, editors, *Americana Norvegica: Studies in Scandinavian-American Interrelations Dedicated to Einar Haugen* (Olso, 1971); a complete compilation of Haugen's publications appears on pages 374–86.

20. Grace Raymond Hebard, "Agnes Mathilde Wergeland," *Dictionary of American Biography*, X (New York, 1936), part 2, 1–2. Perhaps the only biography is Maren Michelet's privately published work of 1916 entitled *Glimpses from Agnes Mathilde Wergeland's Life.* Inspired in part by Miss Wergeland's example, Miss Michelet introduced the study of Norse in the Minneapolis public high schools in 1910. Her efforts were soon augmented by Sigvald Stoylen, Dikka Reque, Pauline Farseth, and others.

21. Eric Blum, editor, *Grove's Dictionary of Music and Musicians*, III, 492–93 (New York, 1954; 5th edition). Carl G. O. Hansen, *My Minneapolis*, 89–91. Willa Cather's *Song of the Lark* is said to have been inspired by the life of Olive Fremstad. Mary Watkins Cushing also relates her story in *The Rainbow Bridge*.

22. Theodore C. Blegen, *Norwegian Migration to America*, II, 572. Leola Bergmann, *op. cit.*, 290.

23. Carl G. O. Hansen, *op. cit.*, 169–70.

24. Carl Söyland, *Skrift i sand*, 56–61.

25. Marion J. Nelson, "Herbjörn Gausta, Norwegian-American Painter," *Americana Norvegica: Studies in Scandinavian-American Interrelations*, III, 105–28. Carl G. O. Hansen reviews Gausta's work in *My Minneapolis*, 170–73.

26. Leola Bergmann, *op. cit.*, 289–90.

27. See Harry A. Stuhldreher, *Knute Rockne, Man Builder* (Philadelphia, Pennsylvania, 1931); Bonnie Skiles Rockne, editor, *The Autobiography of Knute K. Rockne* (Indianapolis, Indiana, 1931); and John Kieran, "Knute Kenneth Rockne," *Dictionary of American Biography*, VIII (New York, 1936), part 2, pages 67–68.

28. "Ernest O. Lawrence" in *Modern Men of Science* (New York, 1966), 286–87, and in Sören C. Röinestad, *A Hundred Years with Norwegians in the East Bay*, 25. Eric Sevareid writes nostalgically of

his home town, Velva, North Dakota, in "You Can Go Home Again," *Collier's* (May 11, 1956), 38–39 and 58–67.

Chapter Thirteen

1. Marcus Lee Hansen, *The Immigrant in American History* (Cambridge, Massachusetts, 1940), 208. Karsten Roedder, *Av en Utvandreravis' Saga: Nordisk Tidende i New York gjennom 75 År* [I], 53.

2. Louis L. Gerson, *The Hyphenate in Recent American Politics and Diplomacy* (Lawrence, Kansas, 1964), 18, 61, and 66.

3. *Decorah-Posten*, July 28 and August 14, 1914. Jon Wefald, *From Peasant Ideals to the Reform State: The Political Ideas and Attitudes of the Norwegians in the American Middle West, 1890–1917*, 163 and 169–74. Wefald cites in particular Chicago's *Skandinaven* of April 17, 1916, and the *Fargo Fram* (Forward) of February 22, 1917.

4. Odd S. Lovoll, "North Dakota's Norwegian-Language Press Views World War I, 1914–1917," *North Dakota Quarterly*, XXXIX (Winter, 1971), 73–84.

5. *Decorah-Posten*, April 10, 1917. Nils P. Haugen, *Pioneer and Political Reminiscences*, 176.

6. Karsten Roedder, *Av en Utvandreravis' Saga* [I], 55. Sverre Norborg, *An American Saga*, 87.

7. Karsten Roedder, *op. cit.*, 55–57.

8. *Ibid.*, 62–72. Brooklyn's *Nordisk Tidende*, February 28, 1918. *New York Times*, June 18, 1917; the *Times* reported that Norway had lost 281 ships since January.

9. Bent Vanberg, "Fifty Years Ago: How the Chr. Hannevig Case Involving Top Legal Brains of U.S. and Norway Became a Classic Contest," *Sons of Norway Viking*, LXIV (1967), 217. A. N. Rygg, *Norwegians in New York, 1825–1925*, 177–80.

10. Karsten Roedder, *op. cit.*, 73. According to Sture Lindmark of Sweden, the governor of Iowa forbade use of all foreign languages, even attempting to ban them on the telephone. See his *Swedish America, 1914–1932: Studies in Ethnicity with Emphasis on Illinois and Minnesota* (Uppsala, 1971), 67.

11. Karsten Roedder, *op. cit.*, 60.

12. Carl G. O. Hansen, *My Minneapolis*, 267. Sverre Norborg, *An American Saga*, 90–92.

13. Carl G. O. Hansen, *op. cit.*, 266. A. N. Rygg, *op. cit.*, 184–85.

14. Louis L. Gerson, *The Hyphenate in Recent American Politics and Diplomacy*, 15. Sverre Norborg, *op. cit.*, 88. Karsten Roedder, *op. cit.*, 61.

15. Karsten Roedder, *op. cit.*, 73–75. A. N. Rygg, *op. cit.*, 190.

16. Kenneth O. Bjork, *Saga in Steel and Concrete*, 355 and 430. For Magnus Swenson's previous accomplishments see chapter 12.

17. Karsten Roedder (*op. cit.*, 75) states that Norwegians of the Bay Ridge section of Brooklyn voted Republican, as usual, but that Norwegian laborers and craftsmen in New York City supported the Democrats. In fear of one-man rule under Wilson, or his replacement James M. Cox, *Nordisk Tidende* again gave its endorsement to the Republican candidates.

18. Louis L. Gerson, *op. cit.*, 108. A study financed by the Carnegie Corporation of New York emphasizes the sympathies of the American people and press toward foreign-language newspapers in the immediate postwar period. See Robert E. Park, *The Immigrant Press and Its Control* (Westport, Connecticut, 1970), 406; originally published in 1922.

19. Karsten Roedder, *op. cit.*, 93 and 101. Carl Söyland, *op. cit.*, 70–77.

20. Karsten Roedder, *op. cit.*, 108, 115–23, and 277. Ragnvald A. Nestos, "Norsemen—in America and at Home," *Review of Reviews*, LXXIII (February, 1926), 175–78. Nestos served as Governor of North Dakota from 1921 to 1925. Carl G. O. Hansen, *op. cit.*, 276–81. The present Leif Erikson Park is located between Fourth and Eighth Avenues, and between 66th and 67th Streets. On July 6, 1939, a Leif Erikson monument was dedicated there by Crown Prince Olav (now King Olav V).

21. For a Swedish-American point of view see Finis Herbert Capps, *From Isolationism to Involvement: The Swedish Immigrant Press in America, 1914–1945* (Chicago, 1966).

22. The friction between British and Norwegian forces in Norway is developed in Sverre Kjeldstadli's "Den norske militære motstand og SOE" (The Norwegian military resistance and SOE), in *Mellom nöytrale og allierte* (Between the neutrals and the allies) (Oslo, 1968), 239–64. SOE was the British Special Operations Executive, which had a Scandinavian branch.

23. Jeffrey G. Peterson "The United States' Changing Attitude toward Norway, 1940–1943," *Sons of Norway Viking*, LXIII (April, 1966), 78–79, 94–95, and 97. Leland Stowe's article appeared in *Life* magazine on May 6, 1940, only four weeks after the invasion. Erik J. Friis supplies a helpful treatment of "The Norwegian Government in Exile, 1940–45," in *Scandinavian Studies* (Seattle, Washington, 1965), 422–44.

24. Arne Kildal on Johan Aasgaard in *Minnesota Posten*, December 4, 1969. Obituary notice on William T. Evjue in *News of Norway*

(Norwegian Information Service, Washington, D.C.), May 1, 1970. Ralph Enger, *The History of the Norwegian Club of San Francisco*, 53, 59, and 65. Erik J. Friis, *The American-Scandinavian Foundation, 1910–1960: A Brief History*, 58.

25. "99th Infantry Battalion U.S. Army," *Sons of Norway Viking*, LXII (January, 1965), 24–25; no author indicated.

26. Leola Bergmann, *op. cit.*, 293. Torger Tokle could claim many records, both in Norway and in the United States. In the 56 ski-jumping meets in which he participated in America, he won first place in 48. *Nord-Norge* (June, 1949), 15–16; published in Grand Forks, North Dakota.

27. Leola Bergmann, *op. cit.*, 265. Kenneth O. Bjork, *Saga in Steel and Concrete*, 392.

28. Leola Bergmann, *op. cit.*, 264. *New Republic*, CXLVII (July 30, 1962), 4.

29. *Milwaukee Journal*, June 4, 1972, from the Associated Press. *Decorah-Posten*, May 25, 1972. A. N. Rygg, *op. cit.*, 210. Balchen died on October 17, 1973, in New York.

30. See "The Foreign Language Press," *Fortune*, XXII (November, 1940), 90–105 *passim*.

Chapter Fourteen

1. Carl J. Hambro, *Amerikaferd: Av Emigrasjonens Historie* (Oslo, 1935), 5 and 95–96. Later appraisals by Hambro may be seen in *Amerika på Skilleveien* (America at the Crossroads), Oslo (1936) and *Powerful America: Streiflys over de Forente Stater Idag* (Glimpses of the United States Today), Oslo (1939). One of Hambro's sons, Edvard, served (1971) as president of the General Assembly of the United Nations. Another son, Johan, has long served as secretary-general of Nordmanns-Forbundet (The League of Norsemen) with headquarters in Oslo.

2. Ingrid Semmingsen, *Veien mot vest*, II, 486 and 490.

3. Ingrid Semmingsen, "Utvandringen og kontakt med Amerika," *Amerika och Norden* (Stockholm, 1964), 65–74; volume 1 of *Publications of the Nordic Association for American Studies*, edited by Lars Åhnebrink.

4. Paul Knaplund, "H. Tambs Lyche: Propagandist for America," *Norwegian-American Studies*, XXIV (1970), 102–11.

5. Arne Kildal, "Nordmenn jeg møtte i Amerika: Lauritz S. Swenson," *Minnesota Posten*, October 30, 1969.

6. Library interrelations are well presented in J. Periam Danton's *United States Influence on Norwegian Librarianship, 1890–1940* (Berkeley and Los Angeles, California, 1957).

7. Arne Kildal, "Pressen og Brobyggingen: Hilsen til *Decorah-Posten* paa 60-Aarsdagen" (The Press and Bridge-building; Greetings to *Decorah-Posten* on its 60th Anniversary), *Decorah-Posten*, September 7, 1934. Karsten Roedder, *Av en Utvandreravis' Saga* [I], 200.

8. Halvdan Koht, "Utsyn til Amerkansk Historie" (Outlook upon American History), *Syn og Segn* (Views and Legends), XVI, 1–11 (Christiania, 1910). *Den Amerikanske Nasjonen i Upphav og Reising* (The American Nation in its Origin and Rise) (Christiania, 1920) and *Pengemagt og Arbeid i Amerika* (Money Power and Labor in America) (Christiania, 1910).

9. Halvdan Koht, *The American Spirit in Europe: A Survey of Transatlantic Influences* (Philadelphia, Pennsylvania, 1949), 274–77.

10. Halvdan Koht, *op. cit.*, 84–98, 166–75, and 242.

11. Halvdan Koht, *Education of an Historian* (New York, 1957), 178–84 and 198–99; translated from the Norwegian by Erik Wahlgren. Sigmund Skard's obituary remarks in *American Studies in Scandinavia*, no. 1 (Summer, 1968), 25; edited by Sune Åkerman and published semiannually in Uppsala, Sweden.

12. Bjørn Gabrielsen, *Martin Tramæl Ser Tilbake* (Martin Tranmael Looks Back), 31–40 (Oslo, 1959). Aksel Zachariassen, *Fra Marcus Thrane til Martin Tranmæl* (Oslo, 1962), 104–28 and 149–50.

13. The quotation is taken from John E. Norton, "Robert Baird, Presbyterian Missionary to Sweden of the 1840s: His View of American Manifest Destiny and His Impact upon Early Swedish Emigration," *The Swedish Pioneer Historical Quarterly*, XXIII (July, 1972), 151–67. Wilhelm Keilhau, *Det norske folks liv og historie*, IX, 135 (Oslo, 1931). In a chapter entitled "Cross Currents" Franklin D. Scott expands upon the theme of American influences; see his *The United States and Scandinavia* (Cambridge, Massachusetts, 1950), 79–88. See also Einar Haugen, "Norway and America: The Ties That Bind," *Wisconsin Magazine of History*, XXXVIII (Spring, 1955), 139–44.

14. *News of Norway*, April 10, 1967; published by the Norwegian Information Service, Washington, D.C.

15. "Vor egen Heimskringla" (Our own Heimskringla), in *Skandinavens Almanak og Kalender* (Chicago, 1935), 43–45.

16. Henriette C. K. Naeseth, "Kristian Prestgard: An Appreciation," *Norwegian-American Studies and Records*, XV (1949), 131–39. Koht's letter appeared in *Decorah-Posten* of April 26, 1945. *En sommer i Norge* was published in Minneapolis in 1928.

17. Karsten Roedder, *Av en Utvandreravis' Saga* [I] 284–86. At the present time only four Norwegian-American newspapers are being published: *Nordisk Tidende*, edited by Sigurd Daasvand; *Vin-*

land, edited by Bertram Jensenius; *Minnesota Posten,* edited by Jenny Alvilde Johnsen; and *Western Viking,* edited by Henning C. Boe. The name of Eyvind J. Evans, contributing editor to *Minnesota Posten,* deserves special recognition. His self-effacing and impressive column, written in nynorsk, has introduced many a neglected figure to older readers especially.

18. See Erik J. Friis, *The American-Scandinavian Foundation, 1910–1960: A Brief History* (New York, 1961).

19. Hellick O. Haugen, "Pioneer of the West," *The Norseman,* no. 3 (1972), 72–75. The article features Snowshoe Thompson. *Decorah-Posten* bade farewell to its readers on December 28, 1972. This weekly would have observed its centennial in 1974.

The Sesquicentennial celebrations in Norway are being arranged by a committee named by the Ministry of Foreign Affairs, with Knut Tredt as chairman. In the U.S. sesquicentennial commissions have been established in Minneapolis, New York, Chicago, and Seattle, in addition to a group in Ottawa, Ill. They cooperate through a National Coordinating Committee, of which Dr. Arthur O. Davidson was Chairman in 1973; Dr. Gordon Mork headed the Committee in 1974; and Dr. Davidson is again at the helm in 1975.

Note should also be taken of the Cleng Peerson Memorial Institute in Stavanger, founded by Georg Joa, which is planned to be a comprehensive library and archive dealing with Norwegian-American immigration to the U.S.

20. Maldwyn Allyn Jones, *American Immigration* (Chicago, 1960), 319. Milton M. Gordon, *Assimilation in American Life: The Role of Race, Religion, and National Origins* (New York, 1964), 139–40. Rudolph J. Vecoli, "Ethnicity: A Neglected Dimension of American History," *American Studies in Scandinavia,* no. 4, 5–7 (Summer, 1970), published in Stockholm and edited by Sune Åkerman.

21. See Franklin D. Scott, "The Study of the Effects of Emigration," *Scandinavian Economic History Review,* VIII (1960), 161–74. For an earlier study see B. J. Hovde, "Notes on the Effects of Emigration upon Scandinavia," *Journal of Modern History,* VI (September, 1934), 253–79.

Selected Bibliography

For additional references to books and articles
see the chapter notes

Monographic and General Works

AGER, WALDEMAR. *Oberst Heg og Hans Gutter.* Eau Claire, Wisconsin, 1916.

ANDERSEN, ARLOW W. *The Immigrant Takes His Stand: The Norwegian Immigrant Press and American Public Affairs, 1847 to 1872.* Northfield, Minnesota, 1953.

—————. *The Salt of the Earth: A History of Norwegian-Danish Methodism in America.* Nashville, Tennessee, 1962.

ANDERSON, RASMUS B. *First Chapter of Norwegian Immigration.* Madison, Wisconsin, 1915.

BENSON, WILLIAM C. *High on Manitou: A History of St. Olaf College, 1874–1949.* Northfield, Minnesota, 1949.

BERGMANN, LEOLA NELSON. *Americans from Norway.* Philadelphia, Pennsylvania, 1950.

BJORK, KENNETH O. *Saga in Steel and Concrete: Norwegian Engineers in America.* Northfield, Minnesota, 1947.

—————. *West of the Great Divide: Norwegian Migration to the Pacific Coast, 1847–1893.* Northfield, Minnesota, 1958.

BLEGEN, THEODORE C. *Grass Roots History.* Minneapolis, Minnesota, 1947.

—————. *Norwegian Migration to America, 1825–1860.* Northfield, Minnesota, 1931.

—————. *Norwegian Migration to America: The American Transition.* Northfield, Minnesota, 1940.

BUSLETT, O. A. *Det Femtende Regiment Wisconsin Frivillige.* Decorah, Iowa, n.d.

CHISLOCK, CARL H. *From Fjord to Freeway: 100 Years of Augsburg College.* Minneapolis, Minnesota, 1969.

CLAUSEN, CLARENCE A., and ANDREAS ELVIKEN. (Eds.) *A Chronicle of Old Muskego.* Northfield, Minnesota, 1951.

COMMAGER, HENRY STEELE. (Ed.) *Immigration in American History: Essays in Honor of Theodore C. Blegen.* Minneapolis, 1961.

[251]

CORSI, EDWARD. *In the Shadow of Liberty: The Chronicle of Ellis Island.* New York, 1937.

DANTON, J. PERIAM. *United States Influence on Norwegian Librarianship, 1890–1940.* Berkeley and Los Angeles, California, 1957.

DIETRICHSON, JOHANNES W. C. *Reise blandt de norske Emigranter i "De forenede nordamerikanske Fristater."* Christiania (Oslo), 1846.

EVJEN, JOHN O. *Scandinavian Immigrants in New York, 1630–1674.* Minneapolis, 1916.

FRIIS, ERIK J. *The American-Scandinavian Foundation, 1910–1960: A Brief History.* New York, 1961.

—————. (Ed.) *The Norwegian Club, Inc., 1904–1964.* Brooklyn, New York, 1964.

GERSON, LOUIS L. *The Hyphenate in Recent American Politics and Diplomacy.* Lawrence, Kansas, 1964.

GJERSET, KNUT. *Norwegian Sailors on the Great Lakes: A Chapter in the History of American Inland Transportation.* Northfield, 1928.

—————. *Norwegian Sailors in American Waters: A Study in the History of Maritime Activity on the Eastern Seaboard.* Northfield, 1933.

HAAGENSEN, ANDREW. *Den Norsk-Danske Methodismes Historie paa begge Sider Havet.* Chicago, 1894.

HAMBRO, CARL J. *Amerikaferd: Av Emigrasjonens Historie.* Oslo, 1935.

HAMSUN, KNUT. *The Cultural Life of Modern America.* Translated from the Norwegian by Barbara G. Morgridge. Cambridge, Massachusetts, 1969. Originally published in Norwegian in 1889.

HANSEN, CARL G. O. *History of the Sons of Norway, 1895–1945.* Minneapolis, 1945.

—————. *My Minneapolis: A Chronicle of What Has Been Learned and Observed about the Norwegians in Minneapolis Through One Hundred Years.* Minneapolis, 1956.

HAUGEN, EINAR. *Norge i Amerika.* Oslo, 1939.

HOLAND, HJALMAR RUED. *De Norske Settlementers Historie.* Ephraim, Wisconsin, 1908.

JENSON, ANDREW. *History of the Scandinavian Mission.* Salt Lake City, Utah, 1927.

JOHNSON, JOHN A. *Det Skandinaviske Regiments Historie.* La Crosse, Wisconsin, 1869.

JONASSEN, CHRISTEN T. *The Norwegians in Bay Ridge: A Sociological Study of an Ethnic Group.* Ph.D. dissertation, New York University, 1947.

Selected Bibliography [253]

KOHT, HALVDAN. *The American Spirit in Europe: A Survey of Trans-atlantic Influences.* Philadelphia, 1949.

LANGELAND, KNUD. *Nordmændene i Amerika: Nogle Optegnelser om De Norskes Udvandring til Amerika.* Chicago, 1888.

LARSON, LAURENCE M. *The Changing West and Other Essays.* Northfield, 1937.

MULDER, WILLIAM. *Homeward to Zion: The Mormon Migration from Scandinavia.* Minneapolis, 1957.

NELSON, DAVID T. *Luther College, 1861–1961.* Decorah, Iowa, 1961.

NELSON, E. CLIFFORD (Ed.). *A Pioneer Churchman. J. W. C. Dietrichson in Wisconsin, 1844–1850.* New York, 1973.

NELSON, E. CLIFFORD, and EUGENE L. FEVOLD. *The Lutheran Church Among Norwegian-Americans: A History of the Evangelical Lutheran Church.* 2 volumes. Minneapolis, 1960.

NORBORG, SVERRE. *An American Saga: A History of the Sons of Norway in the United States and Canada.* Minneapolis, 1969.

PARK, ROBERT EZRA. *The Immigrant Press and Its Control.* New York, 1922.

QUALEY, CARLTON C. *Norwegian Settlement in the United States.* Northfield, 1938.

REIERSEN, JOHAN REINERT. *Veiviser for norske Emigranter til de Forenede Nordamerikanske Stater og Texas.* Christiania, 1844.

ROEDDER, KARSTEN. *Av En Utvandreravis' Saga: Nordisk Tidende i New York gjennom 75 År.* [1] Brooklyn, 1966, II, 1968.

ROHNE, JOHN MAGNUS. *Norwegian American Lutheranism up to 1872.* New York, 1926.

RÖINESTAD, SÖREN C. *A Hundred Years with the Norwegians in the East Bay.* Mimeographed. Oakland, California, 1963.

RÖLVAAG, OLE EDVART. *Giants in the Earth: A Saga of the Prairie.* Translated by Lincoln Colcord from the Norwegian. New York and London, 1927.

RÖNNING, N. N. *The Saga of Old Muskego.* Waterford, Wisconsin, 1943.

RYGG, ANDREW NILSEN. *Norwegians in New York, 1825–1925.* Brooklyn, 1941.

RYNNING, OLE. *True Account of America for the Information and Help of Peasant and Commoner.* Translated and edited by Theodore C. Blegen. Minneapolis, 1926. Originally published in Norwegian in Christiania, 1838.

SCOTT, FRANKLIN D. *The United States and Scandinavia.* Cambridge, Massachusetts, 1950.

SEMMINGSEN, INGRID. *Veien mot Vest: Utvandringen fra Norge til Amerika, 1825–1915.* 2 volumes. Oslo, 1941 and 1950.

STIANSEN, PEDER. *History of the Norwegian Baptists in America.* Wheaton, Illinois, 1939.

STINE, THOMAS OSTENSON. *Scandinavians on the Pacific, Puget Sound.* Seattle, 1900.

SVEJDA, GEORGE. *Castle Garden as an Immigrant Depot, 1855–1890.* Washington, D.C., 1968. An administrative report of the Division of History, Office of Archeology and Historic Preservation, United States Department of the Interior.

WEFALD, JON. *A Voice of Protest: Norwegians in American Politics, 1890–1917.* Northfield, 1971.

WIST, JOHANNES B. (Ed.) *Norsk-Amerikanernes Festskrift 1914.* Decorah, 1914.

Biographical Works

ANDERSON, RASMUS B. *Life Story of Rasmus B. Anderson.* Madison, Wisconsin, 1915.

BERGMANN, LEOLA NELSON. *Music Master of the Middle West: The Story of F. Melius Christiansen and the St. Olaf College Choir.* Minneapolis, 1944.

BLEGEN, THEODORE C. (Ed.) *The Civil War Letters of Colonel Hans Christian Heg.* Northfield, 1936.

BROHAUG, CHRISTOPHER O., and J. EISTEINSEN. *Kortfattet beretning om Elling Eielsens liv og virksomhed.* Chicago, 1883.

CURTI, MERLE. (Ed.) *Paul Knaplund.* Madison, 1967.

DOWD, DOUGLAS F. *Thorstein Veblen.* New York, 1966.

DUUS, OLAUS FREDRIK. *Frontier Parsonage: The Letters of Olaus Fredrik Duus, Norwegian Pastor in Wisconsin, 1855–1858.* Translated by the Verdandi Study Club of Minneapolis, and edited by Theodore C. Blegen. Northfield, 1947.

ECKSTEIN, NEIL T. *The Marginal Man as Novelist: The Norwegian-American Writers, H. H. Boyesen and O. E. Rölvaag as Critics of American Institutions.* Unpublished Ph.D. dissertation, University of Pennsylvania, 1965.

FARSETH, PAULINE, and THEODORE C. BLEGEN. (Eds.) *Frontier Mother: The Letters of Gro Svendsen.* Northfield, 1950.

GLASRUD, CLARENCE A. *Hjalmar Hjorth Boyesen.* Northfield, 1963.

GVAALE, GUDRUN HOVDE. *O. E. Rölvaag: Nordmann og amerikaner.* Bergen, 1962.

HAUGE, ALFRED. *Hundevakt.* Oslo, 1964.

————. *Landkjenning.* Oslo, 1965.

————. *Ankerfeste.* Oslo, 1966. (A fictional trilogy on Cleng Peerson)

HAUGEN, NILS P. *Pioneer and Political Reminiscences*. Reprinted from the *Wisconsin Magazine of History*, XI–XIII (1927–1929). Madison, n.d.

HUSTVEDT, LLOYD. *Rasmus Björn Anderson, Pioneer Scholar*. Northfield, 1966.

JORGENSON, THEODORE, and NORA O. SOLUM. *Ole Edvart Rölvaag: A Biography*. New York, 1939.

KNAPLUND, PAUL. *Moorings Old and New: Entries in an Immigrant Log*. Madison, 1963.

KOHT, HALVDAN. *Education of an Historian*. New York, 1957. Translated from the Norwegian by Erik Wahlgren.

————. *Marcus Thrane. Til Hundreaarsdagen. Oktober 14*. Christiania, 1917.

LARSEN, KAREN. *Laur. Larsen: Pioneer College President*. Northfield, 1936.

LARSON, AGNES M. *John A. Johnson: An Uncommon American*. Northfield, 1969.

LARSON, LAURENCE M. *The Log Book of a Young Immigrant*. Northfield, 1939.

MUNCH, PETER A. and HELENE. (Translators) *The Strange American Way: Letters from Wiota, Wisconsin, 1855–1859 by Caja Munch and An American Adventure, by Johan Storm Munch*. Carbondale, Illinois, 1970.

NAESS, HARALD S. *Knut Hamsun og Amerika*. Oslo, 1969.

NELSON, DAVID T. (Ed.) *The Diary of Elisabeth Koren, 1853–1855*. Northfield, 1955.

NORBORG, SVERRE. *Hans Nielsen Hauge. Biografi*. 2 volumes. Oslo, 1966 and 1970.

ODLAND, MARTIN W. *The Life of Knute Nelson*. Minneapolis, 1926.

OSLAND, BIRGER. *A Long Pull from Stavanger: The Reminiscences of a Norwegian Immigrant*. Northfield, 1945.

QUALEY, CARLTON C. (Ed.) *Thorstein Veblen: The Carleton College Veblen Seminar Essays*. New York, 1968.

RAAEN, AAGOT. *Grass of the Earth: Immigrant Life in the Dakota Country*. Northfield, 1950.

RAEDER, OLE MUNCH. *America in the Forties: The Letters of Ole Munch Raeder*. Translated and edited by Gunnar J. Malmin. Minneapolis, 1929.

REIGSTAD, PAUL. *Rölvaag: His Life and Art*. Lincoln, Nebraska, 1972.

RÖNNING, N. N. *Fifty Years in America*. Minneapolis, 1938.

SÖYLAND, CARL. *Skrift i Sand*. Oslo, 1954.

STRÖMME, PEER. *Erindringer* (Reminiscences). Minneapolis, 1923.

————. *Halvor: A Story of Pioneer Youth.* Translated from the Norwegian by Inga B. Norstog and David T. Nelson. Decorah, 1960.

SWANSEN, H. FRED. *The Founder of St. Ansgar.* Life of Claus L. Clausen. Blair, Nebraska, 1949.

UELAND, ANDREAS. *Recollections of an Immigrant.* New York, 1929.

ULVESTAD, MARTIN. *Nordmændene i Amerika: Deres historie og rekord.* 2 volumes. Minneapolis, 1907 and 1913.

WEINTRAUB, HYMAN. *Andrew Furuseth, Emancipator of the Seamen.* Berkeley, California, 1959.

Articles

AGER, WALDEMAR. "Norsk-Amerikansk Skjönliteratur," *Norsk-Amerikanernes Festskrift* (Decorah, Iowa, 1914), 292–306.

ANDERSEN, ARLOW W. "Knut Hamsun's America," *Norwegian-American Studies,* XXIII (Northfield, Minnesota, 1967), 175–203.

ARESTAD, SVERRE. "Hamsun and America," *Norwegian-American Studies,* XXIV (1970), 148–92.

BENSON, THOMAS I. "Gold, Salt Air, and Callouses," *Norwegian-American Studies,* XXIV (1970), 193–220.

BJORK, KENNETH O. "Literature in Its Relation to Norwegian-American History," *Scandinavian Studies,* XXXVIII (Seattle, Washington, February, 1966), 13–19.

BLEKEN, M. K. "De Norske-Amerikanske Skoler," *Norsk-Amerikanernes Festskrift* (1914), 245–65.

CARLSSON, STEN. "Scandinavian Politicians in Minnesota Around the Turn of the Century," *Americana Norvegica: Studies in Scandinavian-American Interrelations,* III (Oslo, 1971), 237–71.

CLAUSEN, CLARENCE A., and DERWOOD JOHNSON. "Norwegian Soldiers in the Confederate Forces," *Norwegian-American Studies,* XXV (1972), 105–41.

DIESERUD, JUUL. "Nordmænd i det Offentlige og Politiske Liv," *Norsk-Amerikanernes Festskrift,* 307–29.

DRAXTEN, NINA. "Kristofer Janson's Beginning Ministry," *Norwegian-American Studies,* XXIII (1967), 126–74.

ECKSTEIN, NEIL T. "The Social Criticism of Ole Edvart Rölvaag," *Norwegian-American Studies,* XXIV (1970), 112–36.

EGGEN, TH. "Oversigt over den Norsk-Lutherske Kirkes Historie i Amerika," *Norsk-Amerikanernes Festskrift,* 204–44.

FEVOLD, EUGENE L. "The Norwegian Immigrant and His Church," *Norwegian-American Studies,* XXIII (1967), 3–16.

GJERSET, KNUT. "The Norwegian-American Historical Museum," *Norwegian-American Studies and Records,* VI (1931), 153–61.

HAMBRO, JOHAN. "The League of Norsemen," *The Norseman*, no. 4 (Oslo, 1964), 113–17.

HANSEN, CARL G. O. "Det Norske Foreningsliv i Amerika," *Norsk-Amerikanernes Festskrift*, 266–91.

————. "Pressen til borgerkrigens slutning," *Norsk-Amerikanernes Festskrift*, 9–40.

HASSING, ARNE. "Norway's Organized Response to Emigration," *Norwegian-American Studies*, XXV (1972), 54–79.

HAUGEN, EINAR I. "A Critique and a Bibliography of the Writings of Rasmus B. Anderson," *Wisconsin Magazine of History*, XX (1959), 255–68.

————. "Pastor Dietrichson of Old Koshonong," *Wisconsin Magazine of History*, XXIX (1946), 301–18.

————. "Thor Helgeson: Schoolmaster and Raconteur," *Norwegian-American Studies*, XXIV (1970), 3–28.

————. "O. E. Rölvaag: Norwegian-American," *Norwegian-American Studies*, VII (1933), 53–73.

————. "Wisconsin Pioneers in Scandinavian Studies, Anderson and Olson, 1875–1931," *Wisconsin Magazine of History*, XXXIV (1950), 28–39.

HEITMANN, JOHN. "Julius B. Baumann: A Biographical Sketch," *Norwegian-American Studies and Records*, XV (1949), 140–75.

————. "Ole Edvart Rölvaag," *Norwegian-American Studies and Records*, XII (1941), 144–66.

HODNEFIELD, JACOB. "Norwegian-American Bygdelags and Their Publications," *Norwegian-American Studies and Records*, XVIII (1954), 163–232.

HOIDAHL, AAGOT D. "Norwegian-American Fiction, 1880–1928," *Norwegian-American Studies and Records*, V (1930), 61–83.

HOVDE, BRYNJOLF J. "Notes on the Effects of Emigration upon Scandinavia," *Journal of Modern History*, VI (September, 1934), 253–79.

HUSTVEDT, LLOYD. "The Norwegian-American Historical Association and its Antecedents," *Americana Norvegica: Studies in Scandinavian-American Interrelations*, III (Oslo, 1971), 294–306.

JOHNSON, WALTER. "Fifty Years, 1911–1960," *Scandinavian Studies*, XXXII (February, 1960), 1–6.

JORGENSON, THEODORE. "The Main Factors in Rölvaag's Authorship," *Norwegian-American Studies and Records*, X (1938), 135–51.

KILDAL, ARNE. "Torstein Jahr: A Norwegian-American Scholar," *Americana Norvegica: Studies in Scandinavian-American Interrelations*, III (Oslo, 1971), 223–34.

KNAPLUND, PAUL. "Rasmus B. Anderson, Pioneer and Crusader," *Norwegian-American Studies and Records*, XVIII (1954), 23–43.

————. "H. Tambs Lyche: Propagandist for America," *Norwegian-American Studies*, XXIV (1970), 102–11. Translated from the Norwegian by Kenneth O. Bjork from *Nordmanns-Forbundet*, LVII (June, 1964), 119–21.

LARSON, LAURENCE M. "The Norwegian Element in the Northwest," *American Historical Review*, XL (October, 1944), 69–81.

————. "The Norwegian Pioneer in the Field of American Scholarship," *Norwegian-American Studies and Records*, II (1927), 62–77.

LOVOLL, ODD SVERRE. "The Bygdelag Movement," *Norwegian-American Studies*, XXV (1972), 3–26.

————. "North Dakota's Norwegian-Language Press Views World War I, 1914–1917," *North Dakota Quarterly*, XXXIX (Winter, 1971), 73–84.

————. "The Norwegian Press in North Dakota," *Norwegian-American Studies*, XXIV (1970), 78–101.

MALMIN, GUNNAR. (Translator and editor) "Bishop Jacob Neumann's Word of Admonition to the Peasants," *Norwegian-American Studies and Records*, I (1926), 95–109.

MANNING, FLORENCE M. "Carl G. Barth, 1860–1939: A Sketch," *Norwegian-American Studies and Records*, XIII (1943), 114–32.

MULDER, WILLIAM. "Mormons from Scandinavia, 1850–1900: A Shepherded Migration," *Pacific Historical Review*, XXIII (August, 1954), 227–46.

————. "Norwegian Forerunners Among the Early Mormons," *Norwegian-American Studies and Records*, XIX (1956), 46–61.

NAESETH, HENRIETTE C. K. "Kristian Prestgard: An Appreciation," *Norwegian-American Studies and Records*, XV (1949), 131–39.

NAESS, HARALD S. "American Attitudes to Knut Hamsun," *Americana Norvegica: Studies in Scandinavian-American Interrelations*, III (Oslo, 1971), 338–60.

————. "Knut Hamsun and America," *Scandinavian Studies*, XXXIX (November, 1967), 305–28.

NARVESON, B. H. "The Norwegian Lutheran Academies," *Norwegian-American Studies and Records*, XIV (1944), 184–226.

NARVESTAD, CARL T. and AMY. "The Bygdelags of Norse America," *The American-Scandinavian Review*, LVIII (December, 1970), 376–79.

NELSON, DAVID T. "Knut Gjerset," *Norwegian-American Studies*, XXV (1972), 27–53.

NELSON, MARION J. "Herbjörn Gausta, Norwegian-American Painter," *Americana Norvegica: Studies in Scandinavian-American Inter-relations*, III (Oslo, 1971), 105–28.

OLSON, JULIUS E. "Ole Edvart Rölvaag, 1876–1931: In Memoriam," *Norwegian-American Studies and Records*, VII (1933), 121–31.

ORE, OYSTEIN. "Norwegian Emigrants with University Training, 1830–1880," *Norwegian-American Studies and Records*, XIX (1956), 160–88.

PETERSON, JEFFREY G. "The United States' Changing Attitude To-ward Norway, 1940–1943," *Sons of Norway Viking*, LXIII (April, 1966), 78–79, 94–95, and 97.

PREUS, J. C. K. "From Norwegian State Church to American Free Church," *Norwegian-American Studies*, XXV (1972), 186–224.

REYMERT, MARTIN L. "James Denoon Reymert and the Norwegian Press," *Norwegian-American Studies and Records*, XII (1941), 79–90.

SCHAFER, JOSEPH. "Scandinavian Moravians in Wisconsin," *Wisconsin Magazine of History*, XXIV (September, 1940), 25–38.

SCOTT, FRANKLIN D. "American Influence in Norway and Sweden," *Journal of Modern History*, XVIII (March, 1946), 38–44.

––––––. "The Dual Heritage of the Scandinavian Immigrant," *The Swedish Pioneer Historical Quarterly*, XXII (July, 1971), 119–35.

––––––. "The Immigrant Theme in the Framework of National Groups," *Immigration in American History* (Minneapolis, 1961), 115–25.

SEMMINGSEN, INGRID. "Utvandring og kontakt med Amerika," *Amerika och Norden* (Stockholm, 1964), 65–74.

SKÅRDAL, DOROTHY. "The Scandinavian Immigrant Writer in Amer-ica," *Norwegian-American Studies*, XXI (1962), 14–53.

SOLBERG, CARL FREDRIK. "Reminiscences of a Pioneer Editor," *Norwegian-American Studies and Records*, I (1926), 134–46.

STEPHENSON, GEORGE M. "The Mind of the Scandinavian Immigrant," *Norwegian-American Studies and Records*, IV (1929), 63–73.

STILL, BAYRD. "Norwegian-Americans and Wisconsin Politics in the Forties," *Norwegian-American Studies and Records*, VIII (1934), 58–64.

STOYLEN, SIGVALD. "Streiflys over Marcus Thranes Liv og Om-skiftende Virke i Amerika," *Nordisk Tidende* (Brooklyn, March 4, 1965).

SVEINO, PER. "Kristofer Janson and His American Experience," *Americana Norvegica: Studies in Scandinavian-American In-terrelations*, III, (Oslo, 1971), 88–104.

THORSON, GERALD H. "First Sagas in a New World: A Study of the Beginnings of Norwegian-American Literature," *Norwegian-American Studies and Records*, XVII (1952), 108–29.

————. "The Novels of Peer Strömme," *Norwegian-American Studies and Records*, XVIII (1954), 141–62.

TOLO, HAROLD M. "The Political Position of *Emigranten* in the Election of 1852," *Norwegian-American Studies and Records*, VIII (1934), 92–111.

WESTERGAARD, WALDEMAR. (Translator and editor). "Marcus Thrane in America: Some Unpublished Letters, 1880–1884," *Norwegian-American Studies and Records*, IX (1936), 67–76.

WIST, JOHANNES B. "Pressen efter Borgerkrigen," *Norsk-Amerikanernes Festskrift* (1914), 41–203.

WYMAN, ROGER E. "Wisconsin Ethnic Groups and the Election of 1890," *Wisconsin Magazine of History*, LI (Summer, 1968), 269–93.

Norwegian and Norwegian-American Newspapers

Den Norske Rigstidende (Christiania), May 25, 1837.

Christianssandsposten, February 23, 1843.

Stavanger Amtstidende og Adresseavis, October 10, 1844.

Drammens Adresse, May 18, 1847.

Nordlyset (Muskego, Rochester, and Racine, Wisconsin), August 5, 12, and 19; September 2, 1847. April 6, 1848. May 10 and November 8, 1849. March 9, 1850.

Democraten (Racine and Janesville, Wisconsin), July 27, 1850. March 8, 1851.

Emigranten (Inmansville and Madison, Wisconsin), January 23 and July 9, 1852. July 11 and August 15, 1856. May 13, June 24, July 25, August 12, and September 16, 1857. February 21 and October 17 and 24, 1859. January 23 and September 17, 1860. February 16 and November 18, 1861. March 2 and July 20, 1863. February 27, 1865. January 14, 1866.

Arbeider-Foreningernes Blad (Christiania), January 15, 1853.

Morgenbladet (Christiania), January 14, 1854. May 5, 1856.

Den Norske Amerikaner (Madison), June 14, 1856. May 13, 1857.

Nordstjernen (Madison) June 10, 1857.

Folkebladet (Chicago), September 22, 1860.

Fædrelandet (La Crosse, Wisconsin), March 29 and September 6, 1866.

Skandinaven (Chicago), July 26 and September 6 and 20, 1866. October 31, 1867. August 11, May 26, and October 27, 1869.

June 28 and December 20, 1871. June 11 and September 28, 1874. January 9 and 16 and March 2, 1875. June 27, July 11 and 25, August 1, October 17, and November 8 and 14, 1876. February 27 and September 4, 1877. March 5, 1878. April 1, 1896. October 24, 1902. January 14, 1903. August 1, 1906. April 17, 1916.

Dagslyset (Chicago), September, 1870.

Fædrelandet og Emigranten (La Crosse), October 15, 1868. March 16, 1871.

Amerika (Chicago), August 13 and November 4, 1872.

Minnesota (Minneapolis), September 27, 1872.

Skandinaven og Amerika (Chicago), October 2 and November 6, 1873.

Decorah-Posten og Ved Arnen (Decorah, Iowa), November 6 and 10, 1896. November 12, 1912. July 28 and August 14, 1914. April 10, 1917. May 25, 1972.

Nye Normanden (Minneapolis), October 12, 1897.

Fargo Fram, February 22, 1917.

Nordisk Tidende (Brooklyn), February 28, 1918.

Index

Aasen, Ivar, 8-10, 187
Aasgaard, Johan Arnd, 121, 133, 202
Abbott, Lyman, 20
Academies, 134-36
Act of Union (1815), 4, 138
Adams, John Quincy, 27
Addams, Jane, 140
Adventists, 103, 119, 134
Afholds-Basunen (Hillsboro, N. Dakota), 97
Ager, Waldemar, 74, 75, 78, 230-n11; temperance, 97, 147, 160; Norwegian-American writers, 157, 162, 164, 167
Alaska, 86
Alf Brage eller Skolelæreren i Minnesota (Hassel), 159
America letters, 2, 23, 109, 208, 209
American Lutheran Church, 109
American Lutheran Conference, 109
American Protective Association, 93
American-Scandinavian Foundation, 151, 202, 216
American-Scandinavian Review (The), 151, 216
American Spirit in Europe (The), (Koht), 211
Amerika (Chicago), 82, 162
Amerika (LaCrosse), 230n20
Amerika (Madison), 92
Amerikabreve (*see* America letters)
Amerikanske Fantasier (Janson), 159
Amtmandens Dötre (Collett), 8
Amundsen, Roald, 204
Andersen, Arthur E., 178, 179
Andersen, Magnus, 182
Anderson, John, 50

Anderson, Rasmus B., 94, 120; public education, 124, 125, 134, 136; language and literature, 141, 184
Andersonville Prison, 75, 76, 166
Anti-Missourian Brotherhood, 108, 131
Asbjörnsen, Sigvald, 140
Askevold, Bernt, 159, 164
Asserson, Peter C., 229n10
Augsburg College (Minneapolis), 108, 129, 130
Augsburg Seminary (Minneapolis), 108, 128, 130
Augustana College (Sioux Falls, S. Dakota), 126, 127
Augustana Seminary (Chicago), 126
Augustana Synod (Norwegian-Danish), 126
Augustana Synod (Swedish), 110
Aus, Gunvald, 182

Bache, Sören, 51, 105
Bache, Tollef O., 52, 104, 105
Bag Gardinet (Janson), 160
Baird, Robert, 212, 213
Balchen, Bernt, 204
Balling, Hans, 76
Baptist Theological Seminary (Chicago), 114
Baptists, 103, 114, 134
Bare for Moro (Rönning), 164
Barth, Carl G., 178, ·179
Baumann, Julius B., 187; temperance, 160, 162, 163
Bennett law, 125
Benson Grive riot (Iowa), 84
Bergen (Norway), 2, 27, 47, 181, 210, 215
Bergensposten, 11